LIBRARY AND TECHNICAL INFORMATION
GENERAL EDITOR: G CHANDLER

British Official Publications

British Official Publications

SECOND REVISED EDITION

JOHN E. PEMBERTON
B.A., F.L.A.

Librarian, University College at Buckingham

PERGAMON PRESS
Oxford · New York · Toronto
Sydney · Braunschweig

Pergamon Press Ltd., Headington Hill Hall, Oxford

Pergamon Press Inc., Maxwell House, Fairview Park, Elmsford,
New York 10523

Pergamon of Canada Ltd., 207 Queen's Quay West, Toronto 1

Pergamon Press (Aust.) Pty. Ltd., 19a Boundary Street,
Rushcutters Bay, N.S.W. 2011, Australia

Vieweg & Sohn GmbH, Burgplatz 1, Braunschweig

First edition 1971

Second Revised Edition 1973

Library of Congress Cataloging in Publication Data

Pemberton, John E
British official publications.

(Library and technical information)
1. Great Britain – Government publications –
Bibliography. I. Title.
Z2009.P45 1973   015'.42   73-16231
ISBN 0-08-017797-2

Printed in Great Britain by Cambridge University Press

To My Mother and Father

Contents

List of Illustrations

UNLESS otherwise stated, the illustrations are reproduced by kind permission of the Controller of Her Majesty's Stationery Office.

Preface to the Second Edition

For this second edition the text has been revised and updated to take account both of institutional changes, such as the replacement of the National Assembly of the Church of England by the General Synod and the creation of new administrative tribunals like the Value Added Tax Tribunals, and of major new works such as M. F. Bond's *Guide to the Records of Parliament* and *India: the Transfer of Power*. The lists of Royal Commissions, Departmental Committees, Working Parties and Tribunals of Inquiry have been extended to 1972. So too have the various series of publications, for example *Studies in Official Statistics* and *Public Record Office Handbooks*. The guides to further reading which occur throughout the text have similarly been revised as regards new editions and augmented as regards significant new works which have been published in the intervening period. Recent developments have also necessitated the replacement of several facsimile reproductions of specimen pages from key reference publications.

An entirely new chapter on non-H.M.S.O. publications has been added, since this important body of literature is increasing in volume and presents particular problems of access. At the same time the chapter on official publications relating to science, technology and medicine has been deleted, with patents being taken into the new chapter and other materials being covered elsewhere.

My indebtedness to numerous government departments, and in particular to Her Majesty's Stationery Office, continues to increase. I cannot recall an occasion when the response to my requests for information has not been both courteous and extremely efficient. I also wish to thank Mrs Yvonne Hancock, Statistics Librarian of the University of Warwick, for her

valuable comments on the statistics chapter, and to Mrs. Elizabeth Anker, British Official Publications Librarian at Warwick, for considerable bibliographical assistance during the course of this revision.

Buckingham   John E. Pemberton.
September, 1973

CHAPTER 1

British Parliamentary Government

THE CONSTITUTION

There is no single document which contains the text of the British Constitution. It is embodied in the statute law and the records of judicial decisions, and in accepted custom and tradition of which written evidence must be sought in a variety of official and quasi-official publications.

The actual scope of constitutional law cannot be stated in precise terms; certainly there is an undisputed hard core of essential topics — rule of law, separation of powers, parliamentary supremacy, and so forth — but, as an examination of the textbooks clearly reveals, the borders of the subject are ill defined. F. W. Maitland said that "the demarcation of the province of constitutional law is with us a matter of inconvenience" (*Constitutional History*, 1908), and the distinguished constitutional lawyer A. V. Dicey felt obliged to explain in his standard treatise *The Law of the Constitution* (1885), that "before commenting on the law of constitution [the English commentator or lecturer] must make up his mind what is the nature and extent of English constitutional law".

Unmistakably, the traditionalist view of constitutional law, which has been restricted to the consideration of statute law and judicial decisions, is now giving way to a new and wider interpretation under the impetus of Geoffrey Wilson's *Cases and Materials on Constitutional and Administrative law* (1966). According to Wilson, "unless . . . the use of materials other than law reports and decided cases [is] taken for granted, it is impossible to present constitutional law as a coherent subject or relate it in a meaningful way to the functions it has to fulfil or the social and political context in which it has to operate". His collection of materials represents the nearest approach that has yet been made to a written statement of the British Constitution. It draws not only upon statutes and law reports but

1

also upon such documents as White Papers; the reports of Royal Commissions, Select Committees and Inquiries; Official Reports of Debates in the House of Lords and the House of Commons; and even Answers to Parliamentary Questions.

The significance of Wilson's work to those who wish to become informed on all facets of the British Constitution is that they must acquaint themselves with a considerably wider range of official materials than has hitherto been regarded as sufficient — and all of these sources are described in the present volume.

As reliable texts on constitutional law the following can be recommended:

> BAGEHOT, W., *The English Constitution* (rev. edn. 1873, etc.).
> DICEY, A. V., *Introduction to the Study of the Law of the Constitution* (10th Edn. 1959).
> JENNINGS, Sir IVOR, *The British Constitution* (5th edn. 1966).
> MAITLAND, F. W., *Constitutional History of England* (1908).
> MITCHELL, J. D. B., *Constitutional Law* (2nd edn. 1968).
> PHILLIPS, O. HOOD, *Constitutional and Administrative Law* (4th edn. 1967).
> WADE, E. C. S. and PHILLIPS, G. G., *Constitutional Law* (8th edn. 1970).
> WILSON, GEOFFREY, *Cases and Materials on Constitutional and Administrative Law* (1966).

Notwithstanding the varying interpretations of the limits of their subject, all these works agree that the fundamental principle of the British Constitution is the supremacy of Parliament in the making of laws.

SUPREMACY OF PARLIAMENT

The Parliament of the United Kingdom of Great Britain and Northern Ireland consists of the Sovereign, the House of Lords and the House of Commons — each having its own rights and privileges. Together, these three elements constitute the legislature which can legislate for the whole of the United Kingdom, for any part of it or any combination of its parts. It can also legislate for the Isle of Man and the Channel Islands, though these are Crown dependencies and not part of the United Kingdom.

Under the terms of the Parliament Act, 1911, the life of a Parliament is five years, though it may be dissolved before the full term has expired. The period is divided into sessions, each normally lasting for a year and running from November to October. This accounts for the fact that certain categories of Parliamentary Papers which will be described later are known as Sessional Papers.

Unlike the legislative assemblies of those countries which have written constitutions, the British Parliament is not subject to any legal restraints. During its life each assembly can legislate on any matter without hindrance. An official pamphlet on *The British Parliament* (Central Office of Information, H.M.S.O., new edn. 1971) describes its position as follows:

> ... [I]t can make and unmake any law whatsoever; it can legalise past illegalities and make void and punishable what was lawful when done, and thus reverse the decisions of the ordinary law courts; it can destroy the most firmly established convention or turn a convention into binding law; and it has power to prolong its own life beyond the normal period of five years without consulting the electorate.

Having thus described the extent of Parliament's sovereignty, however, it goes on to add that

> In practice, Parliament does not assert its supremacy in this way. Its members bear in mind the common law which has grown up in Britain through the centuries, and they act as far as possible in accordance with precedent and tradition. Moreover, both Houses are sensitive to public opinion and although the validity of an Act of Parliament that has been duly passed, legally promulgated and published by the proper authority cannot be disputed in the law courts, no Parliament would be likely to pass an Act which it knew would receive no public support. The system of party government in Britain ensures that Parliament legislates with its responsibility to the electorate in mind.

POWERS OF THE CROWN

In the British Constitution the Monarchy has no direct authority; its powers are exercised by the Sovereign on the advice of her Ministers or by those Ministers in the Sovereign's name, and the device employed for carrying them into effect is known as the royal prerogative. There are in fact several prerogatives, the two principal being the personal and the political. The latter is the means whereby Parliament is summoned, prorogued and dissolved; by which Ministers, archbishops and bishops are appointed and peers created. In practice, these activities are performed through the issuance of instruments such as Orders in Council, warrants,

writs and proclamations; and even these are the responsibility of the Minister required to countersign them or having custody of the seal necessary for their completion. The legal existence of Parliament, however, depends on the exercise of the royal prerogative. Its business cannot proceed until the Queen's Speech (albeit prepared by her Ministers) has been read from the throne, nor can the legislation it proposes be enacted without the Royal Assent. Members of the House of Commons indeed depend upon the Queen's writ for their very election as the people's representatives in Parliament.

It is always difficult to know precisely what are the powers of a reigning Monarch. A reasonable approach to the question is to consult the studies of immediately preceding Sovereigns and, in using them as a basis of assessing the present position, to make due allowance for the gradual erosion of the powers of the Crown. Books to read, therefore, are:

> NICOLSON, HAROLD, *King George the Fifth: his life and reign* (1952).
> WHEELER-BENNET. J. W., *King George VI: his life and reign* (1958).

These can be supplemented by

> BENEMY, F. W. G., *The Queen Reigns, She does not Rule* (1963).
> HARDIE, F., *The Political Influence of the British Monarchy* (1970).
> PETRIE, Sir C., *Monarchy in the Twentieth Century* (1952) and *The Modern British Monarchy* (1961).

A brief general introduction to the subject is provided by the Central Office of Information reference pamphlet entitled *The Monarchy in Britain.*

THE HOUSE OF LORDS

Membership

Known as the upper House — or, to the Commons, as "another place" — the House of Lords consists of the Lords Temporal and the Lords

Spiritual. Until recent years the former were generally hereditary peers of England, Great Britain and the United Kingdom, but this position has been modified by two important Acts. The first of these was the Life Peerages Act, 1958, which provided for life peers *and peeresses* to be created by the Crown (usually on the recommendation of the Prime Minister). Second was the Peerage Act 1963, which made provision for hereditary peers to disclaim their peerage and assume the rights and status of commoners; removed the disqualification on hereditary peeresses from admission to the House in their own right; and entitled *all* Scottish peers — who hitherto were represented only by sixteen members elected from among themselves — to take their place along with the other peers. Irish peers, however, remain without this right. Under the terms of a much older statute, the Appellate Jurisdictions Act, 1876 (as amended), nine Lords of Appeal in Ordinary — popularly called the Law Lords — are appointed to serve the House in its role as the final court of appeal for civil cases in the whole of the United Kingdom and for criminal cases in England, Wales and Northern Ireland.

The Lords Spiritual are the Archbishops of Canterbury and York, the Bishops of London, Durham and Winchester, and the twenty-one bishops of the Church of England coming next in seniority. They have an important part to play in ensuring that the Lords are properly advised on the General Synod Measures which pass through Parliament (see p. 145)

The first in each session's series of House of Lords Papers is the *Roll of the Lords Spiritual and Temporal* which has three parts: (a) the Roll of the Lords, which lists the peers according to their Roll Number as shown in Fig. 1; (b) an alphabetical list of names (also giving their number in the Roll); and (c) an alphabetical list of the Lords usually addressed by their higher titles as Peers of Ireland, showing their titles in the Roll as Peers of Great Britain and the United Kingdom. At present out of a membership of some 1060, 325 are created peers and 735 peers by succession.

Procedure and Officers

Procedure in the House of Lords is quite different from that in the

ROLL OF THE LORDS

1   His Royal Highness The Prince of WALES.
2   His Royal Highness HENRY WILLIAM FREDERICK ALBERT Duke of
    GLOUCESTER.
3   His Royal Highness EDWARD ALBERT CHRISTIAN GEORGE ANDREW
    PATRICK DAVID Duke of WINDSOR.
4   His Royal Highness EDWARD GEORGE NICHOLAS PAUL PATRICK
    Duke of KENT.
5   ARTHUR MICHAEL Archbishop of CANTERBURY.
6   GERALD AUSTIN Lord GARDINER. (*Lord High Chancellor.*)
7   FREDERICK DONALD Archbishop of YORK.
8   FRANCIS AUNGIER Lord PAKENHAM (*Earl of Longford*). (*Lord
    Privy Seal.*)
9   BERNARD MARMADUKE Duke of NORFOLK. (*Earl Marshal of
    England.*)
10   PERCY HAMILTON Duke of SOMERSET.
11   FREDERICK CHARLES Duke of RICHMOND AND GORDON.
12   CHARLES ALFRED EUSTON Duke of GRAFTON.
13   HENRY HUGH ARTHUR FITZROY Duke of BEAUFORT.
14   CHARLES FREDERIC AUBREY DE VERE Duke of ST. ALBANS.*
15   JOHN ROBERT Duke of BEDFORD.
16   ANDREW ROBERT BUXTON Duke of DEVONSHIRE.
17   JOHN ALBERT EDWARD WILLIAM Duke of MARLBOROUGH.
18   CHARLES JOHN ROBERT Duke of RUTLAND.
19   DOUGLAS Duke of HAMILTON.* (*In another place as Duke of
    Brandon.*)
20   WALTER JOHN Duke of BUCCLEUCH AND QUEENSBERRY.* (*In
    another place as Earl of Doncaster.*)
21   IAN DOUGLAS Duke of ARGYLL.* (*In another place as Duke of
    Argyll.*)
22   GEORGE IAIN Duke of ATHOLL.
23   JAMES ANGUS Duke of MONTROSE.* (*In another place as Earl
    Graham.*)
24   GEORGE VICTOR ROBERT JOHN Duke of ROXBURGHE*. (*In another
    place as Earl Innes.*)
25   DOUGLAS Duke of BRANDON. (*In another place as Duke of
    Hamilton.*)
26   WILLIAM ARTHUR HENRY Duke of PORTLAND.
27   ALEXANDER GEORGE FRANCIS DROGO Duke of MANCHESTER.
28   HENRY EDWARD HUGH Duke of NEWCASTLE.*
29   HUGH ALGERNON Duke of NORTHUMBERLAND.
30   GERALD Duke of WELLINGTON.

FIG. 1. *Roll of the Lords Spiritual and Temporal*

Commons. Unlike the Speaker in the Lower House the Lord Chancellor does not act as an impartial chairman in debates. Maintenance of order is not his responsibility, nor does he, in fact, call upon Members to speak. Matters of procedure and order are determined by the House itself; Members rise to speak and continue to speak (subject to a rarely used curtailment motion) without direction from the chair. Many excellent debates take place in the Lords, often on a *motion for papers* – a technique used for airing subjects without entailing specific resolutions. When a topic has been fully debated the motion is usually withdrawn. *Standing Orders of the House of Lords* do exist. As a result of a Select Committee inquiry, a considerably revised edition was published in 1954, and there have since been amendments and further new editions.

The Lord Chancellor may, and frequently does, speak in debates, but in order to address his peers he has first to enter the Chamber. This he does by moving a few feet away from the Woolsack – a square couch stuffed with wool which is his seat when the House is sitting – which technically lies outside the House.

Several deputy speakers are appointed and most senior among them is the Lord Chairman of Committees.

House of Lords Minutes of Proceedings (which began in 1824) are published daily and along with them are issued the *Notices and Orders of the Day* for the next sitting, in which subjects to be debated for information only are indicated by starring.

Chief of the *permanent* officers is the Clerk of the Parliaments who is appointed by the Crown and who is responsible, among other things, for keeping the records of proceedings and judgements, for advising Members on procedure, endorsing Bills and promulgating Acts of Parliament. His appointment is the subject of the Clerk of the Parliaments Act, 1824.

It is the duty of the Gentleman Usher of the Black Rod to enforce the orders of the House, and it is he who delivers the summons to the Commons that their presence is desired in the upper House. Formerly practised on every occasion the Royal Assent was granted to Bills, but cancelled for this purpose by the Royal Assent Act 1967, Black Rod's summons now only occurs at the beginning and end of each session.

Each bound volume of the *Parliamentary Debates (Hansard): House of Lords Official Report* (popularly called the *Lords Hansard*) contains a list of the principal officers of the House.

Functions and Reform

House of Lords reform is a matter of constant concern to politicians and parliamentarians. Two topics in particular engage their attention: abolition of its hereditary basis and control of its delaying powers over legislation. Bernard Crick's *The Reform of Parliament* (1964) includes a useful introduction to the subject, and a review of past attempts at reform is given in a White Paper entitled *House of Lords Reform* (Cmnd. 3799, 1968) which sets out the Government's legislative proposals in the matter. This paper also lists the present main functions of the House of Lords, apart from providing the supreme court of appeal, as:

"(a) the provision of a forum for full and free debate on matters of public interest;
(b) the revision of public bills brought from the House of Commons;
(c) the initiation of public legislation, including in particular those government bills which are less controversial in party political terms and private members' bills;
(d) the consideration of subordinate legislation;
(e) the scrutiny of the activities of the executive; and
(f) the scrutiny of private legislation."

There is always government representation in the Lords. It is not only because the number of Ministers who may sit and vote in the House of Commons while receiving salaries from the Crown is limited by statute that some are drawn from the upper House; it is also because peers who are in charge of Ministries are able to represent the Government's views and intentions in the second chamber. Certain office-holders, including the Government Whips, are also drawn from the Lords and are able to speak for the Government during debates. The number of peers holding office in the Government can be ascertained from the *Hansard* list noted on p. 9.

P. A. Bromhead's *The House of Lords and Contemporary Politics 1911-1957* (1958) is the most comprehensive book on the upper House, and J. R. Vincent has provided a survey of changes that have occurred in the character of the House since 1957 in an article "The House of Lords" published in *Parliamentary Affairs* (vol. XIX, no. 4. pp. 475–85, 1966).

THE HOUSE OF COMMONS

Membership

The House of Commons is an assembly of 630 elected representatives of the people — 511 for England, 71 for Scotland, 36 for Wales and 12 for Northern Ireland. Members are elected either at a general election after the dissolution of a Parliament or at a by-election caused by a vacancy in the House following the death of a Member or his elevation to the peerage. Members cannot simply resign; they have instead to apply for the office of steward or bailiff of one of Her Majesty's three Chiltern Hundreds of Stoke, Desborough and Burnham, or of the Manor of Northstead — all of which are statutorily designated as disqualifying offices for this specific purpose (House of Commons Disqualification Act, 1957, s. 4).

Certain categories of persons (peers, clergy, bankrupts, etc.) are not qualified to stand for election; but with the further exception of those excluded by the 1957 Act (civil servants, policemen, members of the armed forces, holders of certain judicial offices, etc.) any British subject, aged eighteen or over may stand for election. The elections themselves are governed by the provisions of the Representation of the People Act, 1949, as amended by the Representation of the People Act 1969.

The first issue of *Hansard* for each session contains an Alphabetical List of Members elected at the last general election. As Fig. 2 shows, the Members' constituencies are given and, in the case of the later sessions of a Parliament, amendments occasioned by elevations to the peerage, by-elections and so forth are incorporated in the lists.

Members are also listed both alphabetically and by constituency in the quarterly *Vacher's Parliamentary Companion* (1831–) and the annual *Dod's Parliamentary Companion* (1832–). These also indicate the parties to which Members belong, and in addition contain lists of Ministers, officers of both Houses and the Privy Council, and much other information including the Royal Households, judges and the Parliament of Northern Ireland. Interesting brief profiles of Members can be found in Andrew Roth's *The Business Background of MP's* (1967).

Covering earlier times is *The House of Commons 1754–1790* by Sir Lewis Namier and John Brooke (3 vols., H.M.S.O., 1964), volumes 2 and 3

HOUSE OF COMMONS

ALPHABETICAL LIST OF MEMBERS

[Returned at the General Election, 31st March, 1966]

A

Abse, Leopold (Monmouthshire, Pontypool)

Albu, Austen Harry (Edmonton)

Alison, Michael James Hugh (Yorkshire, West Riding, Barkston Ash)

Allason, Lieutenant-Colonel James Harry, O.B.E. (Hertfordshire, Hemel Hempstead)

Allaun, Frank (Salford, East)

Aldritt, Walter Harold (Liverpool, Scotland)

Allen, Sydney Scholefield, Q.C. (Cheshire, Crewe)

Anderson Donald (Monmouthshire, Monmouth)

Anderson, Miss Margaret Betty Harvie, O.B.E., T.D. (Renfrewshire, East)

Archer, Peter Kingsley (Rowley Regis and Tipton)

Armstrong, Ernest (Durham, North-West)

Ashley, John (Stoke-on-Trent, South)

Astor, Hon. John (Berkshire, Newbury)

Atkins, Humphrey Edward (Merton and Morden)

Atkins, Ronald Henry (Preston, North)

Atkinson, Norman (Tottenham)

Awdry, Daniel Edmund, T.D. (Chippenham)

B

Bacon, Right Hon. Alice Martha, C.B.E. (Leeds, South-East)

Bagier, Gordon Alexander Thomas (Sunderland, South)

Baker, Kenneth Wilfred (Acton) *[By-election, March, 1968]*

Baker, Wilfred Harold Kerton, T.D. (Banff)

Balniel, Lord (Hertfordshire, Hertford)

Barber, Rt. Hon. Anthony Perrinot Lysberg, T.D. (Altrincham and Sale)

Barnes, Michael Cecil John (Brentford and Chiswick)

Beamish, Colonel Sir Tufton Victor Hamilton, M.C. (East Sussex, Lewes)

Beaney, Alan (Yorkshire, West Riding, Hemsworth)

Bell, Ronald McMillan, Q.C. (Buckinghamshire, South)

Bellenger, Rt. Hon. Frederick John (Nottinghamshire, Bassetlaw) *[Died, May, 1968]*

Bence, Cyril Raymond (Dunbartonshire, East)

Benn, Rt. Hon. Anthony Neil Wedgwood (Bristol, South-East)

Bennett, Sir Frederic Mackarness (Torquay)

Bennett, James (Glasgow, Bridgeton)

Bennett, Dr. Reginald Frederick Brittain, V.R.D. (Gosport and Fareham)

Berry, Anthony George (Southgate)

Bessell, Peter Joseph (Cornwall, Bodmin)

Bidwell, Sydney James (Southall)

Biffen, William John (Shropshire, Oswestry)

Biggs-Davison, John Alec (Essex, Chigwell)

Binns, John (Keighley)

Birch, Rt. Hon. Evelyn Nigel Chetwode, O.B.E. (West Flint)

Bishop, Edward Stanley (Nottinghamshire, Newark)

Black, Sir Cyril Wilson (Wimbledon)

Blackburn, Fred (Cheshire, Stalybridge and Hyde)

Blaker, Peter Allan Renshaw (Blackpool, South)

Blenkinsop, Arthur (South Shields)

Boardman, Harold (Leigh)

Boardman, Thomas Gray (Leicester, South-West) *[By-election, November, 1967]*

Body, Richard (Lincolnshire, Holland with Boston)

Booth, Albert Edward (Barrow-in-Furness)

Bossom, Sir Clive, Bt. (Herefordshire, Leominster)

Boston, Terence George (Kent, Faversham)

FIG. 2. *House of Commons Alphabetical List of Members*

of which contain biographies of Members of the second half of the eighteenth century. *The House of Commons 1715–1754* by Romney Sedgwick (2 vols., H.M.S.O., 1971) contains over 2000 biographical studies of Members and over 300 electoral histories of the parliamentary constituencies in England, Scotland and Wales.

Powers

In theory, the Commons have the power to cause the Government's resignation by carrying a *vote of no confidence* or by rejecting a proposal which the Government itself has made a *matter of confidence*. This form of ultimate control has not, however, been exercised for a good many years, and the House relies instead on other means to exert its influence.

Parliamentary Questions

Certain times are set aside (by Standing Order) during which Members may put previously notified questions to the responsible Ministers. Answers are made either orally or in writing, and both kinds are recorded in *Hansard* (see p. 107). Question Time gives Members an opportunity to extract information on the intentions and effects of government policy and to subject the actions of Ministers to close scrutiny − not only through the questions themselves but also through the supplementary verbal questions they are allowed to put.

Adjournment Debates

A further opportunity for Members to raise matters they consider to be of importance either to their own constituents or to the public at large is offered by the motion for the adjournment of the House which occurs at the end of public business on every sitting day (and at other times only in accepted cases of "a specific and important matter that should have urgent consideration", Standing Order No.9). Again, all the exchanges which ensue from these adjournment motions are fully recorded in *Hansard*.

Supply Debates

Financial matters are a particular concern of the Commons; under the terms of the Parliament Act, 1911, so-called *Money Bills* do not even require the assent of the Lords before they can be enacted. Within the Commons itself, debate on the Estimates invariably involves, at the instance of the Opposition, a critical examination of the Government's policies as reflected in the costs which they incur. This is a debate of the House of Commons in Committee of Supply and is indexed in *Hansard* under the heading "Supply".

Parliamentary Commissioner (Ombudsman)

Since April 1967 when the Parliamentary Commissioner Act 1967 was brought into operation M.P.s have been able to refer complaints made by members of the public to the Parliamentary Commissioner for Administration, popularly called the Ombudsman. In general terms the complaints must come from persons claiming to have sustained injustice in consequence of maladministration by government departments. For more precise information on the extent of the Commissioner's jurisdiction, however, the Act itself should be consulted, and a most valuable account of the way in which complaints are handled is contained in the First Report of the Parliamentary Commissioner for Administration (1967–68 H.C. 6). The pre-legislative story of the Ombudsman is largely told in *The Citizen and the Administration: the redress of grievances* by Sir John Whyatt (1961), and in the White Paper (Cmnd. 2767) of October 1965 entitled *The Parliamentary Commissioner for Administration.*

Procedure

Standing Orders

The House of Commons conducts its business from day to day in accordance with a body of prescribed rules and conventions. *Standing Orders of the House of Commons* are published in two parts: *Private Business* and *Public Business,* and appear as House of Commons Papers.

Orders relating to public business are grouped under the following headings (1971–72 H.C. 126):

> Sittings of the House; Arrangement of Public Business; Private Business; Questions; Special Adjournment Motions; Anticipation; Seconders; Bringing in Bills and Nominating Select Committees at Commencement of Public Business; Orders of the Day; Motions for the Adjournment of the House; Supply and Ways and Means; Order of the Day for Committee; Committees of the Whole House; Order in the House; Dilatory Motions; Count of the House; Closure of Debate; Amendments; Divisions; Public Bills; Standing Committees; Select Committees; Committee of Public Accounts; Expenditure Committee; Joint Committee on Consolidation, &c., Bills; Sittings of Committees; Public Money; Packet and Telegraphic Contracts; Public Petitions; Deputy Speaker and Chairmen; Members; Witnesses; Strangers; Letters; Parliamentary Papers; Earlier Meeting of House.

In between revised editions supplements are issued which give the text of new and amended standing orders.

Officers of the House

Certain standing orders relate to the powers and duties of the elected officers of the House, of whom the most important is Mr. Speaker. His powers (in 1973) are covered by twelve orders, and his duties by no less than twenty-four. He is elected by the Members from among their number at the beginning of each new Parliament; though, provided he continues to be returned by the electorate, it is usual for the House to re-elect the Speaker of the preceding Parliament. He regulates the course of debates and ensures the adherence of Members to the rules of procedure, having the ultimate power "In the case of grave disorder ... [to] adjourn the House without putting any question or suspend the sitting to a time to be named by him" (S.O. Public Business, No. 26). Further information on this ancient office may be sought in *The Speakers of the House of Commons* by A. I. Dasent (1911) and *The Office of Speaker* by Philip Laundy (1964).

Second in importance is the Chairman of Ways and Means who presides over the House when it is in committee and who also acts as Deputy Speaker.

Chief *permanent* officer is the Clerk of the House of Commons who has charge of the official records. His office also is an ancient one, dating

back more than three centuries and a half, and over the years successive Clerks have not only been responsible for the records of the House but have also been respected as authorities on procedure. Henry Scobell's *Memorials of Method and Manner of Proceedings of Parliament in passing Bills* (first published in 1656) is a standard work on seventeenth-century procedure; John Hatsell's four-volume *Precedents of Proceedings in the House of Commons under Separate Titles, with Observations* (first edition 1781; best is fourth, 1818) is the authority for the eighteenth century; and the work of Sir Thomas Erskine May, Clerk from 1871 to 1886, entitled *Treatise on the Law, Privileges, Proceedings and Usage of Parliament* has remained the accepted authority on parliamentary procedure since it was first published in 1844. The latest edition (18th, 1971) was edited by the present Clerk, Sir Barnett Cocks and extends to well over one thousand pages. Duties of the Clerk now include advising the Speaker and Members of the House on procedural matters, as well as signing various official documents (votes of thanks, etc.), endorsing Bills and reading items in the House.

Not only the Clerk but the other officers including, for example, the Serjeant-at-Arms (one of whose duties is to maintain law and order within the House), are dealt with in Philip Marsden's *Officers of the Commons, 1363-1965* (1966), and a relevant statute is the House of Commons (Offices) Act, 1812. A list of the principal officers and officials is printed at the beginning of every bound volume of *Hansard* and in Dod's and Vacher's *Parliamentary Companions* already noted.

While May's work is the standard treatise on parliamentary procedure, Eric Taylor's *The House of Commons at Work* (6th edn. 1965) meets the need of those who require an authoritative account which is more concise and readable; published by Penguin, it is also inexpensive.

Two excellent quick reference works are also available: L. A. Abraham and S. C. Hawtrey's *Parliamentary Dictionary* (3rd edn. 1970), and N. Wilding and P. Laundy's *Encyclopaedia of Parliament* (4th edn. 1972). The *Dictionary* comprises concise entries, arranged alphabetically, covering British parliamentary practice. It is a reliable compilation, and the fact that it has a detailed index makes it particularly easy to consult. Strict interpretation of its subject limits can, however, prove frustrating; there are, for example, no entries for either Prime Minister or Cabinet. The *Encyclopaedia* also has an alphabetical arrangement of entries but instead

of an index there are abundant cross-references in the text. It deals not only with every aspect of parliamentary practice but also with parliamentary history under the heading "Parliament" and under the names of Sovereigns from Elizabeth I to Victoria. There are biographies of persons who have helped to determine the powers, privileges and precedents of Parliament; descriptions of political parties; and extended articles under topics like Church and Parliament, Dress in Parliament, Elections, *Hansard*, Irish Parliament, Mace, Sovereign, and Speaker. Lists of office holders and a thirty-eight-page bibliography are included as appendices. Coverage extends to Commonwealth Parliaments.

THE PRIME MINISTER AND THE CABINET

The Prime Minister is the chief executive of the Government: it is he who chooses the Ministers who will form the Cabinet and he, too, who dismisses them. He can recommend the creation of peers and ask the Sovereign to dissolve Parliament. In his book *The Elected Monarch* (1965) F. W. G. Benemy describes the Prime Minister as "The most influential and powerful man in the country, who is for a period of time almost a benevolent dictator." Other people's views of the office can be found in *The British Prime Minister* (1969), an anthology of materials relating to the Premier and the Cabinet over which he presides, edited by J. Murray-Brown.

According to the 1918 Report of the Machinery of Government Committee (Cd. 9230) the Cabinet is "the mainspring of all the mechanism of government", and its main functions may be described as:

(a) the final determination of the policy to be submitted to Parliament;
(b) the supreme control of the national executive in accordance with the policy described by Parliament; and
(c) the continuous co-ordination and delineation of the activities of the several Departments of State.

Members of the Cabinet are listed at the beginning of each new volume of *Hansard*, and in the *List of H.M. Ministers and Heads of Public Departments* published five times a year by H.M.S.O.

Certain matters which require constant review and detailed examination are the special care of Cabinet committees of which some, such as those for Defence and Legislation are standing committees. Publications

CHAPTER 2

Official Publications: Classification and Indexes

PARLIAMENTARY OR NON-PARLIAMENTARY?

It is usual to consider official publications under two headings, Parliamentary and Non-Parliamentary. In general terms Parliamentary Papers are those documents which are required by Parliament in the conduct of its business. The most obvious categories are the standing orders of both Houses and the publications, such as Bills, debates and Acts of Parliament, which relate to the legislative process. In addition there are reports on matters on which legislation is anticipated and, at the other end of the line, reports made to Parliament in pursuance of Acts. Non-Parliamentary Publications, on the other hand, are produced by government departments for use outside the parliamentary context. Good examples are statistical compilations, administrative circulars and the reported decisions of tribunals.

An apparently anomalous situation arises in the case of statutory instruments. In certain instances they are actually required to be laid before Parliament, but because they are not printed for or to the direct order of Parliament they fall into the category of Non-Parliamentary Publications.

The tendency is always towards publication in the Non-Parliamentary category; and this can be traced back to the year 1921 when a move to standardize the page size of Parliamentary Papers was followed by an instruction designed to secure "an immediate reduction in the expenditure on stationery and printing incurred by H.M. Stationery Office on behalf of Public Departments". In April, departments were notified that:

> Mr. Speaker is prepared to accept the proposal that all House of Commons Papers shall in future be printed uniformly in royal octavo and My Lords [Commissioners of His Majesty's Treasury] prescribe this form also in the case of all Command papers. [Treasury Circular No. 19A/21, 25 April 1921.]

There was, however, no intention of making departments adopt this format where there was good reason not to: "Cases may arise, e.g. for certain statistical publications where departments may consider that the proposed royal octavo form is unsuitable." If, however, a department wishes a publication of this kind to be presented to Parliament, "the document presented should be a covering report only, matter unsuitable for presentation in royal octavo form being published as a Stationery Office [i.e. Non-Parliamentary] publication". Then in September arrangements were introduced under which the proportion of Parliamentary Papers would be substantially diminished for reasons other than uniformity of size. Details were set out in a second letter from the Treasury:

> Papers issued by order of either House or in response to an address to the Crown will continue to be printed under the present arrangements. With this exception . . . that the present practice of issuing Departmental publications as Parliamentary Papers should be drastically modified, not only in the urgent interests of economy but to meet the expressed wishes of the Authorities of the House of Commons.
>
> The presentation by Departments to the Houses of Parliament of papers "By Command" should be discontinued except in the cases of documents relating to matters likely to be the subject of early legislation, or which may be regarded as otherwise essential to Members of Parliament as a whole to enable them to discharge their responsibilities. Other documents hitherto issued as Command Papers should in future be issued as Stationery Office publications, or, wherever possible, be discontinued. [Treasury Circular No. 38/21, 6 September 1921].

A further economy measure was a reduction in the number of free copies of official publications distributed to government departments and members of the public. It follows, too, that libraries receiving sets of Parliamentary Papers under deposit or exchange arrangements would thenceforth receive fewer documents due to the transfer of numerous papers to the Non-Parliamentary category.

As a direct result of these various measures 1921 marks a turning point in the life of many series. Statistical compilations were widely affected: a notable example is the *Annual Statement of the Trade of the United Kingdom* which previously had been published as a Command Paper and which now became a Non-Parliamentary Publication. The *United Kingdom Balance of Payments* which was issued as a Command Paper from its inception in 1948 made the change as recently as 1963.

Changes of this kind bring problems for the user: titles which have

figured session by session in the indexes to Parliamentary Papers suddenly fail to appear and the unsuspecting inquirer could be misled into thinking that they had ceased publication. A wise precaution is always to check in the annual catalogues of government publications.

Another unfortunate consequence concerns Royal Commissions. Nowadays, whereas their reports continue to be published as Command Papers, the evidence they receive from witnesses is invariably issued in the form of Non-Parliamentary Publications. This is inconvenient to those libraries which bind all their Parliamentary Papers into the prescribed sessional volumes, as they are thereby obliged to separate reports from evidence. This intolerable situation can only be overcome by buying a second copy of the report to bind with the evidence and other documentary material such as research papers.

Examples of transfers in the reverse direction are less common, but they do occur. The first sixteen issues of *Legal Aid and Advice: report of the Law Society, etc.,* for instance, were Non-Parliamentary: then the seventeenth was published as a Parliamentary Paper (1967-68 H.C. 373).

As regards the reports of departmental committees the choice as to whether or not they are presented to Parliament and published as Parliamentary Papers rests with the responsible Minister. Those which are so presented are known as Command Papers, a very important class of document which is treated separately in Chapter 5.

The principles governing inclusion in one category or the other are dealt with in a Treasury publication entitled *Official Publications* (H.M.S.O., 1958, repr. 1963).

OFFICIAL INDEXES

A folder entitled *H.M.S.O. Catalogue Service* (revised every year) is available free of charge from H.M.S.O., Atlantic House, Holborn Viaduct, London EC1P 1BN

Daily List

The first notice of publication of official papers is in the *Daily List of Government Publications* issued by H.M.S.O. It begins by listing new

DAILY LIST
of Government Publications from
Her Majesty's Stationery Office

Government Bookshops

London: 49 High Holborn, WC1V 6HB (London post orders: PO Box 569, London SE1)

Bristol BS1 3DE: 50 Fairfax Street

Birmingham B1 2HE: 258 Broad Street   Manchester M60 8AS: Brazennose Street

Belfast BT1 4JY: 80 Chichester Street   Edinburgh EH2 3AR: 13a Castle Street   Cardiff CF1 1JW: 109 St Mary Street

Publications may also be ordered through any bookseller

Please quote the full title, price and reference numbers when ordering by post   All prices are net.   Prices in brackets include postage at inland rates

List No. 97   Friday 18th May 1973

All prices shewn in this list are exclusive of VAT

PARLIAMENTARY PUBLICATIONS
(9.5/8in. (244mm) unless otherwise stated)

House of Lords Papers and Bills (Session 1972-73)

(117) Hallmarking Bill. [As Amended in Committee]. (10 411773 7). 44pp.   26½p   (30p)

(119) Land Compensation Bill. Commons Amendments to certain of the Lords Amendments
       and Commons Amendment in lieu of two of the Lords Amendments.   5p   (7½p)
       (10 411973 X). 4pp.

House of Lords Parliamentary Debates (Session 1972-73)

∅ Official Report (Hansard):
   Daily Parts (Unrevised):
     Vol.342. No.82. May 16, 1973. (10 708273 X). Cols. 809-904.   18p   (21½p)

FIG. 3. *Daily List of Government Publications*

Parliamentary Papers and Non-Parliamentary Publications (Fig. 3), and these are followed by particulars of publications reprinted with new prices, publications sold but not published by H.M.S.O., and finally a Statutory Instrument Issue List (see p. 153).

Weekly Select List

To be noted in passing is the *Weekly List of Government Publications from Her Majesty's Stationery Office: a selection of interest to local authorities.*

Weekly Advance List

Also issued weekly is the *List of Non-Parliamentary Publications sent for Printing* which may be used for placing advance orders.

Monthly Catalogue

Next to be issued by H.M.S.O. is *Government Publications issued during* [*e.g.*] *January 1972,* popularly referred to as the "Monthly Catalogue" (Fig. 4). Again Parliamentary Papers come first: House of Lords Papers and Bills, House of Lords Parliamentary Debates (*Hansard* and Standing Committee Debates), House of Commons Bills, Command Papers, Public General Acts, Local Acts, and General Synod Measures. Then comes a Classified List in which Parliamentary and Non-Parliamentary Publications (as well as British and overseas publications sold but not published by H.M.S.O.) are listed by department or issuing organisation. Finally there is an index of names, titles and ISBN's. Statutory instruments are not included (see p. 153).

A loose inset to the catalogue, headed H.M.S.O. Monthly Selection, provides short descriptions of some of the more important publications issued during the month.

Annual Catalogue

Properly referred to as the *Catalogue of Government Publications* [*e.g.*] *1972* this contains all items published by H.M.S.O. during the year, except

GOVERNMENT PUBLICATIONS

issued during December 1972

Her Majesty's Stationery Office/MONTHLY CATALOGUE

Annual Subscription: 50p including postage

To ensure a speedy and efficient service customers are advised to send their orders to the nearest bookshop. (In London area orders should be sent to P.O. Box 569, S.E.1 9NH). Please quote the full title including any reference numbers, and price when ordering by post.

Net prices are quoted. Prices in brackets include postage at Inland rates

Prices and availability are correct at time of going to press, but are subject to alteration without notice.

1 PARLIAMENTARY

The size of Parliamentary Publications, unless otherwise given, is $9\frac{5}{8}''\times 6''$ (244 × 152 mm.)

HOUSE OF LORDS PAPERS AND BILLS

(Session 1971-72)

(160-ix) SELECT COMMITTEE ON THE ANTI-DISCRIMINATION (No. 2) BILL. Minutes of Evidence; Oct. 24, 1972. (10 466572 6). pp. 203-236. 24p ($26\frac{1}{2}$p)

FIG. 4. *Monthly Catalogue of Government Publications*

Statutory Instruments. Section I contains Parliamentary Papers listed numerically in their various series; Section II contains both Parliamentary and Non-Parliamentary Publications, listed under the government departments and other bodies responsible for their preparation which are arranged in alphabetical order. Section III is an alphabetical list of periodicals for which subscriptions may be entered. The volume concludes with an index.

As regards publications sold but not published by H.M.S.O. the Annual Catalogue includes only those which are published in the United Kingdom by public bodies such as the British Museum. Publications of the UN, EEC etc. are listed and indexed in a separately published supplement entitled *International Organisation and Overseas Agencies Publications* (see p. 287).

Figure 5 reproduces a typical page from Part II of the "Annual Catalogue" showing Parliamentary and Non-Parliamentary Publications listed by issuing department. The Parliamentary Papers also appear in their respective series in Section I. Not only are prices given, but also the format of each item and the number of pages it contains. Since 1968 the Standard Book Numbers (now International Standard Book Numbers), by which publications may be ordered either from the government bookshops or any bookseller, are also provided.

Each catalogue includes details of Sectional Lists (see below), the names of bodies for whom H.M.S.O. acts as sales agent, and details of the index cards and supplementary information services which are available.

Pagination is consecutive for five years so that five catalogues may be bound together in one volume (though inadvertently the index for 1953 was paginated separately). Quinquennial consolidated indexes have been issued for the years 1936–40, 1941–45, 1946–50, 1951–55, 1956–60, 1961–65, 1966–70.

Sale catalogues of British official publications first appeared in 1836, though no library appears to have a complete set of the annual cumulative catalogues. A detailed bibliography is provided in K. A. Mallaber's "The sale catalogues of British government publications 1836–1965", *Journal of Librarianship*, vol. 5, no. 2, April 1973, pp. 116–131.

Sectional Lists

Sectional Lists are catalogues of in-print Non-Parliamentary Publications

2. Classified List

NON-PARLIAMENTARY AND PARLIAMENTARY

Excluding Bills, Act, Debates and Measures

Contractions used in this part of the List:—

H.L. = House of Lords Papers; H.C. = House of Commons Papers; Cmnd. = Command Papers.

AGRICULTURAL RESEARCH COUNCIL

(*Each* 9⅝ × 6 in. (244 × 152 mm.) *unless otherwise stated*)

Annual Report:

For the year 1970–71 (H.C. 210) (10 221072 1). 68 pp. 47p (50½p)
For the year ended March 31, 1972 (H.C. 7). (10 200773 X). 76 pp. 47p (50½p)

Sold but not published by H.M.S.O.

Animal Breading Research Organisation. Report January, 1972. (902290 07 X). 9⅝ × 7½ in (244 × 187 mm.). 52 pp., illus. 40p (45½p)

Index of Agricultural and Food Research 1972. (902290 66 5). 132 pp. £1.00 (£1.07)

Institute of Animal Physiology. Babraham, Cambridge. Report for 1970–71. 6th Biennial Report. July, 1972. (902290 67 3). 8⅜ × 5⅜ (211 × 138 mm.). 164 pp., + 8 plates. £1.15 (£1.22)

Letcombe Laboratory. (*Each* 9⅝ × 7¼ in. (244 × 185 mm.)).
Annual Report 1970. (902290 053). 55 pp., illus. 50p (55½p)
Annual Report 1971. June, 1972. (902290 68 1). 64 pp., illus. 67p (73½p)

Weed Research Organization. 4th Report 1969–71. (March 1972). (902290 09 6). 8⅛ × 5⅞ in. (205 × 152 mm.). 104 pp., illus. 48p (54½p)

AGRICULTURE AND FISHERIES, DEPARTMENT OF, FOR SCOTLAND

(*Each* 9⅝ × 6 in. (244 × 152 mm.). *unless otherwise stated*)

Advisory Bulletin:

11. Commercial Tomato Growing in Scotland. (By Miss M. Wilson, N.D.H. and R. E. Johnston, B.Sc., N.D.H.). (11 490771 4). 44 pp., illus. 42p (45½p)

FIG. 5. *Annual Catalogue of Government Publications*

other than statutory instruments. The inclusion in some lists of a selection of Parliamentary Publications, and in a few cases of statutory instruments also, is at departmental behest and is justified by special needs. In some categories (e.g. record works, ancient manuscripts, medical research) where the fact of publication of an item has an historical significance transcending its availability, out-of-print titles (identified as such) are also included. The lists either cover the publications of a particular department (Fig. 6) or collect together the publications of different departments on the same subject. Revisions are issued periodically, for most annually, and all the lists are supplied free of charge. On page 26 is a list of·those currently available.

Sessional Indexes

Prior to 1969–70 the House of Commons Library compiled indexes for each session's collection of Public Bills, House of Commons Papers, and Command Papers. These were for use in conjunction with the bound volumes of sessional papers, in which the documents were re-sorted into four groups, substantially following a scheme prepared under the direction of Speaker Charles Abbott in 1802 as follows:

Group		Kind of papers
I.	Bills	Bills
II.	Reports of Committees:	
	(i.e. House of Commons committees)	House of Commons Papers
III.	Reports of Commissioners:	
	(i.e. extra parliamentary committees,	
	commissions, etc.)	Command Papers – but House of Commons when presented by Act
IV.	Accounts and Papers	House of Commons or Command
	Accounts	House of Commons
	White Papers, Memoranda, etc.	Command
	Treaty Series	Command
	Estimates (of the Public Services)	House of Commons (even though presented by Command)

As from 1969–70 the sessional indexes have been prepared for the House of Commons by the Department of Trade and Industry Library

SECTIONAL LISTS CURRENTLY AVAILABLE

Aeronautical Research Council	8
Agriculture & Fisheries for Scotland (Agriculture), Department of	52
Agriculture and Food	1
Ancient Monuments & Historic Buildings	27
British National Archives	24
Building	61
Central Office of Information	53
Civil Service	44
Defence, Ministry of; Navy Department; Army Department; Air Force Department	67
Education & Science, Department of	2
Employment, Department of	21
Environment, Department of	5
Environment (Transport), Department of	22
Fisheries	23
Forestry Commission	31
Geological Sciences, Institute of	45
Health & Social Security (Health), Department of	11
Health & Social Security (Social Security), Department of	49
HM Treasury & Allied Departments	32
Histories of the First & Second World Wars	60
Home Office	26
Inland Revenue, Board of	29
Land Registry Forms	43
Medical Research Council	12
Meteorological Office	37
Miscellaneous List	50
Official Forms for use on Premises under the Factories Acts	18
Overseas Affairs	69
Periodicals & Subscription Rates	28
Population & Censuses Surveys, Office of	56
Royal Commission on Historical Manuscripts	17
Royal Commissions	59
Scottish Development Department	65
Scottish Education Department	36
Scottish Home & Health Department	66
Trade & Industry, Department of	3
Victoria & Albert Museum	55

Teacher Training and Supply

CIRCULARS

10/60. Teaching Service in The Commonwealth and Other Countries Overseas. (September 12th, 1960) 4*p* (*6½p*)
Addendum No. 1. (January 28th, 1964) 2*p* (*4½p*)

5/68. Recommendation concerning the Status of Teachers, adopted by the Special Inter-governmental Conference on the Status of Teachers, Paris, (October 5th, 1966)
English edition: 16*p* (*18½p*)
Welsh edition: 16*p* (*18½p*)

17/70. Grants to Recognised Students attending Approved Courses of Teacher Training. (SBN 11 270190 6) 20*p* (*22½p*)

REPORTS

National Advisory Council on the Training and Supply of Teachers.

Demand for and Supply of Teachers, 1963–1968. 9th Report of the Council (Chairman: A. L. C. Bullock, M.A.) (April, 1965) (27–381) 37½*p* (*43p*)

General:

Teachers for Further Education. Report of an Advisory Sub-Committee. (Chairman: E. L. Russell, C.B.E., M.A.) (27–347) 6*p* (*8½p*)

Supply and Training of Teachers for Further Education. Report of the Standing Sub-Committee on Teachers for Further Education of the National Advisory Council on the Training and Supply of Teachers. (1966) (27–391) 12½*p* (*15p*)

Women and Teaching. Report on an Independent Nuffield Survey Following-up a Large National Sample of Women who Entered Teaching in England and Wales at Various Dates Pre-war and Post-war. (By R. K. Kelsall, Professor of Sociological Studies, University of Sheffield) (27–366) 20*p* (*22½p*)

Teachers' Copy of Service Book. (Book Form 1a C.R.) (Reprinted 1961, revised price exclusive of purchase tax) 5*p* (*7½p*)

The Training of Teachers. Suggestions for Three Year Training College Course. Ministry of Education Pamphlet No. 34, 1957. (27–265–34) 9*p* (*11½p*)

Further Education

GENERAL

Education and Training for Scientific and Technological Library and Information Work. (By H. Schur and others.) 1968. (SBN 11 270007 1) 37½*p* (*43p*)

Enquiry into Longer-term Postgraduate Course for Engineers and Technologists, 1964–65. (27–385) 22½*p* (*25p*)

Plan for Polytechnics and Other Colleges. (*See page 15.*)

FIG. 6. *Sectional List*

Services, and the documents themselves are now arranged in only two sequences. Bills and other papers — the latter in broad subject groups. Both the indexes and the corresponding title pages and contents lists continue to be published by H.M.S.O.

The *Sessional Index* begins with lists of the three series of papers arranged by their serial numbers in which the appropriate volume and page references are given. Thus in order to locate a particular Command Paper in the sessional volumes one first has to look it up by number in the list of Command Papers to discover its volume and page reference; and the same applies to Bills and H.C. Papers where their numbers are known. Where the serial number is not known recourse has to be had to the alphabetical index which follows the lists, in which the entries are grouped under subject headings as shown in Fig. 7. Cross-references are liberally provided. Finally, access to reports known by the names of authors or committee chairmen is provided by means of a name index.

Sessional Indexes are consolidated into decennial indexes, and these in turn into general indexes each covering a period of fifty years.

General Alphabetical Index 1950 to 1958–59

The most recent decennial index is the *General Alphabetical Index to the Bills, Reports and Papers printed by Order of the House of Commons and to the Reports and Papers presented by Command 1950 to 1958–59* (1962–63 H.C. 96). This is a consolidation of the *Sessional Indexes* for the period, except that the serially ordered tables of Bills, House of Commons Papers and Command Papers are not reproduced. Again there are abundant cross-references. The volume concludes with a select list of chairmen of committees and other authors, where names are quoted in the form in which they were used when the reports were printed, with references from alternative forms.

A specimen page is reproduced in Fig. 8.

General Index 1900 to 1948–49

The latest fifty-year cumulation is the *General Index to the Bills, Reports and Papers printed by Order of the House of Commons and to the*

ALPHABETICAL INDEX

to the Public Bills, Reports, Accounts and Papers of Session 1965-66

EXPLANATION OF REFERENCES

The figures between parentheses (55) &c., refer to the number at the bottom of each separate Bill, Report, Paper, &c., printed by Order of the House of Commons; and those prefixed Cmnd. to the numbers similarly assigned to Papers presented by Command. The volume and page numbers at the end of the Paragraphs refer to the Volumes as arranged for the House of Commons. The words in brackest [passed, cap. 1] inserted in the titles of Bills and National Assembly Measures distinguish those which became law and show their chapter numbers in the volume(s) of Public General Acts.

A

ABERDEEN:

University. See UNIVERSITIES (SCOTLAND) (*Bill*).

ABORTION:

BILLS:

Abortion [H.L.]:
Bill intituled an Act to amend the law relating to termination of pregnancy by registered medical practitioners. [H.L. 51 was brought from the Lords, but not numbered or printed by the House of Commons]; 1965–66 (—) Vol. **i, p. 1.**

Medical Termination of Pregnancy:
Bill to amend and clarify the law relating to termination of pregnancy by registered medical practitioners; 1965–66 (33) Vol. **ii, p. 191.**

ABSENT VOTERS. See ELECTIONS (*Bill*).

ACCOUNTS, PUBLIC:

I. REPORT OF COMMITTEE:
Report from the Committee of Public Accounts: Excess Votes and Atomic Energy Authority; 1965–66 (113) Vol. **iii, p. 1.**

II. PAPER:

Treasury Minute:
Treasury Minute on the Reports from the Committee of Public Accounts, Session 1964–65; 1965–66 Cmnd. 2845. Vol. **viii, p. 291.**

ADMINISTRATION OF ESTATES. See ESTATES OF DECEASED PERSONS.

ADMINISTRATION OF JUSTICE. See COURTS OF LAW.

ADULT OFFENDERS. See PRISONS (*Paper*).

FIG. 7. *Sessional Index*

ALPHABETICAL INDEX

to the Printed Bills, Reports, Accounts and Papers
of Sessions 1950 to 1958-59

EXPLANATION OF REFERENCES

The figures between parentheses (55) &c., refer to the number at the bottom of each separate Bill, Report, Paper, &c., printed by Order of the House of Commons; and those prefixed Cmd. or Cmnd. to the numbers similarly assigned to Papers presented by Command. The volume and page numbers at the end of the Paragraphs refer to the Volumes as arranged for the House of Commons. The words in brackets [passed, cap. 1] inserted in the titles of Bills and National Assembly Measures distinguish those which became law and show their chapter numbers in the volume(s) of Public General Acts.

A

ABERDEEN :

Corporation. See LOCAL GOVERNMENT (S.) (I. *Provisional Order Bills*).
Harbour. See HARBOURS (S.) (I. *Provisional Order Bills*).

ABERDEEN CHARTERED ACCOUNTANTS :

Provisional Order Bill :
  Aberdeen Chartered Accountants' Widows' Fund ; 1950–51 (95) Vol. I, p. 1.

ABORTION :

BILL :

Abortion :
  Bill to amend the law relating to abortion ; 1952–53 (20) Vol. I, p. 5.

ABYSSINIA. See ETHIOPIA.

ACCIDENTS :

I. BILL :

Fatal Accidents :
  Bill [passed, cap. 65] to amend the Fatal Accidents Act, 1846, by enlarging the class of persons for whose benefit an action may be brought thereunder, and to amend the Fatal Accidents (Damages) Act, 1908 ; 1958–59 (29) Vol. I, p. 819.
  Same [as amended by Standing Committee C] ; 1958–59 (67) Vol. I, p. 821.
  Lords Amendments ; 1958–59 (134) Vol. I, p. 825.

II. PROCEEDINGS OF COMMITTEE :

Fatal Accidents Bill :
  Proceedings of Standing Committee C ; 1958–59 (89) Vol. vi, p. 33.

Accidents in Collieries. See COAL.

FIG. 8. *General Alphabetical Index 1950 to 1958–59*

Reports and Papers presented by Command 1900 to 1948—49 (H.M.S.O., 1960). It has a useful introduction in which it is explained that copies of *Decennial Indexes* were used as raw material in its compilation, and that it covers over 40,000 items contained in nearly 2700 volumes of sessional papers. Most of the headings used incorporate parts of titles of particular documents or of names of departments, or of Acts of Parliament; and the reason given for this is that, at least in the House of Commons Library, papers are far more often sought under titles than under subject headings as such. It is further explained that indexes in the earlier part of the period covered sometimes placed a paper under more than one heading: for example, a Treaty Paper would be placed both under the name of the country involved and under the general heading "Treaties"; and that as such double entries were carried forward into the present index some discrepancy of treatment has resulted. Sessional and decennial indexes of the earlier period also occasionally provided useful analyses of comprehensive papers; and where such analauses were found they, too, were carried forward.

General Alphabetical Index 1852—1899

The second fifty-year cumulation is the *General Alphabetical Index to the Bills, Reports, Estimates, Accounts, and Papers, printed by Order of the House of Commons, and to the Papers presented by command, 1852—1899*. Whilst being a useful tool, it unfortunately omits all sessional numbers of papers; and this means that the indexes for 1852—53 to 1868—69 and the following three decennial indexes retain their value.

General Index 1801—1852

Unlike the other fifty-year cumulations this is in three separate volumes, as follows:

(i) *General Index to the Bills printed by Order of the House of Commons 1801—1852;*

(ii) *General Index to the Reports of Select Committees printed by Order of the House of Commons 1801—1822;*

(iii) *General Index to the Accounts and Papers, Reports of Commissioners, Estimates &c. &c. printed by Order of the House of Commons and presented by Command 1801–1852.*

In using these volumes it should be noted that Bills printed before 1836 may be difficult to identify because they lacked short titles by which they could be cited; and that Command Papers did not bear numbers between 1833 and 1869.

Catalogue of Papers 1731–1800

Early in the nineteenth century four sets of Parliamentary Papers were made up at the instance of Speaker Abbot. They consisted of documents which were then available, and should not be considered as complete collections of all published papers. It is important to remember this when using the list which was based on the set preserved in the House, namely the *Catalogue of Papers Printed by Order of the House of Commons, from the year 1731 to 1800 in the Custody of the Clerk of the Journals* (1807, repr. 1954). This has three parts: Bills, Reports, and Accounts and Papers; and within each the papers are arranged first by year, and within year alphabetically by subject. References are given to the location of documents within the collection. There are three separate indexes, one for each of the above categories of papers.

Hansard's Catalogue 1696–1834

Another collection of early papers is the so-called "First Series" or *Reports from Committees of the House of Commons, 1715–1801; forming the Series of Fifteen Volumes of Reports.* It is in fact a reprint of reports which had been printed as separates, together with a list of others whose full text appeared in the *Journals of the House of Commons.* An index based on this collection but extended to cover documents issued during the next thirty years was issued as House of Commons Paper 626 of 1834 with the title *Catalogue of Parliamentary Reports, and a Breviate of their Contents: arranged Under Heads according to the Subjects, 1696–1834.* Entries were grouped under sixteen headings, for example Ecclesiasti-

Judicial.

Fees in Law Courts, 1832 :

1.—[Report from the Select Committee respecting Fees in Courts of Law, 1732.
Journals, vol. 21, p. 892.
Subjects.—Origin of Fees.—Ancient regulations and commissions of inquiry.—Present fees.—Opinions on them.

Expiring Laws, 1796—1802 :

2.—[Report from the Select Committee, in 1796, upon Temporary Laws Expired and Expiring; and, in 1802, upon Laws Expired and Expiring of the United Kingdom. First Series, vol. xiv. pp. 34. 73.
Subjects.—Investigation into the nature, extent and duration of the temporary laws of the realm; also into the propriety of further temporary or permanent renewal of specific statutes.
For the Annual Reports, from 1803 to 1834, *see* General Index to Sessional Papers.

Promulgation of Statutes, 1796—1801 :

3.—[Report from the Select Committee, in 1796, as relating to Great Britain ; and, in 1801, as relating to the United Kingdom. First Series, vol. xiv. pp. 119. 138.
Subjects.—On the most effectual means of promulgating the statutes of the realm; with observations in reference to a preceding inquiry into the state of the temporary laws. *See* likewise under Head IV. No. 96.

Administration of Justice, England :
Chancery Court, 1810—1833 :

4.—Report from the Select Committee on the Lords' Proceedings on the state of Causes in the Court of Chancery. Sess. 1810–11, (194.) vol. 3, p. 923. [1.]

5.—First Report from the Select Committee on the causes that retard the Decision of Suits in the High Court of Chancery.
Sess. 1810–11, (244.) vol. 3, p. 925. [1.]

6.—Second Report from the same Committee. Sess. 1812, (273.) vol. 2, p. 343. [1.]
Subject.—Procrastination of proceedings in Chancery.

7.—Report made to His Majesty by the Commissioners appointed to inquire into the Practice of Chancery. Sess. 1826, (143.) vol. 15, p. 1. [2. 3.]
Subject.—On the present Practice, and proposed Regulations, in the Court of Chancery.

8.—Report of the Lords Commissioners appointed to make a survey of the different Courts in England, Wales and Berwick-upon-Tweed ;—as to the Court of Chancery:—dated 8 November 1740. Sess. 1814–15, (98.) vol. 11, p. 9. [4.]

9.—List of Fees payable to the several Officers of the High Court of Chancery, conformable to the Report of 8th November 1740.
Sess. 1814–15, (183.) vol. 11, p. 111. [4.]

Chancery Offices :

10.—Report from the Select Committee on Chancery Offices.
Sess. 1833, (685.) vol. 14, p. 1.

FIG. 9. *Hansard's Catalogue and Breviate of Parliamentary Papers 1696–1834.*
(By kind permission of Basil Blackwell and Mott Ltd.)

cal Subjects, Judicial, Parliamentary, Trade and Manufactures, Emigration, Poor and Poor-Laws, and Population. There was also a detailed index of subjects and names.

In 1953 this work was reprinted (by Basil Blackwell, Oxford) under the direction of P. and G. Ford who also added a list of House of Lords and House of Commons Papers which were lacking in the original. They gave their reprint the title of *Hansard's Catalogue and Breviate of Parliamentary Papers 1696–1834;* and it is normally this version which is found in libraries.

A specimen page is reproduced in Fig. 9.

NON-OFFICIAL INDEXES

Fords' Breviates and Select Lists

The official indexes are paralleled by a series of select lists and descriptive indexes produced by P. and G. Ford, as follows:

(i) *Select List of British Parliamentary Papers 1955–1964* (1970) (with Diana Marshallsay);

(ii) *A Breviate of Parliamentary Papers 1940–1954: war and reconstruction* (1961);

(iii) *A Breviate of Parliamentary Papers 1917–1939* (1951);

(iv) *A Breviate of Parliamentary Papers 1900–1916: the formation of the Welfare State* (1957).

All the breviates follow the same pattern, comprising abstracts of reports and other material (both Parliamentary and Non-Parliamentary) issued by committees and commissions or similar bodies of investigation into economic, social and constitutional questions, and matters of law and administration. Such things as statistical returns and papers dealing with foreign affairs are omitted. The entries, which are grouped under broad subject headings, each give a full bibliographical reference and a summary of the paper which may be only a few lines or run to more than a page (Fig. 10). Various lists, notably of annual reports of government departments, are added as appendices; and each volume has an alphabetical index of key-

A Breviate of
PARLIAMENTARY PAPERS, 1940-1954
—

I. MACHINERY OF GOVERNMENT

1. The Crown
2. Channel Islands
3. Parliament
4. Ministers
5. Organisation of Departments

6. Civil Service
7. (a) Local Government
   (b) Local Taxation and Financial Administration
8. London

1. THE CROWN
The Title of the Sovereign

pp. 3. 1953

1952-53 Cmd. 8748, xxiv, 847
pres. Feb., 1953

'The existing form of the Royal Title is not in accord with current constitutional relations within the Commonwealth. In particular it is incorrect in its reference to Ireland and it fails to reflect the special position of the Sovereign as head of the Commonwealth. The Prime Ministers and other representatives of the Commonwealth agreed that the various forms of the Title, should, in addition to an appropriate territorial designation, have as their common element the description of the Sovereign as Queen of Her other Realms and Territories and Head of the Commonwealth.' For this country it should be 'Elizabeth the Second, by the Grace of God of the United Kingdom of Great Britain and Northern Ireland and Her other Realms and Territories Queen, Head of the Commonwealth, Defender of the Faith.'

Civil List

Sel. Cttee. Rep., proc. pp. 7. 1947

1947-48 (18) vi, 679
apptd. Nov., o.p. Dec., 1947

The Prime Minister, Anderson, Benson, Butcher, Churchill, Colman (Miss), Corlett, Davies, Eden, Foot, Greenwood, Howard, Kirkwood, Lawson, McGhee, O'Neill, Scott-Elliot, Stanley, Webb, L. Winterton.

'To consider His Majesty's Most Gracious Message of the 18th November relating to Provision for Her Royal Highness the Princess.Elizabeth and Lieutenant Philip Mountbatten, R.N., on the occasion of their marriage, and to the Civil List and other matters connected therewith.'

In his Gracious Message His Majesty desired that provision made for Her Royal Highness and His Royal Highness the Duke of Edinburgh should not impose a burden on the people at a time of grave economic difficulties, and stated that he was willing to make available a sum of £100,000 derived from savings on the Civil List during the war. Recommended that the annuity of £15,000 at present paid to Her Royal Highness the Princess Elizabeth should be raised to £40,000 and to the Duke of Edinburgh an annuity of £10,000.

Civil List

Sel. Cttee. Rep., proc., app. pp. 32. 1952

1951-52 (224) v, 1

FIG. 10 Ford, P. and Ford, G., *Breviate of Parliamentary Papers 1940–1954*.
(By kind permission of Basil Blackwell and Mott Ltd.)

Select List of
British Parliamentary Papers, 1833-1899

I. GOVERNMENT

1. The Crown, Peerage.	4. Civil Service.
2. Parliament.	5. Local Government, Local Taxation.
3. Departments.	6. London.

1. The Crown, Peerage

1833	(646)	vii	Civil List Charges. Sel. Cttee. Rep.
1837	[72]	xxxiv Pt. I	Civil List. Fees, Gratuities, Perquisites and Emoluments. R. Com. Rep.
1837–8	(22)	xxii	Civil List. Accounts and Estimates. Sel. Cttee. Rep.
1837–8	(263)	xxiii	Civil List Pensions. Sel. Cttee. HL. Rep.
	(621)	,,	—— 2nd Rep.
1867	[3885]	xxxi	Oaths. R. Com. Rep., etc.
1867	(191)	lvii	Oath taken by the Sovereign at the Coronation, etc.
	(191–I)	,,	——
1887	(183)	ix	Jubilee Thanksgiving Service (Westminster Abbey). Sel. Cttee. Rep., etc.
1889	(271)	xi	Grants to the Royal Family. Sel. Cttee. Rep., etc.
1837	(365)	xx	Duke of Marlborough's Pension. Sel. Cttee. Reb.
1847	(HL.132)	xxv	Representative Peers of Scotland. Sel. Cttee HL. Rep., mins. of ev.
1874	(HL.140)	viii	Representative Peerage of Scotland and Ireland. Sel. Cttee. HL. Rep., mins. of ev., etc.
1877	(338)	x	Lord Cochrane's Petition. Sel. Cttee. Rep., mins. of ev., etc.
1882	(HL.128)	vii	Law as to Claims and Assumptions of Titles of Peerage. Sel. Cttee. HL. Rep., mins. of ev., etc.
	(HL.128)	,,	—— App.
1895	(302)	x	Earldom of Selborne. Sel. Cttee. Rep., mins. of ev., etc.

2. Parliament

(1) *Elections*

Note. The following list includes documents only on elections generally. For reports on elections in particular constituencies see APPENDIX I.

1834	(591)	ix	Expenses charged by Returning Officers. Sel. Cttee. Rep., mins. of ev., etc.
1835	(547)	viii	Bribery at Elections. Sel. Cttee. Rep., mins. of ev., etc.
1836	(496)	xxi	Controverted elections. Sel. Cttee. Rep.
1837–8	(44)	x	Laws relating to the trial of controverted elections. Sel. Cttee. Rep.
1837	(215)	xii	Fictitious votes in Scotland. Sel. Cttee. 1st Rep.
1837–8	(590)	xiv	—— Sel. Cttee. Rep., mins. of ev., etc.
1837–8	(50)	x	Controverted Election Fees. Sel. Cttee. Rep.
1837–8	(441)	x	Election Petition Recognizances. Sel. Cttee. Rep.
1840	(138)	ix	Controverted elections. Sel. Cttee. Rep., mins. of ev., etc.

FIG. 11. Ford, P. and Ford, G., *Select List of British Parliamentary Papers 1833–1899.* (By kind permission of Basil Blackwell and Mott Ltd.)

words and an index of chairmen and authors. In the select list for 1955–64 no summaries are included.

For the period between *Hansard's Catalogue 1696–1834* and the earliest of their breviates the Fords compiled a *Select List of British Parliamentary Papers 1833–1899* (1953). It covers the same types of papers as the breviates, but there are no summaries. Appendices list reports on election petitions, reports on charities and charitable educational endowments, statistics, and annual reports of government departments; and the volume concludes with an alphabetical index of subjects and names. A specimen page is reproduced in Fig. 11.

King's List 1801–1820

In 1904 P. S. King and Son published a *Catalogue of Parliamentary Papers 1801–1900 with a few of earlier date,* compiled by Hilda Vernon Jones. A supplement for 1901–10 was published in 1912, and a further supplement for 1911–20 in 1922. The work is arranged alphabetically by subject headings with cross references, and every entry is given a series number within square brackets (which should not be read as Command numbers). Years of publication and prices are given, but there are no references to sessional volumes. Most of the important diplomatic correspondence, reports of Royal Commissions and Select Committees are included, and in cases where the title of a paper does not adequately describe its contents annotations are provided. Bills are not included. The first volume is particularly useful for discovering the year of publication of nineteenth-century papers.

Lambert's List, 1701–1750

In 1968 the List and Index Society distributed to subscribers a *List of House of Commons Sessional Papers 1701–1750,* edited by Sheila Lambert. This contains a very useful introduction to the use of eighteenth-century official papers, with references to other bibliographical aids. The list itself is arranged chronologically, session by session; and for each session there are usually three pages, the first showing Bills, the second papers printed separately and the third papers not printed separately but entered in full in the *Journals of the House of Commons.* As regards

Bills, Public Acts are entered first, then Private Acts — both in order of chapter numbers — and finally failed Bills; and in a column for locations abbreviations are given which correspond to those in L. W. Hanson's *Contemporary Printed Sources for British and Irish Economic History, 1701–50* (1963). The next page for each session shows papers that were printed separately, under four headings: Reports of Commissioners, Reports of Committees, Accounts and Papers, and Command Papers. References are given as appropriate to the location of items in the First Series Collection, the Abbot Collection, and the British Museum. For papers not printed separately references are given to their location in the *Journals of the House of Commons*.

Diplomatic Papers

Two volumes cover documents relating to foreign affairs and diplomatic questions:

(i) VOGEL, ROBERT, *A Breviate of British Diplomatic Blue Books 1919–1939* (1963); and

(ii) TEMPERLEY, HAROLD and PENSON, LILLIAN M., *A Century of Diplomatic Blue Books 1814–1914* (1934, rep. 1966).

Temperley and Penson set the pattern which Vogel has continued. Each entry is annotated to show the date on which the paper was laid before Parliament, and the reason for its presentation, i.e. whether by Command or in reply to an Address from one or other of the Houses of Parliament. The date of the Address and that of presentation may be used as a guide to debates in Parliament. Both volumes have good indexes.

A third volume to be noted here is the *Guide to the Principal Parliamentary Papers relating to the Dominions 1812–1911* compiled by M. A. Adam, J. Ewing and J. Munro (1913) which covers Parliamentary Papers relating to Australia, New Zealand, South Africa, emigration and colonization, and miscellaneous dominions.

Chairmen and Authors

Many reports of committees and other bodies are best known by the

BOSANQUET, C. I. C.

1956 Pigs and Bacon. Reorganisation Commission (Chairman: Dr. C. I. C. Bosanquet) Report May 29, 1956.
Session 1955-56: Cmd. 9795.

1964 Demand for Agricultural Graduates. Report of an Interdepartmental Committee. (Chairman: C. I. C. Bosanquet, Esq., M A., D.C.L.). April 30, 1964.
Session 1963-64: Cmnd. 2419.

BOSWORTH, G. S.

1966 Report on Education and Training Requirements for the Electrical and Mechanical Manufacturing Industries. (Chairman: Mr. G. S. Bosworth). (Joint publication of the Dept. of Education and Science, M. of Technology and the Committee on Manpower Resources for Science and Technology.)
Dept. of Education and Science.

BOURDILLON, H. T.

1962 Standards of Public Library Service in England and Wales. Report of the Working Party appointed by the Minister of Education in March, 1961. (Chairman: Mr. H. T Bourdillon, C.M.G.). September 20, 1962.
M. of Education.

BOWEN, R.

1966 Aden. Miscellaneous No. 15 (1966). Report by Mr. Roderic Bowen, Q.C., on Procedures for the Arrest, Interrogation and Detention of Suspected Terrorists in Aden.
November 14, 1966.
Session 1966-67: Cmnd. 3165.

BOWES, H. L.

1958 Inland Waterways. Report of the Committee of Inquiry (Chairman: H. L. Bowes).
June 11, 1958.
Session 1957-58: Cmnd. 486.

BOYD OF MERTON, A. T., Viscount (formerly A. T. LENNOX-BOYD)

1957 Singapore Constitutional Conference held in London in March and April, 1957. Report. (Chairman: Rt. Hon. A. Lennox-Boyd, M.P.).. April 11, 1957.
Session 1956-57: Cmnd. 147.

Nigeria Constitutional Conference. Report by the Nigeria Constitutional Conference held in London in May and June, 1957 (Chairman: Rt. Hon. Alan Lennox-Boyd, M.P.)
June 26, 1957.
Session 1956-57: Cmnd. 207.

1958 Nigeria. Report by the Resumed Nigeria Constitutional Conference (Chairman: Rt. Hon. Alan Lennox-Boyd, M.P.) held in London in September and October, 1958.
October 27, 1958.
Session 1958-59: Cmnd. 569

BOYD ORR, J., Lord

1943 Infant Mortality in Scotland. The Report of a Sub-Committee of the Scientific Advisory Committee. August 20, 1943. (Chairman: Sir John Boyd Orr, D.S.O., M.C., M.D., D.Sc., LL.D., F.R.S.).
Dept. of Health for Scotland.

FIG. 12. Morgan, A. Mary, *British Government Publications: an index to chairmen and authors 1941–1966.* (By kind permission of the Library Association.)

names of their chairmen, and other documents are commonly referred to by their authors. Thus one often refers to the "Willink Commission" instead of the *Royal Commission on the Police* (1960), or the "Newsom Report" instead of *Half our Future: report of the Central Advisory Council on Education* (1963). Chairmen and authors are included in many of the indexes already described, but a compilation exclusively devoted to them is *British Government Publications: an index to chairmen and authors 1941–1966*, edited by A. Mary Morgan (1969) (Fig. 12). This unfortunately had a number of errors and omissions, and a seven-page list of amendments was issued in 1972.

Command Papers

In order to consult a given Command Paper in a library containing the bound volumes of sessional papers it is necessary to know in which session it appeared. This can readily be determined from the concordance on pp. 65-66. Alternatively one may consult the *Numerical Finding List of British Command Papers published 1833–1961/2* compiled by E. Di Roma and J. A. Rosenthal (1967) which prints the number of every Command Paper and against each indicates the session in which it was published, the sessional volume number and the page number within the volume.

Serial Publications

Serial Publications in the British Parliamentary Papers, 1900–1968 by Frank Rodgers (1971) identifies and lists by issuing agency the serials that have occurred in the Sessional Papers and provides a combined subject and agency index to them.

GUIDES TO OFFICIAL PUBLICATIONS

There are four sound general guides to British official publications. They are:

FORD, P. and G., *A Guide to Parliamentary Papers* (3rd edn. 1972).

G.B. Treasury, *Official Publications* (1958, repr. 1963).

OLLE, J. G., *An Introduction to British Government Publications* (2nd edn. 1973)

RODGERS, F. and PHELPS, R. B., *A Guide to British Parliamentary Papers* (1967).

More specialized are:

ARGLES, M., *British Government Publications in Education during the 19th Century* (1971). A twenty-page booklet which includes a chronological list of some of the more important circulars.

GOSDEN, P. H. J. H., *Educational Administration in England and Wales: a bibliographical guide* (1967).

HIGSON, C. W. J., *Sources for the History of Education* (1967). Includes a section on official publications.

MACLURE, J. S., *Educational Documents, England and Wales, 1816–1963* (1965). Reproduces extracts from official reports.

STAVELEY, R. and PIGGOTT, M., *Government Information and the Research Worker* (2nd edn. 1965).

VAUGHAN, J. E., *Board of Education Circulars: a finding list and index* (1972).

VAUGHAN, J. E. and ARGLES, M., *British Government Publications concerning Education* (3rd edn. 1969).

CHAPTER 3

Parliamentary Proceedings

ORDER PAPER OF THE HOUSE OF COMMONS

For the House of Commons to get through its considerable work load its Members must adhere to a detailed agenda and conduct their business according to precisely specified procedures. Standing orders of the House were dealt with in Chapter 1; as for the day's agenda this is printed in a document called the *Order Paper*. It starts with questions for oral answer and questions for written answer, the former being asterisked (Fig. 17). These set in motion the research necessary to enable departments of the Civil Service to provide their Ministers with the information upon which to base their replies. As will be seen later (p. 107) Answers to Parliamentary Questions are published in the *Official Report of Debates (Hansard)* and constitute a valuable source of factual data.

Under the heading "Orders of the Day and Notices of Motions" are listed the stages of Bills which are to be taken and motions put down by Members for debate.

Further questions and motions occur under the heading "Notices of Questions and Motions given on [date]". Questions are listed under future dates, and again those for oral answer are asterisked. Motions appear either under a particular date or under the heading "An Early Day"; in each case the motion appears in full along with the names of Members supporting it. Every Monday there appears a cumulation of "Notices of Motions and Orders of the Day which now stand in the Order Book of the House of Commons". It begins with questions for oral answer (under dates), goes on to notices of motions (under dates), then lists notices of motions for which no dates have been fixed and provides an index to them.

Another section of the *Order Paper* is devoted to "Notices of Amendments" to Bills which Members intend to move. Those which actually are

moved can be ascertained and their outcome discovered from the minutes of proceedings of standing committees (see pp. 49-50).

VOTES AND PROCEEDINGS

The work of the House itself and of its standing committees is minuted in the *Votes and Proceedings* (1680–). Issued daily while Parliament is in session they record all the business that was transacted on the previous day. They do not, however, normally record what was actually said – debates are reported in *Hansard* and the *Standing Committee Debates* described in Chapter 8. The only exceptions to this are instances when the House specially orders statements to be entered and, by ancient custom, the inclusion of the Speech from the Throne both on the opening and the prorogation of Parliament. Another addition to the usual contents is the order passed by the House early in the session which gives the Speaker the necessary authority to appoint a printer for the *Votes and Proceedings* (invariably nowadays the Controller of Her Majesty's Stationery Office) and at the same time forbids any other person to print them.

Reports of *Standing Committee Proceedings* form a separate section; they differ from the minutes of proceedings of standing committees in that the latter include division lists which name Members and how they voted, while the former, on the other hand, simply state, for example, "Negatived on division".

Also included in the *Votes and Proceedings* are particulars of accounts and papers which have been presented. Entries take the following form:

Community Relations Commission, – Copy *presented,* of Report of the Commission for the period 1st January 1968 to 31st March 1969 [by Act]; to lie upon the Table and to be *printed.* [No. 259]

If the document is not to be printed then this last statement and the document number are omitted. Also, when a paper is laid upon the Table by the Clerk of the House the words "to lie upon the Table" are omitted.

DIVISION LISTS

Along with the *Votes and Proceedings* go the *Division Lists* which record the names of those Members who voted with the "Ayes" and those with the "Noes" (Fig. 13). It should be noted, however, that this information also appears in *Hansard*, which is the source more usually consulted for details of divisions (see p. 107).

BILLS

The *Public Bill List* and *List of Private Bills* are described on pp. 93, 95 and 97.

THE BLUE PAPER

Together, the *Order Paper*, the *Votes and Proceedings* (including the *Standing Committee Proceedings*) and the *Division Lists* make up what is commonly referred to as the *Blue Paper*, so named because some of the items are printed on blue tinted paper. It is printed overnight, and the Vote Office arranges for it to be delivered by hand early in the morning to Members residing within three miles of the House, and to be posted to the rest.

It is not usual for libraries which receive copies of the *Blue Paper* to preserve them beyond the current session of Parliament. They have limited research value; divisions and answers to parliamentary questions are recorded in *Hansard*, and proceedings in the *Journals*.

JOURNALS OF THE HOUSE OF COMMONS

The *Journals*, published sessionally, are the permanent official records of the House. As such one of their principal uses is as an authority on points of procedure; and the Clerks at the table have recourse to them when advising the Speaker on matters of precedent. They are printed by H.M.S.O. under the direction of the Clerk of the House.

With the exception of the period 1581–1602 a complete set is available back to 1547; and it is interesting to note in passing that Samuel

6.59 Before Midnight   **DIVISION LIST**   9

Monday 2nd May 1966

Number 3

Building Control Bill,—Order for Second Reading read ;

Motion made, and Question put, That the Bill be now read a second time :—The House *divided :* Ayes 279, Noes 181.

AYES

Abse, Leo
Albu, Austen
Allaun, Frank (*Salford, E.*)
Alldritt, Walter
5 Allen, Scholefield
Anderson, Donald
Archer, Peter
Armstrong, Ernest
Ashley, Jack
10 Atkins, Ronald (*Preston, N.*)
Atkinson, Norman (*Tottenhm*)
Bacon, Rt Hon Alice
Bagier, Gordon A. T.
Barnett, Joel
15 Baxter, William
Bence, Cyril
Benn, Rt Hn Anthony Wedgw'd
Bennett, J. (*Glasgow, Bridgeton*)
Bidwell, Sydney
20 Binns, John
Bishop, E. S.
Blackburn, F.
Boardman, H.
Booth, Albert
25 Boston, Terence
Bowden, Rt Hon Herbert
Boyden, James
Braddock, Mrs E. M.
Bray, Dr Jeremy
30 Brooks, Edwin
Broughton, Dr A. D. D.
Brown, Bob (*Newcastle, W.*)
Buchan, Norman
Butler, Herbert (*Hackney, C.*)
35 Butler, Mrs. Joyce (*W'd Gr'n*)
Cant, R. B.
Carter-Jones, Lewis
Castle, Rt Hon Barbara
Chapman, Donald
40 Coe, Denis

C

Coleman, Donald
Concannon, J. D.
Corbet, Mrs Freda
Cousins, Rt Hon Frank
45 Craddock, George (*Bradford, S.*)
Crawshaw, Richard
Crosland, Rt Hon Anthony
Cullen, Mrs Alice
Dalyell, Tam
50 Davidson, A. (*Accrington*)
Davies, Dr Ernest (*Stretford*)
Davies, G. Elfed (*Rhondda. E.*)
Davies, Ednyfed H. (*Conway*)
Davies, Harold (*Leek*)
55 Davies, Ifor (*Gower*)
Davies, Robert (*Cambridge*)
Davies, S. O. (*Merthyr*)
Delargy, Hugh
Dell, Edmund
60 Dempsey, James
Dewar, D. C.
Diamond, Rt Hon John
Dickens, J. M. Y.
Dobson, Ray
65 Doig, Peter
Donnelly, Desmond
Dunn, James A.
Dunnett, Jack
Dunwoody, Mrs G. P. (*Exeter*)
70 Dunwoody, Dr John (*Falm'th*)
Eadie, Alex
Edwards, Rt Hn Ness (*Caerphilly*)
Edwards, William (*Merioneth*)
Ellis, John
75 English, Michael
Ennals, David
Ensor, David
Evans, Albert (*Islington, S.W.*)
Faulds, Andrew
80 Fernyhough, E.

Fitch, Alan (*Wigan*)
Fletcher, Raymond (*Ilkeston*)
Fletcher, Ted (*Darlington*)
Floud, Bernard
85 Foley, Maurice
Foot, Michael (*Ebbw Vale*)
Ford, Ben
Forrester, John
Fowler, Gerry
90 Fraser, J. D. (*Norwood*)
Fraser, Rt Hn Tom (*Hamilton*)
Freeson, Reginald
Galpern, Sir Myer
Gardner, A. J.
95 Garrett, W. E.
Garrow, Alex
Ginsburg, David
Gordon Walker, Rt Hon P. C.
Gourlay, Harry
100 Gray, Dr Hugh
Gregory, Arnold
Griffiths, David (*Rother Valley*)
Griffiths, Rt Hon J. (*Llanelly*)
Griffiths, Will (*Exchange*)
105 Hale, Leslie (*Oldham. W.*)
Hamilton, James (*Bothwell*)
Hamilton, William (*West Fife*)
Harper, Joseph
Harrison, Walter (*Wakefield*)
110 Hart, Mrs Judith
Haseldine, Norman
Hattersley, Roy
Healey, Rt Hon Denis
Henig, Stanley
115 Herbison, Rt Hon Margaret
Hilton, W. S.
Hobden, Dennis (*Kemptown*)
Hooley, Frank
Horner, John
120 Houghton, Rt Hon Douglas

FIG. 13. *Division List*

Richardson, the novelist, supervised the retrospective printing of volumes for 1547 to 1741 in his role as Printer to the House of Commons. Material for these early years were derived from the records which had been made by various Clerks to the House, notably John Seymour, Clerk from 1548 to 1567 and Fulk Onslow, Clerk from 1567 to 1602. The House itself first expressed concern for the preservation of its records in 1604 when a warrant was drawn up requiring "that a Room, or Place, be provided near at hand, with convenient Presses and Shelves, for the Disposing and Preserving of the said Register, Papers, and Entries; and for the Clerk and his Servants to attend upon all Occasions, for the Service for the said House". (*Journals of the House of Commons,* vol. 1, 1547–1628, p. 215.)

Prior to session 1801 committee and other reports were printed in the body of the *Journals,* but on an instruction from Speaker Abbot they began, with volume 56, 1801, to be printed as appendices. However, with the increasing output of separately printed and numbered papers a good deal of duplication occurred, and the appendices were discontinued after volume 89, 1834.

Each printed volume has an index, and in addition there are cumulative indexes as follows: 1547–1714, 1714–74, 1774–1800, 1801–20, 1820–37, 1837–52, 1852–65, 1866–79. Thereafter, beginning with 1880–90, there are regular decennial indexes (Fig. 14).

The *Journals* were first placed on sale to the public in 1836, and a useful account of their history appears in Appendix II of the *Report of the Committee on Publications and Debates Reports* (1914–16 H.C. 321).

Today, the *Journals* are made up largely from the *Votes and Proceedings,* but the content is not entirely the same. For example, whilst particulars of papers presented to the House are listed again in the *Journals,* division lists are not carried forward.

MINUTES OF PROCEEDINGS OF THE HOUSE OF LORDS

The *Minutes of Proceedings* (1824–) perform for the Lords what the *Blue Paper* performs for the Commons. After the minutes themselves come division lists, and these are followed by the headings "Causes" and "Appeal Committee" which refer to the House's legal functions. Then comes a section devoted to "Notices and Orders for the Day" in which entries are grouped under future dates followed by those for which no

GENERAL INDEX

TO THE JOURNALS OF THE HOUSE OF COMMONS

Volume 206, 1950-51, to Volume 215, 1959-60

ABANDONMENT OF ANIMALS:

[1959-60.] Bill to prohibit the abandonment of animals; and for purposes connected therewith; presented, 36. (*Cited as Abandonment of Animals Act*, 1960) R.A., 250.

ABERDEEN CHARTERED ACCOUNTANTS' WIDOWS' FUND ORDER CONFIRMATION:

[1950-51.] Bill to confirm a Provisional Order under the Private Legislation Procedure (Scotland) Act, 1936, relating to Aberdeen Chartered Accountants' Widows' Fund; presented, 186. (*Cited as Aberdeen Chartered Accountants' Widows' Fund Order Confirmation Act*, 1951) R.A., 213.

ABERDEEN CORPORATION ORDER CONFIRMATION:

[1955-56.] Bill to confirm a Provisional Order under the Private Legislation Procedure (Scotland) Act, 1936, relating to Aberdeen Corporation; presented, 49. (*Cited as Aberdeen Corporation Order Confirmation Act*, 1955) R.A., 88.

[1956-57.] Bill to confirm a Provisional Order under the Private Legislation Procedure (Scotland) Act, 1936, relating to Aberdeen Corporation; presented, 213. (*Cited as Aberdeen Corporation Order Confirmation Act*, 1957) R.A., 262.

ABERDEEN EXTENSION ORDER CONFIRMATION:

[1951-52.] Bill to confirm a Provisional Order under the Private Legislation Procedure (Scotland) Act, 1936, relating to Aberdeen Extension; presented, 326. (*Cited as Aberdeen Extension Order Confirmation Act*, 1952) R.A., 353.

ABERDEEN HARBOUR ORDER CONFIRMATION:

[1952-53.] Bill to confirm a Provisional Order under the Private Legislation Procedure (Scotland) Act, 1936, relating to Aberdeen Harbour; presented, 194. (*Cited as Aberdeen Harbour Order Confirmation Act*, 1953) R.A., 210.

[1955-56.] Bill to confirm a Provisional Order under the Private Legislation Procedure (Scotland) Act, 1936, relating to Aberdeen Harbour; presented, 378. (*Cited as Aberdeen Harbour Order Confirmation Act*, 1956) R.A., 406.

[1957-58.] Bill to confirm a Provisional Order. under the Private Legislation Procedure (Scotland) Act, 1936, relating to Aberdeen Harbour; presented, 12. (*Cited as Aberdeen Harbour Order Confirmation Act*, 1957) R.A., 37.

[1959-60.] Bill to confirm a Provisional Order under the Private Legislation Procedure (Scotland) Act, 1936, relating to Aberdeen Harbour; presented, 31. (*Cited as Aberdeen Harbour Order Confirmation Act*, 1959) R.A., 77.

ABERDEEN HARBOUR (SUPERANNUATION) ORDER CONFIRMATION:

[1956-57.] Bill to confirm a Provisional Order under the Private Legislation Procedure (Scotland) Act, 1936, relating to Aberdeen Harbour (Superannuation); presented, 213. (*Cited as Aberdeen Harbour (Superannuation) Order Confirmation Act*, 1957) R.A., 262.

ABINGDON CORPORATION:

[1950-51.] Bill to extend the boundaries of the borough of Abingdon; to empower the Mayor Aldermen and Burgesses of the borough to acquire and use lands; to provide for the extinction of common or commonable rights over Abingdon Common; to make provision with regard to fishing in and in the neighbourhood of the borough; to provide for the dissolution of a joint committee appointed by the Council of the borough and the Parish Council of the parish of Saint Helen Without; to make further provision for the improvement health local government and finances of the borough; and for other purposes; presented, 76. (*Cited as Abingdon Corporation Act*, 1951) R.A., 319.

ABORTION:

[1952-53.] Bill to amend the law relating to abortion; presented, 24.

ACCOMMODATION AGENCIES:

[1952-53.] Bill to prohibit the taking of certain commissions in dealings with persons seeking houses or flats to let and the unauthorised advertisement for letting of houses or flats; ordered; presented, 65. (*Cited as Accommodation Agencies Act*, 1953) R.A., 273.

FIG. 14. *Journals of the House of Commons: General Index 1950–51 to 1959–60*

date has been named. Next there are "Questions for Written Answer", and finally lists of "Bills in Progress". (see p. 95), "Special Orders in Progress" and "Special Procedure Orders in Progress".

A specimen page is reproduced in Fig. 19.

JOURNALS OF THE HOUSE OF LORDS

The *Journals of the House of Lords* date back to 1509 and are substantially similar to the Commons *Journals*. There are differences, however. For instance, division lists are included, and each day's proceedings are preceded by a list of Members present. Also, since the Lords do not commit Bills to standing committees for detailed consideration a much greater proportion of *Journals* is devoted to giving the texts of amendments and recording the outcome of deliberations thereon.

Each sessional volume has its own index, and in addition there are cumulative indexes as follows: 1509–1649 (Commonwealth), 1660–1714, 1714–79, 1780–1819, 1820–33, 1833–52/3. Thereafter, beginning with 1854–63, there are regular decennial indexes.

CHAPTER 4

Commons and Lords Papers

HOUSE OF COMMONS PAPERS

Whenever the House of Commons requires the submission of a report, and orders it to be printed the resultant document is issued in a numbered series of House of Commons Papers. The series in fact includes papers presented to both Houses as well as to the Commons alone. House of Commons Papers arise in different ways, as follows:

(i) "Returns" are printed in response to a direction of the House to obtain certain information. Returns from departments headed by a Secretary of State are called for by the House by means of a Humble Address to Her Majesty: those from other departments by means of an Order of the House;

(ii) "Act Papers" comprise reports or accounts required to be laid before Parliament under the provision of certain Acts; though Act Papers of less general interest to Members are printed as Non-Parliamentary Publications, and others are simply laid open to inspection by Members in typescript form;

(iii) Reports are made by select committees appointed by the House to inquire into special matters. The examination of witnesses is usually recorded in Minutes of Evidence, and papers submitted to a committee are usually published as appendices to its report; and

(iv) Minutes are printed of proceedings of standing committees appointed to examine Bills.

House of Commons Papers are identified by their serial numbers which are printed without brackets at the bottom left of their title pages. A fresh sequence of numbers begins each session; and citations must therefore include the session, e.g. 1968–69 H.C. 126. Naturally the annual *Cata-*

logue of Government Publications, which lists papers issued during the *calendar* year, includes H.C. Papers from each of two consecutive sessions. Each H.C. Paper nowadays (since 1949) normally appears twice in the catalogue: once in a numerical sequence of papers, and again under the department or other body responsible for producing it.

In its classified list the annual catalogue includes a heading for the House of Commons itself, and the following is an abbreviated list of the items which appeared under that heading in the 1967 catalogue:

House of Commons Members' Fund. Accounts 1965–66 (H.C. 346)
Minutes of Proceedings, e.g.
    Agriculture Bill. Standing Committee A (H.C. 248)
    Companies Bill [Lords]. Standing Committee E (H.C. 519)
    Countryside (Scotland) Bill. Scottish Standing Committee (H.C. 523)
    Criminal Law Bill [Lords]. 2nd Reading Committee (H.C. 374)
    Estimates Committee (H.C. 670)
    Refreshment Houses Bill [Lords]. Standing Committee H (H.C. 515)
    Rural Development in Wales and Monmouthshire. Welsh Grand Committee (H.C. 387)
    Water (Scotland) Bill [Consideration of Principle]. Scottish Grand Committee (H.C. 333)
Parliamentary Commissioner for Administration. Session 1967–68:
    1st Report (H.C. 6)
    2nd Report (H.C. 47)
    3rd Report (H.C. 54)
Public Bills. Return for 1966–67 (H.C. 676)

Reports of Committees:
    Estimates
        Session 1966–67: *e.g.*
            6th Report. Building and Natural Resources (H.C. 274)
            9th Report. Economic Affairs (H.C. 548)
            14th Report. Defence and Overseas Affairs (H.C. 666)
        Session 1967–68: *e.g.*
            1st Report. Winter Supplementary Estimates (H.C. 56)
Report from the Committee of Privileges. Session 1966–67 (H.C. 462)

Public Accounts. Session 1966—67: *e.g.*

  3rd Report. Excess Votes (H.C. 369)

  4th Report. Virement between Votes of Service Departments (H.C. 529)

Select Committee on Agriculture. Session 1966—67: *e.g.*

  1st Special Report (H.C. 349)

  Minutes of Evidence *16 items*

Select Committee on Agriculture. British Agriculture, Fisheries and Food and the European Economic Community.

  Vol. I. Report (H.C. 378-XVII)

  Vol. II. Appendices, Minutes of Evidence, Annexes and Index (H.C. 378-XVIII)

Select Committee on House of Commons (Services).

  Session 1966—67: *e.g.*

    9th Report. House of Commons Telephone Service (H.C. 376)

    14th Report. Closed Circuit Television Annunciator System (H.C. 651)

    15th Report. New Parliamentary Buildings (H.C. 652)

  Session 1967—68:

    1st Report. Refreshment Department, House of Commons (H.C. 46)

Select Committee on Nationalised Industries.

  Session 1966—67: *e.g.*

    1st Report. The Post Office:

      Vol. I. Report and Proceedings of the Committee (H.C. 340)

      Vol. II. Minutes of Evidence, Appendices and Index (H.C. 340—I)

Select Committee on Nationalised Industries Sub-Committee A.

  Minutes of Evidence *13 items*

Select Committee on Procedure. Session 1966—67: *e.g.*

  2nd Report. Standing Order No. 9; Urgent and Topical Debates (H.C. 282)

  3rd Report. Methods of Voting (H.C. 283)

Select Committee on Procedure. Sub-Committee A.

  Public Bill Procedure, etc. 6th Report (H.C. 539)

Select Committee on Science and Technology

  Minutes of Evidence *17 items*

Select Committee on Statutory Instruments.

    Session 1966–67: *e.g.*

        3rd Report. The Rate Support Grant Order 1966 (H.C. 303)

        Minutes of Evidence. March 7, 1967 (H.C. 386–I)

Special Reports of Committees.

    Estimates:

        Session 1966–67: *e.g.*

            5th Special Report. Police (H.C. 275)

            9th Special Report. Government Statistical Services (H.C. 444)

        Session 1967–68: *e.g.*

            2nd Special Report. Manpower Training for Industry (H.C. 57)

    Public Accounts:

        Session 1966–67: *e.g.*

            Special Report on Parliament and the Control of University Expenditure (H.C. 290)

Select Committee on Nationalised Industries:

    Session 1966–67: *e.g.*

        1st Special Report. The Post Office (H.C. 576)

Select Committee on Science and Technology:

    Session 1966–67: *e.g.*

        1st Special Report (H.C. 330)

    Session 1967–68:

        1st Special Report (H.C. 32)

Standing Orders of the House of Commons.

    Session 1966–67:

        Private Business 1967 (H.C. 668)

        Public Business 1966 (H.C. 284)

        Public Business. Standing Orders relating to Ways and Means, as amended on 24 October, 1967 (H.C. 675)

    Session 1967–68:

        Public Business. New Standing Orders made and Standing Orders amended on 14 November, 1967 (H.C. 16)

There are several observations which can be made about this list. The first, and most important, is that some of the H.C. Papers cited here belong to session 1966–67 and some to 1967–68. This is because the calendar year 1967 covered by the annual catalogue includes the latter end of the 1966–67 session and the earlier part of the 1967–68 session. In fact the

higher numbers belong to the earlier session and the lower numbers to the later session. This is well brought out in the case of the Special Reports of the Select Committee on Science and Technology; and it shows the importance of including mention of the session when citing a House of Commons Paper.

Secondly, at the beginning of the list are minutes of proceedings of standing committees. These complement the standing committee debates (see p. 108) and include particulars of amendments moved in committee. The first notice of amendments appears in the *Order Paper*, and the outcome of these can be traced in the minutes of proceedings.

The list also shows that whereas select committees, being parliamentary, must of necessity begin and end in the same session, many in fact are reappointed each session on a continuing basis. Also, when dealing with the Estimates Committee,* one should note that its papers appear under two headings: Reports of Committees and Special Reports of Committees. And on the matter of finance, a good many more House of Commons Papers are listed under the Treasury: items such as the Civil Appropriation Accounts, the Civil Estimates,† the Public Accounts (Defence) Votes and the Vote on Account.

What the list does not show are the annual reports which are listed under the appropriate departments. It may also be recalled that the Fords' breviates and select lists described in Chapter 2 include lists of annual reports with full references.

More technical matters such as the method of presenting papers to Parliament are dealt with in the Treasury's booklet *Official Publications* (1958, repr. 1963) where, for example, it is stated that House of Commons Papers can be printed only by order of the House, and that in practice the authority to order the printing of papers is delegated to the Librarian. House of Commons Papers may be presented only when the House is in session, and as they must be presented, ordered to be printed, and numbered by the House before they can finally be printed, the practice of presenting "in dummy" has grown up. In cases where a report has not been completed before a recess a piece of paper bearing only its title is presented, and this allows the full version to be published as soon as it is ready. Presentation consists of sending two copies of the paper to the Votes

* Now Expenditure Committee.
† Now Supply Estimates.

and Proceedings Office (and two copies to the Clerk of the Parliaments, House of Lords, if presentation is also being made to that House). Receipt is noted in the *Votes and Proceedings* as described in the previous chapter.

All H.C. Papers are bound into the volumes of sessional papers which are described on pp. 25, 28.

HOUSE OF LORDS PAPERS

House of Lords Papers are distinguished by their serial numbers which are printed in curved brackets at the bottom left of their title pages. As with H.C. Papers, it is essential to include mention of the session when making a citation, e.g. 1968—69 H.L. 1.

Unlike the Commons series, House of Lords Papers and House of Lords Bills are numbered in the same series. Also, unlike the Commons method of publishing amendments to Bills, is the practice in the Lords of publishing such amendments separately, and numbering them individually in the H.L. series. Often there is also a marshalled list of amendments.

The majority of papers in the series in fact relate to Bills and these are excluded from the list which appears under the House of Lords heading in the annual *Catalogue of Government Publications.* A special case are Consolidated Bills of which the Reports by Joint Committees of the House of Lords and of the House of Commons do appear.

Following, by way of example, is an abbreviated version of the entries in the 1967 catalogue:

Consolidated Bills. Reports by the Joint Committee of the House of Lords and of the House of Commons.

Session 1966—67: *e.g.*

4th Report. Teachers' Superannuation Bill [H.L.] together with the Proceedings of the Committee and Minutes of Evidence (H.L. 18-IV, 151-I) (H.C. 268-I)

10th Report. Road Traffic Regulation (H.L. 264) (H.C. 514) Road Traffic Regulation Bill [H.L.] (H.L. 18-X, 264-I) (H.C. 514-I)

Session 1967—68: *e.g.*

Provisional Collection of Taxes Bill [H.L.] and the Capital Allowances Bill [H.L. together with the proceedings of the Committee

and Minutes of Evidence (H.L. 20-I, 30-I) (H.C. 30-I)

Reports of Committees.

House of Lords Offices.

Session 1966–67:

3rd Report (H.L. 195)

4th Report (H.L. 323)

Session 1967–68:

1st Report (H.L. 23)

Joint Committee on Censorship of the Theatre. Report together with the Proceedings of the Committee. Minutes of Evidence, Appendices and Index (H.L. 255) (H.C. 503)

Joint Committee on the Forestry Bill [H.L.] Special Report (H.L. 162) (H.C. 311)

Procedure of the House

4th Report (H.L. 177)

5th Report (H.L. 254)

Select Committee Reports.

Select Committee on Televising the Proceedings of the House of Lords.

Session 1966–67: 1st Report, etc. (H.L. 190)

2nd Report, etc. (H.L. 284)

Session 1967–68: 1st Report, etc. (H.L. 27)

Select Committee on the Tees Valley and Cleveland Water Bill (H.L. 172)

Standing Orders of the House of Lords relative to Private Bills Provisional Order Confirmation Bills, Special Procedure Orders and Special Orders. Amendments (H.L. 334)

Special Orders Committee of the House of Lords.

Session 1966–67: *e.g.*

15th Report (H.L. 160)

27th Report (H.L. 331)

Session 1967–68: *e.g.*

1st Report (H.L. 14)

Roll of the Lords Spiritual and Temporal (H.L. 1)

Where a paper bears both an H.L. and an H.C. number it is interesting to note that the annual *Catalogue of Government Publications* lists it only under House of Lords Papers; whereas it appears in the *Sessional Index*

under House of Commons Papers, and provision is made for binding it in the volumes of sessional papers, which include only Commons documents.

A complete numerical list of House of Lords Papers and Bills appears at the beginning of the annual *Catalogue of Government Publications*, and tables of contents are available from H.M.S.O. for libraries wishing to bind their sessional sets of papers. There have been three cumulative indexes only: 1801–1859 (1860), 1869–1870 (1872), and 1871–1884/5 (1890).

A description of surviving sets is given in K. A. Mallaber's "The House of Lords Sessional Papers", *Journal of Librarianship*, vol. 4, no. 2, April 1972, pp. 106–114.

CHAPTER 5

Command Papers

NATURE AND SCOPE

A large number of Parliamentary Papers — over three hundred each year — state on their title-pages that they were presented to Parliament "By Command of her Majesty". As with many other parliamentary affairs carried out in the name of the Sovereign, the Queen is never personally involved in this procedure. It is a purely technical device used by Ministers to introduce documents to Parliament which did not have their origin there, and the formula used has led to these items being referred to as Command Papers. Some nineteenth-century papers indicate that they were "printed by Command", but they are not classed as Command Papers since they were not *presented* by Command.

Unlike House of Commons Papers, Command Papers may be printed before presentation to Parliament and they may, in fact, be "presented" during a recess. The relevant House of Commons Standing Order reads:

> If during the existence of a Parliament, papers are commanded by her Majesty to be presented to this House at any time, the delivery of such papers to the Votes and Proceedings Office shall be deemed to be for all purposes the presentation of them to this House.

They again differ from House of Commons Papers in that no order to print is required from the House, and numbering is a matter solely for H.M. Stationery Office. It is usual for Command Papers to be presented on the day before publication, but presentation may take place earlier in the same session. It is, a duty of the Stationery Office to ensure that copies are available for Members of both Houses in the Vote Office on the date of publication previously agreed between H.M.S.O. and the issuing department, and that the public does not have prior access to them.

Normally, Command Papers are discretionary; that is, it is up to the

head of a department to decide, in the light of the paper's importance to Parliament, whether or not it should be presented "By Command". In making this decision, a Minister may consider whether the subject of the paper is one upon which legislation is anticipated. The Treasury Circular No. 38 of 1921 (quoted on p. 18) directed that the presentation of papers by Command should be discontinued except in the cases of "documents relating to matters likely to be the subject of early legislation, or which may be regarded as otherwise essential to Members of Parliament as a whole to enable them to discharge their responsibilities". The Government regularly presents statements of policy to Parliament by means of Command Papers, and this is a particular instance when the term "White Paper" is used. When questioned on the difference between a Green Paper (see p. 228) and a White Paper the Prime Minister replied: "A White Paper indicates the broad lines of the legislation the Government intend to introduce and, very often, of executive action that will be taken." (*H.C.Deb.* vol. 783, 13 May 1969, col. 1220.) Among the 1965–66 Command Papers listed on pp. 59-63 are a number of "Policy White Papers", e.g.

Cmnd.   2852 The Adult Offender
2864 The Scottish Economy
2916 Leasehold Reform in England and Wales
2922 A University of the Air
2928 Leisure in the Countryside, England and Wales

Statements of this kind provide the factual basis for debates in Parliament and offer other interested parties an opportunity to study the Government's intentions and to express the extent of their agreement and the nature of their divergence of opinion. Quotations from some of the papers just noted illustrate these points. *The Adult Offender,* for example, claims to set out "the Government's broad proposals for early reform in our treatment of offenders", and goes on to say that "the present White Paper is published for purposes of discussion". The introduction to *The Scottish Economy* says: "This White Paper sets out the Government's plans for the expansion of the Scottish economy, within the framework of the National Plan, in the period up to 1970." Legislative intent is also clearly expressed. In *Leasehold Reform in England and Wales* it is stated that "The Government will . . . introduce a Bill to give leaseholders . . . greater security and to enable them to acquire the freehold on fair terms."

An exceptional case is that of the Annual Estimates which, although presented by Command, are by their nature so much a part of the business of the House that they are published, on its authority, as House of Commons Papers.

Annual reports of government departments may be published as Command Papers; examples of long standing are the Report of the Commissioners of Her Majesty's Customs and Excise and the Report of the Commissioners of Her Majesty's Inland Revenue. Precedent, however, is no sure guide: although the education report had been issued as a Command Paper for more than a century, *Education and Science in 1969* appeared as a Non-Parliamentary Publication.

The great blue books which describe the social conditions of the nineteenth and early twentieth centuries and record the nation's foreign affairs were also published by Command. The term "blue book" has no significance other than to indicate that the volume in question is provided with a stout paper cover tinted blue. Nowadays, although economists refer to the annual *National Income and Expenditure* (see p.261 as "the blue book", the words are actually printed on only one document published by H.M.S.O., namely *Carriage of Dangerous Goods by Sea (The Blue Book)*.

A large number of the Command Papers in each session are State Papers presented by the Foreign Office, and as these will be described later they have been excluded from the following list. The session 1965—66 has been used for the purpose of exemplifying the nature and scope of Command Papers. This was a short session, due to the General Election of 31 March 1966, and therefore produced a more manageable — though still representative — list of papers.

Command Papers 1965—66 (Excluding State Papers)

Cmnd.

2807 Southern Rhodesia. Documents relating to the negotiations, November 1963—November 1965

2808 Prices and Incomes Policy: an "Early Warning" system

2809 Export of Works of Art, 1964—1965. Twelfth Report of Reviewing Committee

2813 Explosion at Cambrian Colliery, Glamorgan. Report

Cmnd.

2815 Criminal Statistics, England and Wales, 1964

2823 British Broadcasting Corporation. Annual Report and Accounts, 1964–65

2824 Roumanian Property. Accounts, 1964–65

2825 Hungarian Property. Accounts, 1964–65

2826 Bulgarian Property. Accounts, 1964–65

2827 Gift of Stores to the Government of Malta. Treasury Minute

2835 Patents. United Kingdom Patent Law: the effects of the Strasbourg Convention of 1963

2836 Welfare of Animals kept under Intensive Livestock Husbandry Systems. Report of the Technical Committee

2837 Scottish Housing Programme, 1955–1970

2838 The Housing Programme, 1965–1970

2839 National Board for Prices and Incomes. Report no. 6: Salaries of Midland Bank Staff.

2841 Housing Summary. 31st October, 1965

2842 Customs and Excise. Report for 1964–65

2845 Public Accounts Committee. Treasury Minute on the Reports, Session 1964–65

2846 University Grants Committee. Annual Survey, academic year 1964–65

2847 Assessment of Disablement. Report of the Committee

2848 Public Boards. List of Members, as at 1st November, 1965, with Salaries and Allowances

2849 British Guiana Independence Conference. Report

2852 The Adult Offender

2853 Aircraft Industry. Report of the Committee of Inquiry

2855 Re-organisation of the Army Reserves

2856 The Training of Justices of the Peace in England and Wales

2859 Road Safety Legislation, 1965–6

2861 Oversea Migration Board. Statistics for 1964

2862 National Board for Prices and Incomes. Report No. 7: Electricity and Gas Tariffs

2863 Housing Summary. 30th November, 1965

2864 The Scottish Economy, 1965–1970: a plan for expansion

2867 Commonwealth Medical Conference, 1965. Communiqué

Cmnd.

Cmnd.

2902   Defence, 1966–67. Statement on the Defence Estimates, 1966. Part II

2903   Service Pay and Pensions

2905   Industrial Courts Act, 1919. Report of a Court of Inquiry into . . . the dispute between employees in membership of Longbridge Group of Delivery Agents and their employees

2906   Police Areas of the County of Devon and the City of Exeter. Report of an Inquiry in respect of the Objections to the proposed Compulsory Amalgamation

2907   Rents of Houses owned by Local Authorities in Scotland, 1965

2913   Agriculture in Scotland. Report for 1965

2914   Scottish Education Department. Education in Scotland in 1965

2915   Public Expenditure: Planning and Control

2916   Leasehold Reform in England and Wales

2917   Conference on Electoral Law. Letter dated 8th February, 1966 from Mr. Speaker to the Prime Minister

2918   Wales 1965

2919   National Board for Prices and Incomes. Report No. 12: Coal Prices

2920   Housing Summary. 31st January, 1966

2921   Local Government Finance in Scotland

2922   A University of the Air

2923   Local Government Finance in England and Wales

2926   Army (Pensions, etc.) Royal Warrant

2927   Air Service (Pensions, etc.) Order by Her Majesty

2928   Leisure in the Countryside, England and Wales

2929   Bechuanaland Independence Conference, 1966. Report

2931   Post Office Prospects, 1966–67

2932   Conference on Electoral Law. Letter dated 7th March, 1966 from Mr. Speaker to the Prime Minister

2933   Agriculture Acts. Annual Review and Determination of Guarantees, 1966

2934   Legal Aid in Criminal Proceedings Committee. Report

2935   Industrial Courts Act, 1919. Report of a Court of Inquiry into . . . the dispute between Motor Vehicle Collections Ltd. and Avon Car Transporters Ltd.

2936   Statutory Smallholdings Committee. First Report

2937   Shipbuilding Inquiry Committee. Report

NUMBERING

The history of Command Papers dates back at least to the beginning of the eighteenth century. As well as appearing as separate documents they were also at one time printed as appendices to the *Journals of the House of Commons*. The early papers were not, however, serially numbered. The first numbered list occurs in the 1836 index to Parliamentary Papers and shows number one to have been issued in 1833. Unlike House of Commons Papers and Bills, Command Papers are not numbered sessionally, but are issued in long series of which so far there have been five. Citation in the first of these is simply by means of a serial number within square brackets (the numbers were not printed on the documents themselves); in the last four the number is preceded by an abbreviation of the word Command, as follows:

1st Series	*4th Series*
[1]-[4222] 1833–1869	[Cmd. 1]-Cmd. 9889 1919–1956
2nd Series	*5th Series*
[C. 1]-[C. 9550] 1870–1899	Cmnd. 1- 1956–
3rd Series	
[Cd. 1]-[Cd. 9239] 1900–1918	

The square brackets were introduced in the 1836 index in order to draw the distinction between items presented by Command and House of Commons Papers which had their own serial numbers. Although the introduction of the initial C in 1870 rendered the brackets superfluous they continued to be used until 1922.

In order to locate a Command Paper in the sessional volumes it is necessary to know the session in which it appeared. On occasion documents occur out of sequence; the 1959–60 volumes, for instance, contain Cmnd. 846–1195, except for Cmnd. 1103, 1151, 1160 and 1194 which appeared in the following session. Given a Command number the appropriate session can be identified by means of the concordance on pp. 65-66. Precise references to the location of papers within the sessional volumes are provided by the *Numerical Finding List of British Command*

Papers published 1833–1961/2 compiled by E. Di Roma and J. A. Rosenthal (1967).

STATE PAPERS

State Papers constitute a distinct category of Command Papers: in fact they make up about one half of the total every session. They are always collected together into volumes at the end of each set of sessional papers (see p. 25) and are there grouped under two headings — State Papers: General and International, and State Papers: Treaties. (Some are also reproduced in the volumes of *British and Foreign State Papers* which are described on pp. 232-3). Under the broad heading of State Papers issued by Command there are three separate series: Treaty, Country and Miscellaneous; and to these are added various other documents such as reports of proceedings of certain United Nations conferences and the texts of international conventions not yet ratified by the United Kingdom.

Treaty Series

It is possible for the Treaty Series to be dealt with as a separate entity as each document has a serial number and the series as a whole has its own bibliographic apparatus. There are both annual indexes and consolidated indexes each covering three or four years. The former are arranged in parts, the first of which is a General List in which items are listed in order of their T.S. (Treaty Series) numbers; Command Paper numbers are given and further information provided under the headings Nature of Instrument (with Signatories), Place and Date of Signature, and Date of Entry into Force for U.K. Part II is a Subject Index; Part III an index of Multilateral Treaties; Part IV an index of Bilateral Treaties with Foreign States (excluding the Republic of Ireland); and Part V an index of Agreements with Other Commonwealth Countries and the Republic of Ireland. The *General Index to Treaty Series* was, until recently, arranged in two parts: I — General Treaties, II — Bilateral Treaties and Index of Subjects. However, beginning with the volume for 1968–1970, this division has been discontinued and the index now consists simply of one combined listing under subject headings (Fig. 15). Against each entry there are full particulars of

CONCORDANCE OF COMMAND PAPERS 1833–1972

1	1833	2007–2147	1856	7581–7916	1895
2–7	1834	2148–2205	1857 (Sess. 1)	7917–8276	1896
8	1835	2206–2288	1857 (Sess. 2)	8277–8647	1897
9–12	1834	2289–2451	1857–58	8648–9043	1898
13–19	1835	2452–2517	1859 (Sess. 1)	9044–9550	1899
20–22	1836	2518–2585	1859 (Sess. 2)	Cd.	
23–25	1835	2586–2753	1860		
26	1836	2754–2904	1861	1–428	1900
27–28	1835	2905–3069	1862	429–785	1901
29	1836	3070–3238	1863	786–1385	1902
30–31	1835	3239–3419	1864	1386–1765	1903
32–44	1836	3420–3579	1865	1766–2235	1904
45–47	1835	3580–3751	1866	2236–2681	1905
48	1834	3752–3952	1867	2682–3282	1906
49–51	1836	3953–4085	1867–68	3283–3726	1907
52–53	1835	4086–4222	1868–69	3727–4445	1908
54–56	1836	C.		4446–4961	1909
57	1835			4962–5464	1910
58–62	1836	1–230	1870	5465–6004	1911
63	1835	231–347	1871	6005–6664	1912–13
64	1834	347(I)	1873	6665–7047	1913
65–67	1835	348–461	1871	7048–7619	1914
68–102	1837	462–676	1872	7620–8168	1914–16
103–147(1)	1837–38	677–879	1873	8169–8431	1916
147(2)	1840	880–1112	1874	8432–8972	1917–18
148–150	1837–38	1113–1375	1875	8973–9239	1918
151	with 137	1376–1563	1876	Cmd.	
152–210	1839	1564	1877		
211–212	1840	1565–1635	1876	1–507	1919
213	1839	1636–1894	1877	508–1102	1920
214–285	1840	1896–2179	1878	1103–1552	1921 (Sess. 1)
286–333	1841 (Sess. 1)	2181–2456	1878–79	1553–1561	1921 (Sess. 2)
334–348	1841 (Sess. 2)	2457–2738	1880	1562–1584	1922 (Sess. 1)
349–423	1842	2739–3097	1881	1585	1922 (Sess. 2)
424–520	1843	3098–3453	1882	1586–1612	1922 (Sess. 1)
521–598	1844	3454–3828	1883	1613	1922 (Sess. 2)
599–676	1845	3829–4198	1884	1614–1740	1922 (Sess. 1)
677–757	1846	4199–4602	1884–85	1741–1747	1922 (Sess. 2)
758–875	1847	4603–4912	1886	1748	1922 (Sess. 1)
876–1006	1847–48	4913–5245	1887	1749–1782	1922 (Sess. 2)
1007–1129	1849	5246–5617	1888	1783	1923
1130–1292	1850	5618–5889(V)	1889	1784	1922 (Sess. 2)
1293–1424	1851	5890–6204	1890	1785–1786	1923
1425–1539	1852	6205–6548	1890–91	1787	1922 (Sess. 2)
1540–1697	1852–53	6550–6841	1892	1788–2005	1923
1698–1854	1854	6842–7291	1893–94	2006–2273	1924
1855–2006	1854–55	7292–7580	1894	2274–2569	1924–25

CONCORDANCE OF COMMAND PAPERS 1833–1972 *(cont.)*

2570–2786	1926	7517–7547	1948	1152–1159	1959–60
2787–3006	1927	7548–7852	1948–49	1160	1960–61
3007–3177	1928	7853–8076	1950	1161–1193	1959–60
3178–3338	1928–29	8077–8387	1950–51	1194	1960–61
3339–3651	1929–30	8388–8683	1951–52	1195	1959–60
3652–3962	1930–31	8684–8984	1952–53	1196–1501	1960–61
3963–4196	1931–32	8985–9325	1953–54	1502	1961–62
4197–4456	1932–33	9326–9467	1954–55	1503	1960–61
4457–4490	1933–34	9468–9889	1955–56	1504	1961–62
4491	1932–33			1505–1512	1960–61
4492–4740	1933–34	Cmnd.		1513–1515	1961–62
4741–5015	1934–35			1516–1517	1960–61
5016–5297	1935–36	1–285	1956–57	1518–1843	1961–62
5298–5574	1936–37	286–521	1957–58	1844–2162	1962–63
5575–5876	1937–38	522	1958–59	2163–2478	1963–64
5877–6135	1938–39	523–540	1957–58	2479–2805	1964–65
6136–6235	1939–40	541	1958–59	2806–2937	1965–66
6236–6322	1940–41	542	1957–58	2938–3435	1966–67
6323–6403	1941–42	543	1958–59	3436–3799	1967–68
6404–6486	1942–43	544	1957–58	3800–4182	1968–69
6487–6572	1943–44	545–845	1958–59	4183–4734	1969–70
6573–6659	1944–45	846–1102	1959–60	4735–4801	1970–71
6660–6951	1945–46	1103	1960–61	4802–5124	1971–72
6952–7231	1946–47	1104–1150	1959–60		
7232–7516	1947–48	1151	1960–61		

dates, acceptances, signatures and ratifications, as well as references giving both Treaty Series and Command Paper numbers; and whilst Part II gives details of bilateral treaties it also includes the titles of multilateral treaties with references back to the full entries for these items in Part I. Cumulations have been published as shown on p. 69. Each year *Supplementary Lists of Ratifications, Accessions, Withdrawals, etc.,* are compiled by the Foreign and Commonwealth Office and published in the Treaty Series as Command Papers (see numbers 2828 and 2897 on p. 70). Their purpose is to supplement the data given in the individual treaty documents and not, as might be inferred from their title, to update some master list of ratifications. The new information they provide is digested in the consolidated indexes which thus to some extent supersede them.

Treaty Series documents are also listed and indexed in the monthly and annual catalogues of government publications issued by H.M.S.O. and in the indexes to the volumes of sessional papers already mentioned.

An *Index of British Treaties 1101–1968* compiled and annotated by

GENERAL INDEX TO TREATY SERIES*
1968-1970

N.B. The texts of reservations, declarations, etc., are not included. Such texts may be found in the relevant Treaty Series publications, indicated in the right-hand columns of this Index. Except where otherwise stated the dates given herein are the dates of deposit of the ratifications, accessions, etc., and are not necessarily the effective dates, which should be determined from the relevant provisions of the instruments concerned.

	Date	Treaty Series No.	Command No.
ABU DHABI—			
Exchange of Notes concerning the Guarantee by the United Kingdom and the Maintenance of the Minimum Sterling Proportion by Abu Dhabi (Sterling Area Agreement)	London, 24 Sept., 1968	118/1968	Cmnd. 3834
ADOPTION—			
European Convention on the Adoption of Children	Strasbourg, 24 Apr., 1967	51/1968	Cmnd. 3673
Signatures—			
Denmark	24 Apr., 1967		
France	24 Apr., 1967		
Germany, Federal Republic of	24 Apr., 1967		
Greece (with declaration)	19 May, 1967		
Ireland, Republic of	25 Jan., 1968		
Italy	24 Apr., 1967	51/1968	Cmnd. 3673
Luxembourg	24 Apr., 1967		
Malta	24 Apr., 1967		
Norway (with declaration)	24 Apr., 1967		
Sweden	24 Apr., 1967		
United Kingdom	24 Apr., 1967		
Ratifications—			
Ireland, Republic of (with declaration) ...	25 Jan., 1968	51/1968	Cmnd. 3673
Malta	22 Sept., 1967		
Sweden	26 June, 1968	106/1968	Cmnd. 3861
United Kingdom	21 Dec., 1967	51/1968	Cmnd. 3673
AFGHANISTAN—			
Cultural Convention	Kabul, 19 Apr., 1965	7/1968	Cmnd. 3501
AIR SERVICES—			
Convention for the Unification of Certain Rules relating to International Carriage by Air ...	Warsaw, 12 Oct., 1929	11/1933	Cmd. 4284
Accessions—			
Afghanistan	20 Feb., 1969	129/1969	Cmnd. 4272
Ecuador	1 Dec., 1969	81/1970	Cmnd. 4468
Gabon	15 Feb., 1969	129/1969	Cmnd. 4272
Libya	16 May, 1969		
Paraguay	28 Aug., 1969	130/1969	Cmnd. 4362
Saudi Arabia	27 Jan., 1969	129/1969	Cmnd. 4272

* For list of previous General Indexes see final page of this volume.

FIG. 15. *General Index to Treaty Series 1961–1964: General Treaties*

CHRONOLOGICAL LIST

Tel Aviv/Jerusalem, *4 November/29 December 1959*. Entry into force: immediately.
[T.S. 11(1960), Cmnd. 968; P. (1959-60) XXXVI 509; 360 U.N.T.S. 390.]

1960

Convention establishing the EUROPEAN FREE TRADE ASSOCIATION.
Signed at Stockholm *4 January 1960*. Ratifications deposited at Stockholm: United Kingdom, Austria, Denmark, Norway, Portugal, Sweden, Switzerland 3 May 1960. Applies only to European territories of the parties.
Extensions: Liechtenstein by Protocol of 4 January 1960; Greenland 1 July 1961; Faroe Islands 1 January 1968*. Entry into force: 3 May 1960. Duration: terminable on 12 months' notice. Supplemented by Protocol of 28 July 1960 from 22 March 1961. Authentic texts: English and French.
[T.S. 30(1960), Cmnd. 1026; P. (1959-6) XXXIV 213; 370 U.N.T.S. 3.]

Protocol relating to the application of the Convention of 4 January 1960 establishing the EUROPEAN FREE TRADE ASSOCIATION to the Principality of LIECHTENSTEIN.
Signed at Stockholm *4 January 1960*. Ratifications deposited at Stockholm: United Kingdom, Austria, Denmark, Liechtenstein, Norway, Portugal, Sweden, Switzerland 3 May 1960. Entry into force: 3 May 1960. Authentic texts: English and French.
[T.S. 30(1960), Cmnd. 1026; P. (1959-60) XXXVI 426; 420 U.N.T.S. 130.]

Agreement between the Government of the United Kingdom and the UNITED NATIONS SPECIAL FUND concerning assistance from the Special Fund.
Signed at New York *7 January 1960*. Extended to the Federation of Rhodesia and Nyasaland by Exchange of Notes of 28 June 1960; to Bahrain and Qatar by Exchanges of Notes of 18 January 1968. Entry into force: immediately. Duration: terminable on 60 days' notice.
[T.S. 15(1960), Cmnd. 995; P. (1959-60) XXXV 903; 348 U.N.T.S. 177.]

Agreement between the Government of the United Kingdom and the Government of the CZECHOSLOVAK REPUBLIC for air services between and beyond their respective territories.
Signed at Prague *15 January 1960*. Entry into force: immediately. Duration: terminable on 12 months' notice. Authentic texts: English and Czech.
[T.S. 26(1960), Cmnd. 1036; P. (1959-60) XXXVI 209.]

FIG. 16. *Index of British Treaties 1101–1968*

CUMULATIVE INDEXES TO TREATIES

Years	Treaty Series No.	Command No.	
1892–1896	2 (1897)	C.	8336
1897–1901	2 (1902)	Cd.	913
1902–1906	18 (1907)	Cd.	3605
1907–1911	4 (1912)	Cd.	6036
1912–1916	4 (1917)	Cd.	8466
1917–1921	14 (1922)	Cmd.	1746
1922–1926	24 (1927)	Cmd.	2935
1927–1929	27 (1930)	Cmd.	3639
1930–1932	12 (1933)	Cmd.	4312
1933–1935	12 (1936)	Cmd.	5193
1936–1938	28 (1939)	Cmd.	6031
1939–1946	22 (1947)	Cmd.	7098
1947–1951	49 (1953)	Cmd.	8908
1952–1954	6 (1958)	Cmnd.	368
1955–1957	6 (1961)	Cmnd.	1285
1958–1960	121 (1961)	Cmnd.	1748
1961–1964	100 (1965)	Cmnd.	2871
1965–1967	23 (1970)	Cmnd.	4343
1968–1970	89 (1972)	Cmnd.	5044

Clive Parry and Charity Hopkins was published by H.M.S.O. in three volumes in 1970 and is a complete consolidated index to the Treaty Series. Volume 1 is arranged by subject and volumes 2 and 3 by date (see Fig. 16).

Following is a list of Treaty Series items published in the short 1965–66 session which shows the nature of these documents.

Treaty Series 1965–66

Cmnd.

2806 Air Services Agreement with Panama

2810 International Convention and Additional Protocol concerning the Carriage of Goods by Rail (CIM)

2811 International Convention and Additional Protocol concerning the Carriage of Passengers and Luggage by Rail (CIV)

2812 International Convention for the Safety of Life at Sea

2814 Agreement amending the Agreement Establishing the South Pacific Commission

Cmnd.

2818 Supplementary Agreement with the European Organisation for the Development and Construction of Space Vehicle Launchers

2819 Agreement with Germany concerning the Conduct of Manoeuvres and other Training Exercises in the Saltau-Lüneburg Area

2820 Agreement with Malaysia concerning certain Overseas Officers serving in Sabah and Sarawak

2821 Double Taxation Agreement with Jamaica

2828 Third Supplementary List of Ratifications, Accessions, Withdrawals, etc., for 1965

2832 Protocol for the Extension of the International Wheat Agreement, 1962

2833 Consular Convention with Japan

2840 Agreement with Japan for the Exchange of Money Orders

2843 Exchange of Notes with Jordan concerning the Further Allocation of Interest-Free Loan

2844 Agreement with Australia and New Zealand relating to the Territory of Nauru

2850 Memorandum of Agreement with the Netherlands for certain Air Services

2851 Exchange of Notes with Burma amending the Air Transport Agreement

2857 Notes to Belgium, etc., reimposing the Visa Requirement for their respective nationals travelling to Southern Rhodesia

2869 Loan Agreement with Turkey

2870 Amendments to Annexes I and III to the European Interim Agreement on Social Security Schemes relating to Old Age, etc.

2871 General Index to Treaty Series, 1961–1964

2872 Loan Agreement with Chile, with Exchange of Notes

2894 Declarations made by the United Kingdom recognising the competence of the European Commission of Human Rights, etc.

2896 Exchange of Notes with France extending the Convention on Social Security to the Islands of Guernsey, etc.

2897 Fourth Supplementary List of Ratifications, Accessions, Withdrawals, etc., for 1965

2898 Film Co-Production Agreement with France

Cmnd.

2900 Amendments to Articles 23, 27 and 61 of the Charter of the United Nations

2908 Exchange of Notes with the United States concerning the reciprocal granting of licences to amateur radio operators

2911 Exchange of Notes with France on the Payment of Family Allowances to Persons going from Guernsey to France or from France to Guernsey for Seasonal Agricultural Work

2912 Additional Regulations amending the International Sanitary Regulations

2925 Agreement with Venezuela concerning the Frontier between British Guiana and Venezuela

Country Series

Documents in the Country Series are serially numbered by country; that is, the first to relate to, say, Italy in a particular year is numbered Italy No. 1 (1965), the second Italy No. 2 (1965) and so on. The short 1965–66 session again provides a sample list of convenient size.

Country Series 1965–66

Cmnd.

2930 Republic of Ireland No. 1 (1966). Agreement on Social Security

2816 Italy No. 1 (1965). Exchange of Notes concerning the Exemption from Customs Duties of Material imported by Cultural Institutes in the United Kingdom and Italy

2817 Italy No. 2 (1965). Exchange of Notes concerning the Exemption from Local Taxation of the Premises of Cultural Institutes in the United Kingdom and Italy

2866 Morocco No. 1 (1966). Agreement for Air Services

2830 Netherlands No. 1 (1965). Agreement relating to the Delimitation of the Continental Shelf under the North Sea between the two countries.

2831 Netherlands No. 2 (1965). Agreement relating to the Exploitation of Single Geological Structures extending across the Dividing Line on the Continental Shelf under the North Sea

2910 Soviet Union No. 1 (1966). Consular Convention

2909 Sweden No. 1 (1966). Protocol amending the Extradition Treaty
2854 United Arab Republic No. 1 (1966). Cultural Convention
2899 United States No. 1 (1966). Twelfth Annual Report of the Marshall Aid Commemoration Commission for the year ending September 30, 1965.
2924 Yugoslavia No. 1 (1966). Cultural Convention

Miscellaneous Series

A fresh numerical sequence is started each year for items in the Miscellaneous Series of State Papers, but they are not separately indexed. Sectional List No. 69, *Overseas Affairs* indicates those in print and indicates those which have been superseded by a Treaty Series version. The following list includes representative titles.

Miscellaneous Series 1965–1966

Cmnd.
2822 The Antarctic Treaty, and the Recommendations of subsequent Consultative Meetings, 1961–64
2829 Ninth Annual Report of the Council of Association with the High Authority of the European Coal and Steel Community
2834 Documents relating to the British Involvement in the Indo-China Conflict, 1954–65
2860 Fifteenth Annual Report of the Foreign Compensation Commission for 1965–65
2895 Amendments to Article 28 of the Convention of the Inter-Governmental Maritime Consultative Organisation
2904 Convention on the Prevention and Punishment of the Crime of Genocide

Other State Papers 1965–66

Cmnd.
2858 Republic of Ireland. Agreement with Ireland establishing a Free Trade area

ROYAL COMMISSIONS AND TRIBUNALS OF INQUIRY

The reports of Royal Commissions and Tribunals of Inquiry are issued as Command Papers and are dealt with in Chapters 6 and 11 respectively.

CHAPTER 6

Royal Commissions

CHARACTER AND PURPOSE

A Royal Commission is a body, set up by the issue of a Royal Warrant, whose purpose is to carry out an investigation of a specified subject and to make recommendations thereon for the Government's consideration. The Royal Warrant is issued by the Sovereign and countersigned by one of the principal Secretaries of State; it sets out the Commission's terms of reference and authorizes it to call for "persons and papers". Chairmen of Royal Commissions are appointed as such, not elected from among the members; they have particular qualifications which may relate to their knowledge of the subject in question or to their known ability to draw conclusions from a mass of assembled evidence. Often a commission and its report are popularly referred to by the name of the chairman: thus we have the "Donovan Commission" (on Trade Unions and Employers' Associations) and the "Todd Report" (of the Royal Commission on Medical Education). Commissioners' names are given in the report; prior to its publication they can usually be found in *Hansard* or in *The Times,* which has its own bi-monthly index.

Every Royal Commission is served by a secretariat, normally drawn from the Civil Service, and particulars of current commissions are given in the *British Imperial Calendar and Civil Service List* (see p. 233). Their funds are detailed in the Civil Appropriation Accounts and, should the need arise, in the Civil Contingencies Fund — both are published as House of Commons Papers. All reports of Royal Commissions since 1920 have included a statement of their cost; the total cost of the 1969 Royal Commission on Local Government in Greater London, for instance, was given as £44,645, of which £11,954 represented the cost of printing and publishing the Report and the Minutes of Evidence. This practice of pub-

lishing costs arose at the instigation of a Major Entwistle who cited Australian reports as a precedent (*H.C.Deb.* vol. 131, 8 July 1920, col. 1683).

Royal Commissions may be considered as part of the pre-legislative process: for, although a Government is not bound by a commission's findings it is generally with the purpose of providing information needed in the formation of legislative policy that commissions are set up. In 1910 a Departmental Committee on the Procedure of Royal Commissions under the chairmanship of Lord Balfour of Burleigh (Cd. 5235) expressed themselves to be "disposed to deprecate the appointment of Royal Commissions on subjects as to which there is no reasonable prospect of early legislation". They saw their particular value as "the elucidation of difficult subjects which are attracting public attention, but in regard to which the information is not sufficiently accurate as to form a preliminary to legislation". They are a device which enables Ministers to draw upon a wider range of information and expert opinion than is available to them in the departments of the Civil Service. It should, however, be noted that although Royal Commissions have a greater prestige than departmental advisory committees this does not necessarily mean that their subjects are correspondingly more important than those investigated by the latter.

Whereas a parliamentary select committee must report before the end of the session in which it is set up, a Royal Commission has no such limitation and may last over two or three years. Nor is its membership restricted to Members of Parliament as is necessarily the case with select committees; part of its success derives from the wide range of expertise which exists among its members.

Since Royal Commissions originate outside Parliament their reports, which are formally addressed to the Sovereign, are presented to Parliament "By Command". Volumes of documentary and oral evidence and any research papers which might have been prepared are, however, published as Non-parliamentary Publications. At least, that is the position at present: it was the practice up to the first part of this century to issue these documents, too, as Command Papers. It should be noted that the minutes of evidence of Royal Commissions are not entered separately in the indexes to the H.M.S.O. annual *Catalogue of Government Publications.* Thus, for example, the Law Society's evidence to the Royal Commission on Trade Unions and Employers' Associations (see p. 85) does not appear in the index to the 1967 catalogue.

Following is a list of the Royal Commissions which have reported since 1900. It reveals the wide variety of subjects which have been investigated, ranging from matters of national importance such as coal production to ones of very local concern such as university education in Dundee. The titles also reflect the changing political and social climate: the poor laws were studied in the first decade of the century, agriculture in India and London squares in the twenties, equal pay in the years after the Second World War, and trade unions in the sixties. There are some surprises, too: reports on alien immigration in 1907, London traffic in 1905, and decimal currency in 1920.

ALPHABETICAL LIST OF ROYAL COMMISSIONS, 1900–72

The first date is the year in which the Commission was appointed, and the second the date of its report. The name in brackets is that of the Commission's Chairman. Chairmen are included in the index at the end of the volume. C., Cd., Cmd., Cmd. = Command Paper. The number quoted is that of the Commission's Final Report, unless otherwise stated.

Accidents to Railway Servants   1899–1900
    (Lord Hereford) Cd. 41
Administration of the Port of London   1900–02
    (Lord Revelstoke) Cd. 1151
Afforestation. *see* Coast Erosion, etc.
Africa: *see* East Africa; Martial Law Sentences in South Africa; Military Hospitals in South Africa; War in South Africa; War Stores in South Africa
Agricultural Industry in Great Britain   1919
    (H. Peat) Interim Report Cmd. 473 (Final Report not published)
Agriculture in India   1926–28
    (Marquis of Linlithgow) Cmd. 3132
Alien Immigration   1902–03
    (Lord James) Cd. 1741
Arms: *see* Private Manufacture of and Trading in Arms
Arrest and Subsequent Treatment of Mr. Francis Sheehy Skeffington, Mr. Thomas Dickson and Mr. Patrick James McIntyre   1916
    (Sir J. Simon) Cd. 8376

Civil Service: *see also* Superannuation in the Civil Service; Superior
    Civil Service in India
Coal Industry   1919
    (Lord Sankey) Cmd. 360
Coal Industry   1925—26
    (Sir H. Samuel) Cmd. 2600
Coal Mines: *see* Safety in Coal Mines
Coal Supplies   1901—05
    (Lord Allerton) Cd. 2353
Coast Erosion, Reclamation of Tidal Lands, and Afforestation in the
    United Kingdom   1906—11
    (I. C. Guest) Cd. 5708
Common Land   1955—58
    (Sir William Ivor Jennings) Cmnd. 462
Congestion in Ireland   1906—08
    (Lord Dudley) Cd. 4097
Court of Session and the Office of Sheriff Principal (Scotland)   1926—27
    (Lord Clyde) Cmd. 2801
Cross-River Traffic in London   1926
    (Lord Lee of Fareham) Cmd. 2772
Currency: *see* Decimal Currency
Death Penalty: *see* Capital Punishment
Decimal Currency   1918—20
    (Lord Emmott) Cmd. 628
Deferred Rebates: *see* Shipping "Rings" and Deferred Rebates
Delay in the King's Bench Division   1912—13
    (Lord St. Aldwyn) Cd. 7177
Dentists: *see* Doctors' and Dentists' Remuneration
Despatch of Business at Common Law   1934—36
    (Earl Peel) Cmd. 5065
Distribution of the Industrial Population   1937—39
    (Sir Montague Barlow) Cmd. 6153
Divorce: *see* Following title and Marriage and Divorce
Divorce and Matrimonial Causes   1909—12
    (Lord Gorell) Cd. 6478
Doctors' and Dentists' Remuneration   1957—60
    (Sir Henry Pilkington) Cmnd. 939 Supp. to Report: Cmnd. 1064

Dominions: *see* Natural Resources, Trade and Legislation of the
    Dominions
Dublin University: *see* Trinity College, Dublin
Dundee: *see* University Education in Dundee
Durham: *see* University of Durham
Duties of the Metropolitan Police   1906–08
    (D. B. Jones) Cd. 4156
East Africa   1953–55
    (Sir Hugh Dow) Cmd. 9475
Ecclesiastical Discipline   1904–06
    (Sir M. Hicks Beach) Cd. 3040
Education: *see* Oxford and Cambridge Universities; Trinity College,
    Dublin; titles beginning University
Elections: *see* Existence of Corrupt Practices at the last Election for the
    City of Worcester; Proportional Representation
Electoral Systems   1908–10
    (R. F. Cavendish) Cd. 5163
Environmental Pollution   1970–
    (Sir Eric Ashby) 3rd Report Cmd. 5054
Equal Pay   1944–46
    (Sir Cyril Asquith) Cmd. 6937
Examination of Assizes and Quarter Sessions   1966–69
    (Lord Beeching) Cmnd. 4153
Existence of Corrupt Practices at the last Election for the City of
    Worcester   1906
    (E. T. Atkinson) Cd. 3268
Feeble-Minded: *see* Care and Control of the Feeble-Minded
Finance and Currency (East Indies)   1913–14
    (A. Chamberlain) Cd. 7236
Fire Brigades and Fire Prevention   1921–23
    (Sir P. Laurence) Cmd. 1945
Fishing Industry: *see* Salmon Fisheries
Food: *see* Following title and Supply of Food, etc., in Time of War
Food Prices   1924–25
    (Sir A. Geddes) Cmd. 2390
Gaming: *see* Betting, Lotteries and Gaming

Health and Safety of Miners   1906—07
    (Lord Monkswell; H. H. S. Cunynghame) Cd. 5561
Honours   1923
    (Lord Dunedin) Cmd. 1789
Housing of the Industrial Population of Scotland, Rural and Urban
    1912—17
    (G. Ballantyne) Cd. 8731
Howth: *see* Landing of Arms at Howth
Immigration: *see* Alien Immigration
Income Tax   1919—20
    (Lord Colwyn) Cmd. 615
Incomes: *see* Equal Pay; Taxation of Profits and Income
India: *see* Following titles and Agriculture in India; Finance and Currency
    (East India); Labour in India; Public Services (East Indies); Superior
    Civil Services in India
Indian Currency and Finance   1925—26
    (E. Hilton Young) Cmd. 2687
Indian Decentralisation   1907—08
    (Sir H. Primrose; C. Hobhouse) Cd. 4360
Indian Expenditure   1896—1900
    (Lord Welby) Cd. 131
Indian Statutory Commission   1927—30
    (Sir J. Simon) Cmd. 3568 (Survey); Cmd. 3569 (Recommendations)
Inland Waterways: *see* Canals and Inland Navigations
Insurance *see* National Health Insurance; Unemployment Insurance
Inventors: *see* Awards to Inventors
Ireland: *see* Congestion in Ireland; Rebellion in Ireland; Trinity College,
    Dublin; University Education in Ireland
Jackson: *see* Sir John Jackson Ltd.
Justices of the Peace   1946—48
    (Lord Du Parcq) Cmd. 7463
Justices of the Peace: *see* also Selection of Justices of the Peace
King's Bench Division: *see* Delay in the King's Bench Division
Labour in India   1929—31
    . (J. Whitley) Cmd. 3883
Land: *see* Common Land

Land Drainage in England and Wales   1927
    (Lord Bledisloe) Cmd. 2993
Land Transfer Acts   1908–11
    (Lord St. Aldwyn) Cd. 5483
Landing of Arms at Howth on July 26th, 1914   1914
    (Lord Shaw) Cd. 7631
Law Relating to Mental Illness and Mental Deficiency   1954–57
    (Lord Percy of Newcastle) Cmnd. 169
Licensing (England and Wales)   1929–31
    (Lord Amulree) Cmd. 3988
Licensing (Scotland)   1929–31
    (Lord Mackay) Cmd. 3894
Lighthouse Administration   1906–08
    (G. W. Balfour) Cd. 3923
Local Government   1923–29
    (Earl of Onslow) Cmd. 3436
Local Government. *see also* Following titles and Existence of Corrupt
    Practices at the last Election for the City of Worcester
Local Government in England   1966–69
    (Lord Redcliffe-Maud) Cmnd. 4040; Memo of dissent. Cmnd.
    4040–I
Local Government in Greater London   1957–60
    (Sir Edwin Herbert) Cmnd. 1164
Local Government in Scotland   1966–69
    (Lord Wheatley) Cmnd. 4150
Local Government in the Tyneside Area   1935–37
    (Sir A. Scott) Cmd. 5402
Local Government of Greater London   1921–23
    (Viscount Ullswater) Cmd. 1830
Local Taxation   1896–1901
    (Lord Balfour of Burleigh) Cd. 638
Locomotion and Transport in London: *see* London Traffic
London: *see* Following entries and Administration of the Port of London;
    Cross-River Traffic in London; Local Government in Greater London;
    University Education in London
London Squares   1927–28
    (Marquis of Londonderry) Cmd. 3196

London Traffic   1903–05
    (Sir D. Barbour) Cd. 2597
Lotteries and Betting   1932–33
    (Sir S. Rowlatt) Cmd. 4341
Lotteries: *see also* Betting, Lotteries and Gaming
Lunacy and Mental Disorder   1924–26
    (H. Macmillan) Cmd. 2700
Malta (Finances, Economic Position, and Judicial Procedure) 1911–12
    (Sir F. Mowatt) Cd. 6090
Malta   1931–32
    (Lord Askwith) Cmd. 3993
Marriage and Divorce   1951–55
    (Lord Morton of Henryton) Cmd. 9678
Martial Law Sentences in South Africa   1902
    (Lord Alverstone) Cd. 1364
Matrimonial Causes: *see* Divorce and Matrimonial Causes
Mauritius   1909–10
    (Sir F. Swettenham) Cd. 5185
Meat Export Trade of Australia   1914–15
    (P. Street) Cd. 7896
Medical Education   1965–68
    (Lord Todd) Cmnd. 3569
Mental Illness: *see* Care and Control of the Feeble-Minded; Law Relating
   to Mental Illness; Lunacy and Mental Disorder
Merthyr Tydfil   1935
    (Sir A. Lowry) Cmd. 5039
Mesopotamia War   1916–17
    (Lord Hamilton) Cd. 8610
Metalliferous Mines and Quarries   1910–14
    (Sir H. Cunynghame) Cd. 7476
Military Hospitals in South Africa   1900–01
    (Sir R. Romer) Cd. 453
Militia and Volunteers   1903–04
    (Duke of Norfolk) Cd. 2061
Mines   1907–11
    (Lord Monkswell) Cd. 5561

Mines: *see also* Following title and Coal Industry; Health and Safety of Miners; Metalliferous Mines and Quarries; Safety in Coal Mines

Mining Subsidence   1923–37
    (Lord Blanesburgh) Cmd. 2899

Motor Cars   1905–06
    (Lord Selby) Cd. 3080

Museums: *see* National Museums and Art Galleries

National Health Insurance   1924–26
    (Lord Lawrence) Cmd. 2596

National Museums and Art Galleries   1927–30
    (Lord d'Abernon) Cmd. 3463

Natural Resources, Trade and Legislation of the Dominions   1912–17
    (E. Vincent) Cd. 8462

Newfoundland   1933
    (Lord Amulree) Cmd. 4480

Nyasaland: *see* Rhodesia–Nyasaland

Oxford and Cambridge Universities   1919–22
    (H. Asquith) Cmd. 1588

Palestine   1936–37
    (Earl Peel) Cmd. 5479

Penal System in England and Wales   1964 wound up 1966
    (Viscount Amory)

Physical Training (Scotland)   1902–03
    (Lord Mansfield) Cd. 1507

Poisoning by Arsenic   1901–03
    (Lord Kelvin) Cd. 1848

Police   1960–62
    (Sir Henry Willink) Cmnd. 1728

Police: *see also* Duties of the Metropolitan Police

Police Powers and Procedure   1928–29
    (Lord Lee) Cmd. 3297

Pollution: *see* Environmental Pollution

Poor Laws and Relief of Distress   1905–09
    (Lord Hamilton) Cd. 4499; Ireland: Cd. 4630; Scotland: Cd. 4922

Population   1945–49
    (Viscount Simon; Sir Hubert Douglas Henderson) Cmd. 7695

Population: *see also* Distribution of Industrial Population

Tyneside: *see* Local Government in the Tyneside Area
Unemployment Insurance   1930–32
    (Holman Gregory) Cmd. 4185
University Education in Dundee   1951–52
    (Lord Tedder) Cmd. 8514
University Education in Ireland   1901–03
    (Lord Robertson) Cd. 1483
University Education in London   1909–13
    (Lord Haldane) Cd. 6717
University Education in Wales   1916–18
    (Lord Haldane) Cd. 8991
University of Dublin: *see* Trinity College, Dublin, and the University of Dublin
University of Durham   1934–35
    (Lord Moyne) Cmd. 4815
Venereal Diseases   1913–16
    (Lord Sydenham) Cd. 8189
Vivisection   1906–12
    (Lord Selby: A. J. Ram) Cd. 6114
Volunteers: *see* Militia and Volunteers
Wales: *see* Merthyr Tydfil; University Education in Wales
War in South Africa   1902–04
    (Earl of Elgin) Cd. 1789
War Stores in South Africa   1905–06
    (Sir G. Farwell) Cd. 3127
West Indies   1938–39
    (Lord Moyne) Cmd. 6607
West Indies: *see also* Trade Relations between Canada and the West Indies
Whiskey and other Potable Spirits   1908–09
    (Lord Hereford) Cd. 4796
Worcester *see* Existence of Corrupt Practices at the last Election for the City of Worcester
Workmen's Compensation   1938–44
    (Sir Hector Hetherington) Cmd. 6588

Further reading is provided by Charles J. Hanser's *Guide to Decision: the Royal Commission* (1965), a comprehensive book covering the whole

subject from appointment, procedure and functions of commissions to detailed case studies. An appendix gives details (excluding chairmen) of the Royal Commissions between 1900 and 1964. *The Role of Commissions in Policy-Making* (1973), edited by Richard A. Chapman, analyses the work of five recent Royal Commissions and Departmental Committees and concludes with a chapter which examines their function and effect. There are two guides covering the nineteenth-century: B. L. Gabiné's *A Finding-List of British Royal Commission Reports 1860–1935* (1935) and H. M. Clokie and J. W. Robinson's *Royal Commissions of Inquiry* (1937), which includes a list for 1800–1936. *Whitaker's Almanack* gives particulars of current commissions including their addresses, dates of setting up, terms of reference, chairmen, members and secretaries.

CHAPTER 7

Bills

INTRODUCTION

A Bill is a draft version of a proposed Act of Parliament, a document containing the text of a piece of legislation as it passes through both Houses. There may in fact be more than one version of a Bill, reflecting modifications made to it during its passage. Some Bills will never be enacted at all, being either abandoned or rejected en route. Of these a number will reappear in another session of Parliament; but each time they must start again at the beginning of the legislative process.

This chapter relates mainly to Public Bills (which will become Public General Acts). Private Bills (which follow a different procedure to become Private Acts) are not published by H.M.S.O., but are available from the MP's who introduce them.

DRAFTING

Bills themselves have draft versions. Drafting is a very exact art and, in the case of Government Bills, is carried out by lawyers of the Parliamentary Council to the Treasury. These draftsmen remain responsible for the wording of any amendments which may subsequently be made. (Members of Parliament who introduce their own so-called Private Members' Bills have to arrange drafting for themselves, and the engagement of parliamentary lawyers of requisite skill can be very expensive.)

A few copies of a draft Bill are printed before the Bill is ever introduced into the House. They are passed to members of the Government and to certain officials, and only when the Government is satisfied with the wording will the draft be passed to the Public Bill Office. There it is examined by the Clerk of Public Bills who checks it for compliance with

the rules of the House which are very precise, especially where the proposed legislation would involve a charge on public funds. If any irregularities are discovered after the Bill has actually been presented the Speaker may order that it shall be withdrawn. It is unusual for draft Bills to be published: an example is *A Programme for Controlling Inflation: a draft bill,* Cmnd. 5200 (1972)

STAGES

First Reading

When a Bill is to be presented it appears on the *Order Paper* for the day, following the list of Parliamentary Questions (Fig. 17). A Public Bill is introduced either upon an order of the House or upon presentation by a Minister, or it may be "brought down" from the House of Lords. The first stage is known as First Reading which is a purely formal affair entailing the reading of the Bill's short title by the Clerk of the House.

The document used on this occasion is a "dummy" Bill, a piece of buff paper which simply records the title of the Bill and the names of Members presenting and supporting it. At the time of First Reading an order is made for the Bill to be printed and a date is named for the next stage to be taken in the House. Usually there is no debate at the time a Bill is introduced.

Second Reading

This is the stage at which the principle of a Bill is discussed; if it fails to pass this test it cannot proceed further. The debate is reported in *Hansard* with particulars of any division which may arise.

Committee Stage

A Bill which passes its Second Reading is then sent "upstairs" to a standing committee where it is examined in detail, certainly clause by clause if not word by word. An exception is the case of Bills involving

No. 10   **Order Paper: 10th November 1969**   **383**

QUESTIONS FOR ORAL ANSWER—*continued*

✳ 80 **Mr James Dickens** (Lewisham, West): To ask Mr Chancellor of the Exchequer, if, taking 1964 as 100, he will state the percentage increase in gross domestic product at factor cost and in public expenditure, in the subsequent years up to and including 1968.

✳ 81 **Sir Frederic Bennett** (Torquay): To ask Mr Chancellor of the Exchequer, what was the dollar value of the United Kingdom's gold and currency reserves, including Her Majesty's Government's dollar portfolio in October 1964; on what dates and at what dollar values this portfolio was absorbed into the reserves; and what was the total value of the reserves in October 1969.

✳ 82 **Sir Frederic Bennett** (Torquay): To ask Mr Chancellor of the Exchequer, what was the sterling value of all travellers cheques and foreign currency issued to United Kingdom residents for foreign travel for holiday purposes, on medical grounds, for business reasons and in other specified categories, respectively, during the 12 months or the nearest convenient annual period before the introduction of the current £50 restriction; and what were the equivalent figures for the last 12 months or in a similar convenient period on the same seasonal basis.

✳ 83 **Mr John Tilney** (Liverpool, Wavertree): To ask the Secretary of State for Education and Science, what is his policy for increasing the number of technically trained entrants to industry by securing a reduction in number of those who drop out from the lower stages of their technological training; and whether he has considered the evidence of Dr J. Gardner of Bradford Technical College in his Survey of Students' Reading 1964, a copy of which has been sent to him.

✳ 84 **Mr David Steel** (Roxburgh, Selkirk and Peebles): To ask the Secretary of State for Employment and Productivity, how many of the 8,500 vouchers available under the Commonwealth Immigrants Act were taken up in 1968; and how many of these were for persons from Malta.

AT THE COMMENCEMENT OF PUBLIC BUSINESS

Notice of Presentation of Bills

1 Mr Anthony Wedgwood Benn

INDUSTRIAL DEVELOPMENT (SHIPS): Bill to restrict the power of the Minister of Technology to make grants under section 5(1) of the Industrial Development Act 1966 and enable the Parliament of Northern Ireland to restrict, by reference to certain matters, the power of the Ministry of Commerce for Northern Ireland to make grants under section 6(1) of the Industrial Development (General Assistance) Act (Northern Ireland) 1966.

2 Mr Anthony Greenwood

LOCAL AUTHORITIES (GOODS AND SERVICES): Bill to make further provision with respect to the supply of goods and services by local authorities to certain public bodies, and for purposes connected therewith.

FIG. 17. *Order Paper of the House of Commons*

finance which are considered in detail in a committee of the whole House. Though it has no power to reject the whole Bill a committee can amend particular clauses, which may have virtually the same effect.

Reports of standing committee debates are published separately and not as part of *Hansard* (see p. 108).

Report Stage

If a Bill is not amended during the Committee Stage the Report Stage is a formality, the Bill then moving straight to Third Reading. If the Bill has been amended the House considers it in its amended form. It may be sent back to a standing committee, a committee of the whole House or a select committee for further consideration before it can proceed.

Third Reading

The debate on a Bill at this stage is normally much more limited than during Second Reading, and when it passes the vote at the end of the proceedings it has successfully passed through the Commons.

Lords Stage

After its journey through the Commons a Bill next has to pass the scrutiny of the House of Lords. Should the Lords not wish to make any amendments it has only to await the Royal Assent in order to become an Act. All Bills which are amended in the Lords and all Bills involving finance (whether amended or not) are sent back to the Commons.

Consideration of Lords Amendments

Amendments proposed by the Lords are examined one by one in the Commons. Should they be approved the Lords are notified and the Bill is ready to receive the Royal Assent. Should they not be approved the Commons will notify the Lords of their reasons and possibly forward their own amendments to the Lords amendments. This exchange can be pro-

longed, but eventually agreement should be reached which will then clear the way for granting of the Royal Assent.

VERSIONS OF A BILL

The first version of a Bill to be issued is that which is ordered to be printed at the time of First Reading. Often it will have been printed already and kept in sealed bundles in the Vote Office; or at least it will have been set up in type. Following First Reading the Public Bill Office advises the Vote Office that it may now release copies to Members of Parliament, all of whom automatically receive copies of Public Bills. At the same time the Bill is placed on sale by H.M.S.O.

It is quite common for another version to be printed incorporating amendments made in standing committee, and there may perhaps be yet another on report. (For notices of amendments and minutes of proceedings of standing committees see p. 53). Each new version of a Bill has its own number; all, however, are brought together in the sessional volumes of Parliamentary Papers. When a Bill passes to the Lords it is reprinted. Lords amendments are printed separately, and are incorporated into subsequent versions of the Bill.

CITATION OF BILLS

Bills are printed on pale green tinted paper and each bears a serial number at the bottom left-hand side of its first page. The number on Bills originating in the Commons appears within square brackets, and those originating in the Lords within curved brackets.

As new numerical sequences begin each session it is essential that references made to Bills should include the session as well as the Bill number, e.g.:

    H.C. Bill 1966–67 [10],
    H.L. Bill 1966–67 (10).

RECORDS OF THE PASSAGE OF BILLS

The stages through which a Bill passes are all recorded in the *Votes and*

PUBLIC BILL LIST

Session 1968-69

Saturday 21st June 1969

*Bills marked thus * are Government Bills*   † *Given precedence by the Government*   § *Not printed*

Title of Bill	Brought in by	Progress
*Administration of Justice [*Lords*] [60] [143]	Mr Attorney General	As amended, in the Standing Committee, to be considered, Mon., June 23
Age Level of Employment [124]	Mr Edward Milne	2nd Reading [*Dropped*]
*Age of Majority (Scotland) [*Lords*] [90]	Mr Secretary Ross	Committed to a Standing Committee, Apr. 15
Agricultural Training Board (Abolition) [50]	Mr John Farr	2nd Reading [*Dropped*]
*Agriculture (Spring Traps) (Scotland) [10] [58] [127]	Mr Secretary Ross	Lords Amendments *agreed to*, June 10
*Air Corporations [134] [180]	Mr Anthony Crosland	As amended, in the Standing Committee, to be considered, Mon., June 23
§Air Transport Licensing Act 1960 (Amendment) [88]	Mr Kenneth Lewis	2nd Reading [*Dropped*]
Animal Breeding Establishments [165]	Mr Peter Bessell	2nd Reading, Fri., June 27
Anti-Discrimination [92]	Mrs Joyce Butler	2nd Reading [*Dropped*]
Architects Registration (Amendment) [72] [138]	Mr Arnold Shaw	As amended, in the Standing Committee, to be considered, Mon., June 23
*Army Reserve [102]	Mr Secretary Healey	*Royal Assent*, May 16
Auctions (Bidding Agreements) [93] [122]	Mr Costain	*Passed*, May 2
Auctions (Bidding Agreements) Act 1927 (Amendment) [35]	Mr Costain	*Withdrawn*, Feb. 21
Betting, Gaming and Lotteries (Amendment) [*Lords*] [149]	Mr Albert Roberts	*Royal Assent*, May 16
Borders Development (Scotland) [68]	Mr David Steel	2nd Reading [*Dropped*]
British Broadcasting Corporation [100]	Mr Peter Bessell	2nd Reading *negatived*, Apr. 18
British Standard Time Act (Repeal) [48]	Mr Ronald Bell	2nd Reading, Fri., June 27
*Children and Young Persons [91] [158]	Mr Secretary Callaghan	*Passed*, June 9
Children and Young Persons Act 1963 (Amendment) [129]	Mr Hugh Jenkins	2nd Reading [*Dropped*]

[27]

FIG. 18. *Public Bill List*

1008   **H. L.**   **14° *Julii***   ***A.* 1969**

QUESTIONS FOR WRITTEN ANSWER—*continued*

The Lord Barnby — To ask Her Majesty's Government whether they will—
  (*a*) give values recording the export to and import from Denmark for 1968 and the first six months of 1969;
  (*b*) state what proportion of total imports of bacon into the United Kingdom for those periods was supplied by Denmark.

[8th July.]

The Earl of Lauderdale — To ask Her Majesty's Government what research they have sponsored to discover uses for industrial, agricultural, fisheries or other waste which, if scarcely profitable by themselves, might be nationally profitable in terms of the balance of payments through release of other resources for the export drive.   [10th July.]

The Earl of Harrowby — To ask Her Majesty's Government whether, in view of the fact that the Boundary Commissions' Report would add to the list, given in their written answer to a question in this House on 24th November 1964, of " Parliamentary boroughs " which embrace large rural areas, they will either reconsider the policy of calling such constituencies " Boroughs " or arrange for the rural areas to be removed into " County " constituencies.   [11th July.]

BILLS IN PROGRESS

Parliament [H.L.],
Gaming (Amendment) (No. 2) [H.L.],
Personal Records (Computers) [H.L.],
Trustee Investments (National Debt Commissioners) Amendment [H.L.],
Iron and Steel,
National Insurance (No. 2),   } Waiting for Second Reading.
Employer's Liability (Compulsory Insurance),
Ministry of Housing and Local Government Provisional Order (King's Lynn),
Welland and Nene (Empingham Reservoir) and Mid-Northamptonshire Water,

Greater London Council (Money),
West Bromwich Corporation,   } Committed to the Committee on Unopposed Bills.
Essex River and South Essex Water,

Walsall Corporation,
Wolverhampton Corporation,   } Committed to Select Committees.
Greater London Council (General Powers),

Statute Law (Repeals) [H.L.],   } Referred to the Joint Committee on Consolidation Bills.
Sea Fish Industry [H.L.],

Development of Tourism,   – Committed to a Committee.

Divorce Reform,
Housing,
Housing (Scotland),   } Committed to a Committee of the Whole House.
Architects Registration (Amendment),
Air Corporations,

Trustee Savings Banks [H.L.],   } Re-committed to a Committee of the Whole House.
Late Night Refreshment Houses [H.L.],

Street Offences [H.L.],
Conservation of Seals [H.L.],
Children and Young Persons,
Auctions (Bidding Agreements),   } Waiting for Report.
Transport (London),
Calderdale Water [H.L.],
London Transport,
Cardiff Corporation,

FIG. 19. *House of Lords Minutes of Proceedings*

Proceedings, from a notice of its introduction on the *Order Paper* (see Fig. 17) to the granting of Royal Assent.

On Saturday each week the *Votes and Proceedings* contain a Public Bill List (Fig. 18) which gives the title of each Bill before the House and indicates by whom it was brought in and the present stage of its progress. The list also includes a statement of the status of Bills in standing committee, giving the date on which they were committed or withdrawn, or that on which the relevant committee reported.

Every issue of the *House of Lords Minutes of Proceedings* also includes a statement of Bills in Progress in which Bills are grouped according to the degree of their advancement (Fig. 19).

A non-official publication which reports progress on Bills is *Review of Parliament and Parliamentary Digest,* which is published weekly whilst Parliament is sitting.

At the end of each session a return is prepared which lists the Public Bills that have been introduced and shows what happened to them. Its full title is:

> Return of the number of Public Bills, distinguishing Government from other Bills, introduced into this House, or brought from the House of Lords, during Session –, showing: (1) the number which received the Royal Assent; (2) the number which did not receive the Royal Assent, indicating those which were introduced into but not passed by this House, those passed by this House but not by the House of Lords, those passed by the House of Lords but not by this House, those passed by both Houses but Amendments not agreed to; and distinguishing the stages at which such Bills were dropped, postponed or rejected in either House of Parliament, or the stages which such Bills had reached by the time of the Prorogation or Dissolution.

Not only are the numbers of Bills in these categories recorded, but their titles also. Figure 20 is reproduced from 1966–67 H.C. 676 and shows, in addition to a summary statement of the numbers of each type of Public Bill which were enacted, part of the list of titles of those Bills which were introduced into the Commons but which – for one reason or another – were not passed. Out of eighty-one Bills in the full list no less than twenty-nine were not printed.

A list of Private Bills is published as part of the *Order Paper* (Private Business) at the end of each session. The progress of each Private Bill is tabulated under headings for each stage of the legislative process, from First Reading to Royal Assent (Fig. 21).

4   RETURN RELATING TO PUBLIC BILLS, SESSION 1966-67

SUMMARY OF BILLS WHICH RECEIVED THE ROYAL ASSENT

Government Bills	103
Other Bills	24
Provisional Order Bills	8
Order Confirmation Bills	9
	——
Total	144
	——

II. BILLS WHICH DID NOT RECEIVE THE ROYAL ASSENT

§ Not printed

BILLS INTRODUCED INTO, BUT NOT PASSED BY, THE COMMONS

TITLE OF BILL	STAGE AT WHICH DROPPED, POSTPONED, REJECTED, OR PROGRESS ENDED
Air Pollution	Withdrawn.
Aircraft Noise	2nd Reading (Prorogation).
Animals (Control of Intensified Methods of Food Production)	Withdrawn.
Areas of Special Scientific Interest	2nd Reading (Dropped).
§Broadcasting Enabling	Withdrawn.
§Business Interests of Members of Parliament (Register)	2nd Reading (Prorogation).
Clients' Money (Accounts)	Adjourned Debate on 2nd Reading (Dropped).
§Control of Sewage	2nd Reading (Prorogation).
Criminal Responsibility	2nd Reading (Dropped).
Department of World Security	2nd Reading (Dropped).
§Development of Play-Groups	Withdrawn.
Development of Play-Groups (No. 2) ...	2nd Reading (Prorogation).
Dismissal Appeals Board	2nd Reading (Dropped).
§Disused Graveyards	2nd Reading (Dropped).
§Election of Regional Economic Planning Councils	2nd Reading (Dropped).
Employees Protection	2nd Reading (Dropped).
Employment Agencies	As amended, in the Standing Committee, to be further considered (Prorogation).
§Erosion Prevention	Withdrawn.
§Erosion Prevention (No. 2)	2nd Reading (Dropped).
Export Encouragement	2nd Reading (Dropped).
Export of Animals for Research	2nd Reading (Dropped).
Feuduties, Multures and Long-leases (Scotland)	2nd Reading (Dropped).
Freedom of Publication Protection	2nd Reading (Dropped).
Government of Wales	2nd Reading (Dropped).
Hearing Aids	Adjourned Debate on 2nd Reading (Dropped).
Highways (Straying Animals)	2nd Reading (Dropped).
House Buyers Protection	2nd Reading (Dropped).
House of Lords (Abolition of Delaying Powers)	2nd Reading (Dropped).
Importation of Animals	2nd Reading (Dropped).
§Insurance Companies ... ...'	Withdrawn.
Justices of the Peace (Subsistence Allowances)	Withdrawn.
Labelling of Food	2nd Reading (Dropped).
§Law of Contempt (Press and Broadcasting) ...	2nd Reading (Dropped).

FIG. 20. *Return Relating to Public Bills*

SESSION 1968-69

LIST OF PRIVATE BILLS

AND PROCEEDINGS THEREON

22nd October 1969

Name of Bill	Bill read first time	Bill read second time	Bill committed	Committee to which Bill is referred	Bill reported	Bill, as amended, considered	Bill read third time	Royal Assent
Barclays Bank	Jan. 22	Jan. 28	Feb. 25	Unopposed	Mar. 12	Mar. 24	Mar. 27	May 16
Barnsley Corporation [Lords]	Mar. 18	April 1	April 1	Unopposed	April 2	April 16	April 22	April 24
Bedford Corporation [Lords]	June 10	July 1	July 1	Unopposed	July 9	July 15	July 21	July 25
Blackpool Corporation [Lords]	April 17	April 29	April 29	Opposed	July 8	Oct. 16 at 7 o'clock	Oct. 16	Oct. 22
Bournemouth Corporation	Jan. 22	Jan. 28	Jan. 28	Unopposed	Feb. 19	Feb. 25	Mar. 4	April 17
Bradford Corporation [Lords]	June 24	July 8	July 8	Unopposed	July 16	July 21	July 24	July 25
Brighton Corporation	Jan. 22	Mar. 17 at 7 o'clock†	Second Reading Negatived		—	—	—	
Bristol Clifton and West of England Zoological Society [Lords]	May 7	May 20	May 20	Unopposed	June 18	Not amended	June 24	June 25
British Railways	Jan. 22	Feb. 18	Feb. 25	Unopposed	Mar. 19	Mar. 26	April 1	July 25
British Transport Docks [Lords]	Mar. 26	April 15	April 15	Unopposed	May 7	May 14	May 20	June 25
Calderdale Water [Lords]		Suspended		.	.	.	.	.
Cardiff Corporation	Jan. 22	Jan. 28	Jan. 28	Opposed	May 2	May 13	May 20	July 25
Chelsea College, University of London [Lords]	Mar. 11	Mar. 25	Mar. 25	Unopposed	April 2	Not amended	April 16	April 17
City of London (Various Powers)	Jan. 22	Feb. 11	Feb. 11	Unopposed	Mar. 12	Mar. 25	May 20	July 25
Corn Exchange [Lords]	Mar. 20	April 22	April 22	Unopposed	May 14	May 20	June 10	June 25
Covent Garden (Suspended Bill)	Nov. 4	Nov. 4					Nov. 4	Mar. 6
Coventry Corporation [Lords]	Mar. 4	Mar. 18	Mar. 18	Unopposed	April 2	Not amended	April 16	April 17
Derby Corporation	Jan. 22	Jan. 28	Jan. 28	Unopposed	Feb. 19	Feb. 25	Mar. 4	April 17
Derbyshire County Council	Jan. 22	Jan. 28	Jan. 28	Unopposed	Feb. 12	Feb. 18	Feb. 25	Mar. 27
Dudley Corporation [Lords]	June 12	June 24	June 24	Opposed	July 14	Oct. 15	Oct. 15	Oct. 22
Essex River and South Essex Water	Jan. 22	Jan. 29	Mar. 25	Unopposed	May 14	June 11	June 17	July 25

7 B

FIG. 21. *List of Private Bills*

INDEXES

Bills are first listed in the *Daily List of Government Publications* issued by H.M.S.O. They then reappear in the *Monthly Catalogue* and the *Annual Catalogue,* both of which are indexed.

Public Bills are collected together in the first two or three volumes of the sessional papers and are there arranged in alphabetical order of their titles. Furthermore, different versions of and amendments to a particular Bill appear together. Thus, if one knows the session in which a Bill was introduced and its title one can quickly locate it in the sessional volumes. Failing this, recourse can be had to the general index to these volumes in which Bills are indexed under subjects.

OUTLAWRIES BILL

At the beginning of each new session, before the debate on the Address by the Sovereign, a Bill is introduced which has a special significance regarding the constitutional principle of parliamentary supremacy. This is the Outlawries Bill, of which mention will regularly be found in the *Journals of the House of Commons* in the following terms: "A Bill for the more effectual preventing Clandestine Outlawries was read the first time; and ordered to be read a second time."

Normally nothing more is heard of it. In 1946, however, a Member did try to initiate a debate, but the Speaker ruled him out of order. Thereupon another Member rose to support his colleague on the grounds "that the purpose of the Outlawries Bill is to insist upon the right of the House to discuss some item or other of its own business before going on to consider the King's Speech" (*H.C.Deb.* vol. 430, 12 Nov. 1946, col. 4). In 1968 a Member further asserted its purpose as being "to show that in this House we have the right to give priority to discussion of matters other than Government business" (*H.C.Deb.* vol. 766, 18 June 1968, col. 917). Despite these protestations, on neither occasion were further proceedings allowed.

CHAPTER 8

Parliamentary Debates

Reports for the period from the Norman Conquest down to 1803 are contained in *The Parliamentary History of England*, a work in thirty-six volumes begun by William Cobbett and completed by J. Wright. The compilers used a number of sources, of which the principal ones are listed in the first issue of *Hansard* each session: "the *Constitutional History*, 24 vols.; *Sir Simonds D'Ewes' Journal; Debates of the Commons in 1620 and 1621; Chandler and Timberland's Debates*, 22 vols., *Grey's Debates of the Commons, from 1667 to 1694*, 10 vols.; *Almon's Debates*, 24 vols.; *Debreet's Debates* 63 vols.; *The Hardwicke Papers; Debates in Parliament by Dr. Johnson*, etc., etc."

These and other early sources are described in *A Bibliography of Parliamentary Debates of Great Britain* (House of Commons Library Document No. 2, H.M.S.O., 1956). Supplementary material is noted by A. Aspinall in an essay on "The reporting and publishing of the House of Commons' Debates, 1771–1834" in *Essays Presented to Sir Lewis Namier* (R. Pares and A. J. P. Taylor, eds., 1956).

HISTORY OF HANSARD

Although the name *Hansard* has consistently been used through the years to indicate the report of debates in Parliament, Hansard the man neither originated the publication, nor has he any connection with it today. It was William Cobbett who in 1803 began publishing a record of the proceedings of Parliament in an acceptably unbiased form under the title of "Cobbett's Parliamentary Debates" in his *Political Register*. This he continued to do until in 1811 he sold out his interest in this venture to

Thomas Curson Hansard the son of Luke Hansard, printer to the House of Commons. Under Hansard the report was published monthly. It was not a verbatim account but was pieced together from reports which appeared in the press. It took the name *Hansard's Parliamentary Debates* for the first time in 1829. The next landmark was in 1855 when the Stationery Office was instructed by the Treasury to subscribe to 150 sets for the benefit of government offices. In 1878 Parliament set up a select committee (1878 H.C. 327)' to inquire into the reporting of its debates. It did not favour the idea of an official publication but Parliament's real concern for an accurate record was expressed by the practical measure of paying a subsidy through the Stationery Office which enabled Hansard to engage a reporter to attend in the House and thus contribute to a raising in the accuracy of his publication's reports. In 1888 a joint select committee (1888 H.C. 284) again looked into the matter and this time it was recommended that Parliament should exercise greater control over the publication by putting the work out on tender to a contractor who would be expected to employ a staff of reporters sufficient to ensure full-time attendance at debates. The following year Hansard's sold out and the task of producing reports was undertaken by a number of different contractors. Eventually, in 1907, yet another select committee (1907 H.C. 239) considered the problem and as a result of its recommendations the House of Commons assumed responsibility for reporting its own debates and appointed a staff specifically for the purpose; the first *Official Report* appeared in 1909. The old family name, however, continued to be used in parliamentary and scholarly circles and in 1943 the House bowed to popular usage and the word *Hansard* was again included on the title-page of its *Official Report of Debates.*

Since 1803 there have been five series:

1st Series 1803—20
2nd Series 1820—30
3rd Series 1830—91
4th Series 1892—1908
5th Series 1909—

OFFICIALITY OF HANSARD

On the matter of the official character of *Hansard* helpful statements

made by the Speaker are reported in vol. 461, cols. 1146–7 (16 Feb. 1949) and cols. 1347–50 (17 Feb. 1949). There it is said that *Hansard* is official to the extent that it is a report by people who are officially appointed as part of the staff of the House of Commons. But there is a sense in which the *Journals* and the *Votes and Proceedings* on which·they are based are more official. The Speaker quoted the fact that under the Evidence Act, 1845, copies of the *Commons Journals* are admitted in evidence without proof of the printing: whereas copies of *Hansard* are not so admitted as evidence of facts therein stated. The two publications, of course, serve different purposes: *Hansard* reports the debates in the House; the *Journals* record the business transacted by the House. *Hansard* reports what was said: the *Journals* record what was done.

LORDS DEBATES

Debates in the House of Lords have been reported and published separately since 1909; before then a summary had been published in the same volumes as the Commons debates. Currently they are published in daily parts, in weekly parts and in bound volumes. There is a weekly index, and the bound volume covering the last part of a session contains a sessional index. A new cumulative index was introduced in the 1965–66 session. Hitherto indexing had been limited to the services just mentioned; this new index, published about nine times a year, progressively covers all the debates of the session and greatly assists research.

FORM OF CITATIONS

As there is no single, commonly accepted form of reference to the *Official Report of Debates,* it is necessary to be familiar with the various forms in common use. The Treasury's *Official Publications* (H.M.S.O., 1958, repr. 1963, p. 18) says that references to *Hansard* "usually take the form of, e.g. 520 HC (or HL) DEB 1955/56 Col. 1234 or 522 HC DEB 1955/56 Col. *123.* These refer respectively to Column 1234 of Volume 520 in the 5th Series, and to Column *123* of the Written Answers to

Questions in Volume 522 in the 5th Series."

In their *Guide to Parliamentary Papers,* P. and G. Ford simply say:

The official method of citation is as follows:

vol. no.	/	House	/	series	/	date	/	col. no.
213		H.C.Deb.		5s.		8 Feb., 1928		col. 136.

It may be observed that inclusion of the year in the citation really obviates the need to make mention of the series; and that since the pages of *Hansard* are not numbered no ambiguity can arise from omitting mention of the word "column" in the citation.

PRESENT-DAY REPORTING PRACTICE

The recording of debates in Parliament is a very demanding task, and one which requires special skills. Reporters work in short spells of about ten minutes each. At the end of a spell the reporter dictates his shorthand notes to a typist, and this continuous process of transcription goes on until the end of the day's business. There are a few moments of respite; at Question Time, for instance, both the Questions and the Answers are available in advance: the Questions from the *Order Paper* and Answers from the departments concerned. Against this, the reporting of Supplementary Questions can be particularly difficult, but reporters are free to consult with Members involved in the interest of accurate reporting.

It is not, in fact, strictly true to say that *Hansard* constitutes a verbatim transcript of what was said in the House. Reporters are allowed the licence of making grammatical corrections, of inserting the proper forms of reference to Members of the House and of effecting limited stylistic improvements. Above all, the *sense* of what was said must not be tampered with; and this applies particularly in those circumstances where Members themselves are allowed to suggest amendments. These arise after publication of the daily edition of *Hansard.* The type for this edition is set up as transcripts are received in H.M. Stationery Office; printing and making up into issues is done overnight and copies are rushed to the Post Office in the early hours for delivery to Members (as far as possible) by first post. Even copies destined for departments and government bookshops are available by about nine o'clock. Clearly there is little time for editing, and Members are entitled to suggest amendments to reports of their speeches, either to

correct what they claim to be errors of transcription or to improve the grammar of their utterings for the sake of improving their intelligibility. Here, above all, the utmost care has to be taken to preserve the sense of what was originally said. Those amendments which are admitted are carried into the bound volumes of *Hansard* which are recognized as constituting the official record of what was said.

Altogether, there are three editions of *Hansard*. Firstly there are the daily reports; these are numbered serially, a fresh series beginning each session. Then there is a weekly edition, the *Weekly Hansard* for which a *Weekly Index* is also published. Finally there are the bound volumes. A new volume is begun at the beginning of each new session of Parliament, and subsequent volumes appear throughout the session so as to produce volumes of approximately uniform thickness. Each session's output concludes with a sessional index (Fig. 22).

BROADCASTING OF PROCEEDINGS IN PARLIAMENT

Over the years the tendency has been towards an increasingly liberal policy over publicizing the proceedings of Parliament. The Opening of Parliament was first broadcast, both on radio and television, on 28 October 1958, and in 1966 proceedings in the House of Lords were televised on closed-circuit by way of an experiment. In 1968 the Select Committee on House of Commons (Services) recommended that "edited summarised" broadcasts of proceedings should be made during a four-week experiment (1967–68 H.C. 152). Later in the year the Select Committee reported that its Sub-committee on Broadcasting were of the opinion that the experiment proved that radio broadcasting is feasible and would be "a most effective method of bringing Parliament to the public" (1967–68 H.C. 448). At the beginning of the 1968–69 session the new Select Committee on House of Commons (Services), however, suggested that "present financial circumstances preclude any recommendation for expenditure on a project which is known to be controversial" (1968–69 H.C. 48). But despite continued opposition from some quarters a greater amount of broadcasting would seem to be inevitable in the future.

Useful discussions of the topic are Robin Day's *The Case for Televising Parliament* (1963) and Colin Seymour-Ure's "An examination of the pro-

GENERAL INDEX
TO THE
PARLIAMENTARY DEBATES
(OFFICIAL REPORT)

FIFTH SERIES   **VOLUME 752**

First Session of the Forty-fourth Parliament of the United
Kingdom of Great Britain and Northern Ireland.
Elizabeth II, 1966–67

TWENTY-SIXTH VOLUME OF SESSION 1966–67

18th April, 1966 — 27th October, 1967
EXPLANATION OF ARRANGEMENT AND ABBREVIATIONS

Bills: Read First, Second or Third Time = 1R, 2R, 3R.   *Amendt.*=Amendment.   *Com.*=Committee.
    Rep.=Report.
All entries refer to Questions except those headed *Debate*.
Column Numbers in *italics* refer to Written Questions at end of Volume.
Where in the Index * is added with Reading of a Bill, or a Vote in Committee of Supply, it indicates that
    no Debate took place on that stage of the Bill, or on that Vote.
Subjects discussed in Committee of Supply are entered under their headings, and also under Members'
    Names, without reference to the actual Vote before the Committee.
(S) after an entry denotes that the subject was discussed in Committee of Supply.
Questions are indexed under subject headings and under the names of Members asking and Ministers
    replying.
Ministerial statements are indexed under subject headings, under "Ministerial Statements" and under
    the names of the Ministers making them.

Debates on Bills, Motions, etc. are indexed under subject headings and under the names of Members
    and Ministers who speak.

Where the Number of a Volume is not repeated, it will be understood that the reference is the same
    as the previous Volume quoted.

A.1, Long Bennington Bypass :
Debate
[728] 1082-92.

Abattoirs :
Standards, [751] 734.

Abbotsham Primary School :
Toilets, [735] *323 ;* [745] *130.*

Abbotsinch Airport :
Near collision, [733] *358-9.*
Radar control system, [731] *239-40 ;* [732]
105.

Abbotsinch and Prestwick Airports :
Report, [747] 22.

Abbotsinch and Turnhouse Airports :
Diversions, [746] *237.*

Abercynon and Aberdare :
Bypasses, [750] 2455-6.

Aberdeen :
[745] 1609-10.
Advance factories, [730] 2180-1 ; [735]
381-2 ; [737] 1563-4 ; [745] *97.*
College of Zoology, University inquiry,
[735] *359 ;* [741] *273-4.*

Aberdeen :—*cont.*
Craiginches Prison, overcrowding, [746] *215.*
Deaf children's hostel, [741] *273.*
Ellon Hospital, [733] *353.*
Export intelligence facilities, [728] 583.
Fatal accident, Aberdeen University, legal
aid, [735] *284.*
Foresterhill College, [733] *352-3.*
Grammar School and High School for Girls,
co-education, [735] *281.*
Industrial expansion, [728] *283-4.*
Industrial Liaison Centre, [751] *422-3.*
Liner trains, [738] *100-1.*
New factories, [749] *258-9.*
Ports, deep water berth, [729] *105.*
Road schemes, [745] *108.*
Royal Infirmary:
Extensions, [748] *274.*
Visitors, [731] *202-3.*
Shipping:
Transport services, Aberdeen and
Northern European ports, [727] *138.*
Ships, Aberdeen Harbour, collision, [728]
1538.
Skilled workers, [727] *154.*
Trade with Northern Europe, [740] 498-9.
Unemployment, [728] 30-6 ; [734] *94-6 ;*
[740] *208 ;* [744] 732-4.

Aberdeen and Deeside :
Tourist resorts, [728] *83.*

1

FIG. 22 *House of Commons Debates (Hansard): General Index*

posal to televise Parliament" (*Parliamentary Affairs,* vol. XVII, no. 2, Spring 1964).

USING HANSARD

There are some points to note about the bound volumes which affect the user's success in consulting them. Undoubtedly the most important of these is the different type used for numbering the columns of debates and the columns containing the written answers to questions. In the House of Commons *Hansard,* written answers are collected together at the end of each volume and their column numbers printed in italics. These italic numbers are also used in the index, and one has to be alert to this when looking up references. It is all too easy to overlook the fact that a particular column reference in the index is printed in italics and to search the corresponding column of debates fruitlessly for mention of the subject sought.

Other peculiarities in the index are the symbols used for indicating the various stages of the legislative process. These are as follows:

1 R	= First Reading of a Bill
2 R	= Second Reading
3 R	= Third Reading
Amendt.	= Amendment
Com.	= Committee
Rep.	= Report

When in the index an asterisk (*) is added with the reading of a Bill it indicates that no debate took place on that stage.

Several other features of the indexing system should be noted. They are:

(i) all entries refer to Questions except those headed "Debate";

(ii) subjects discussed in Committee of Supply are entered under the appropriate headings, and also under Members' names without reference to the actual Vote before the Committee;

(iii) (S) after an entry denotes that the subject was discussed in Committee of Supply;

(iv) Questions are indexed under subject headings and under the names of Members asking and Ministers replying;

(v) ministerial statements are indexed under subject headings, under "Ministerial Statements" and under the names of the Ministers making them;

(vi) debates on Bills, Motions, etc., are indexed under subject headings and under the names of Members and Ministers who speak.

THE QUEEN'S SPEECH

A debate of particular interest for the purpose of obtaining a general view of the Government's policy is that which follows the Queen's Speech from the Throne. The speech, which is actually prepared by the Government, enumerates the principal subjects on which it is intended to introduce legislation in the new session; and the ensuing debate in the House lasts for some two weeks and reveals many of the policy differences existing between the major parties. Both speech and debate (the Debate on the Address) are reported in *Hansard,* where they are indexed under "Queen's Speech on the Opening of Parliament". The Address is also published separately by H.M.S.O. under the title *Her Majesty's Most Gracious Speech to both Houses of Parliament.*

THE BUDGET

A very full debate always follows the Budget speech which is made by the Chancellor of the Exchequer at an early date in the financial year. Both the speech and the debate are recorded in *Hansard.* The speech made by Mr. Callaghan in 1966, for example, appeared in vol. 727, 1966–67 cols. 1429–61; and the debate extended to nearly 300 columns. The Budget speech sets out in detail the proposed taxation for the year, and immediately following it the *Financial Statement and Budget Report* is made available to Members. This, in fact, is one of the exceptional cases when a document is released so quickly, and it involves a special arrangement whereby copies are sent in advance under seal to the Vote Office in the House with instructions that they are not to be distributed until authorized. After the introduction of the Budget resolutions are made in the House which eventually form the basis for the Finance Bill; and this Bill again engenders a considerable volume of debate.

DIVISIONS

In the House of Commons Members who vote for a motion are the *Ayes,* those against the *Noes;* in the Lords they are the *Contents* and the *Not Contents.* When a vote is taken in the Commons and it is not clear from the voicing of "Ayes" and "Noes" which is in the majority, a division may be called in which case the two sides separate and file into lobbies whose doors are locked until the result of the count is declared. *Division Lists* record the voting. These are printed with the Order Papers (see p. 44) and are also recorded in *Hansard,* but not in the *Journals of the House of Commons.* Lists were first officially published by the Commons in 1836, but Cobbett's *Parliamentary History* gives details of many important votes of the eighteenth century. A useful document on this period, which includes a bibliography, is *The Parliamentary lists of the Early Eighteenth Century: their compilation and use: the proceedings of a colloquium held at Leicester on 16 May 1970* edited and introduced by Aubrey Newman (Leicester University Press, 1973).

A memorandum on the use of mechanical methods of voting in the House of Commons appears as Appendix 9 of the Report from the Select Committee on Procedure, 1958–59, H.C. 92-I. In 1966 the Select Committee investigated the possibility of introducing an electromechanical system of voting in the House of Commons, but made a recommendation against its adoption (1966–67 H.C. 283).

Division Lists also appear in the House of Lords *Hansard,* the *House of Lords Minutes of Proceedings* and the *Journals of the House of Lords.*

PARLIAMENTARY QUESTIONS

In addition to reporting debates – which in themselves are an important source of data – *Hansard* contains authoritative information on an extremely wide range of subjects in the form of answers to parliamentary questions. These are recognized, for example, as a source of statistical information of a kind not easily found elsewhere. *Trade and Industry* makes a regular feature of parliamentary answers culled from *Hansard.* Ministers have very substantial departmental facilities which they use in framing their replies to questions, and they may also include references to other sources of information.

DIGEST OF DEBATES

In November 1971 publication began of the non-official journal *Debate: a digest of parliamentary debates and questions.* There are ten issues plus an annual volume, all of which have indexes.

STANDING COMMITTEE DEBATES

Quite distinct from the official report of debates of the House are the standing committee debates (1909–). These are verbatim reports of the debates of the standing committees appointed to consider Bills following their Second Reading. They are first published as daily parts (unrevised), and each part reports the proceedings of one or more sittings of the committee concerned with a particular Bill. In due course the daily parts are bound into volumes; for the session 1966–67, for example, there were thirteen bound volumes. Here the reports are first arranged by the committee: that is to say the reports of Standing Committee A come first followed by B, C, D, etc., with the Scottish and Welsh committees coming last. Each volume is indexed (with each Bill treated separately) but there is no general index to the sessional set, and it is therefore necessary to discover which standing committee considered a Bill before the report of its debate can be located. This is done using the H.M.S.O. annual catalogue of *Government Publications* where, immediately following the particulars of *Hansard* and under the heading Standing Committees Official Reports, the debates are listed alphabetically by names of Bills with the standing committee indicated in each case.

CHAPTER 9

Acts and Measures

ROYAL ASSENT

Having passed through all the stages of the legislative process in both Houses, a Bill receives the Royal Assent to become an Act. The Queen herself is no longer present at this ceremony; the Sovereign in fact only attends personally at the opening of each new session of Parliament when she reads the Speech from the Throne (see p. 106). The manner of signifying Royal Assent is prescribed in the Royal Assent Act 1967 (Fig. 23) which repealed the Royal Assent by Commission Act, 1541.

Immediately following Royal Assent an Act becomes the law of the land, unless it embodies a statement making some other specific provision for bringing it into operation. In the case of the Protection of Birds Act 1967, for instance, section 12 (4) states that "This Act shall come into force at the expiration of a period of six months beginning with the day on which it is passed." Often the power to name the day on which an Act shall come into operation is delegated to some other authority. A good example of this is the Decimal Currency Act of 1967 which makes provision that on an "appointed day" the currency denominations will be the pound sterling and the new penny, and further specifies that this day "means such day in the year 1971 as the Treasury may by order made by Statutory instrument appoint". It was the case up to 1793 that when no indication of commencement was given in the Act the courts considered it to have become law as from the first day of the session.

It is a duty of the Clerk of the Parliaments (under the terms of the Acts of Parliament (Commencement) Act, 1793, to mark the official copies of every new Act with the day, the month and the year when it received the Royal Assent. Acts are printed by Her Majesty's Stationery Office whose Controller is then acting in his capacity as Queen's Printer of Acts of

Royal Assent Act 1967

1967 CHAPTER 23

An Act to amend the law relating to the signification of Her Majesty's Royal Assent.   [10th May 1967]

B E IT ENACTED by the Queen's most Excellent Majesty, by and with the advice and consent of the Lords Spiritual and Temporal, and Commons, in this present Parliament assembled, and by the authority of the same, as follows:—

1.—(1) An Act of Parliament is duly enacted if Her Majesty's Assent thereto, being signified by Letters Patent under the Great Seal signed with Her Majesty's own hand,— *Signification of Royal Assent.*

   (a) is pronounced in the presence of both Houses in the House of Lords in the form and manner customary before the passing of this Act; or

   (b) is notified to each House of Parliament, sitting separately, by the Speaker of that House or in the case of his absence by the person acting as such Speaker.

(2) Nothing in this section affects the power of Her Majesty to declare Her Royal Assent in person in Parliament, or the manner in which an Act of Parliament is required to be endorsed in Her Majesty's name.

2.—(1) This Act may be cited as the Royal Assent Act 1967. *Short title and repeal.*

(2) The Royal Assent by Commission Act 1541 is hereby repealed. *1541 c. 21.*

FIG. 23. *Royal Assent Act 1967*

Parliament, an office to which appointment is made by the Crown by letters patent.

It is presumed in law that every Act from the thirteenth century to the present day is known by every citizen. The lists of Acts promulgated in 1967 which appear in the following pages will, however, give some indication of the magnitude of the task which faces those who would acquaint themselves with the whole of the statute law of the land.

TYPES OF ACTS

Quite apart from the obvious differences of subject content between one Act and another, there are differences of character and extent of operation. For instance, Acts which confer powers the exercise of which is either obligatory or discretionary are known as *enabling legislation,* a general term used to distinguish them from peremptory or prohibitory Acts. Acts which do not come into operation automatically but which have to await adoption by the authorities they concern are called *adoptive Acts;* when adopted they only apply to that authority's area. There are a number of technical classifications, too, which relate to the way in which statutes are interpreted; and a useful survey of the different types, with ample references to further sources, is provided in Halsbury's *Laws of England* at the beginning of the section devoted to statutes.

Queen's Printer's Classification

Acts of Parliament are classified by the Queen's Printer according to their provenance, that is to say into those originating in Public Bills and those originating in Private Bills. The former are published as *Public General Acts* and the latter as *Local and Personal Acts.*

Public General Acts

Normally when one speaks of Acts of Parliament one is referring to the Public General Acts. Following is a list of those promulgated in 1967; the starred (*) titles are those which recur each session. The list illustrates the volume and diversity of the Government's legislative programme.

Abortion Act
Aden, Perim and Kuria Muria Islands Act
Advertisements (Hire-Purchase) Act
Air Corporations Act
Agriculture Act
Anchors and Chain Cables Act
Antarctic Treaty Act
*Appropriation Act
Bermuda Constitution Act
Civic Amenities Act
Coal Industry Act
Commonwealth Settlement Act
Companies Act
*Consolidated Fund Act
Consolidated Fund (No. 2) Act
Control of Liquid Fuel Act
Criminal Justice Act
Criminal Law Act
Countryside (Scotland) Act
Dangerous Drugs Act
Decimal Currency Act
Deer (Amendment) (Scotland) Act
Development of Inventions Act
Education Act
*Expiring Laws Continuance Act
Export Guarantees Act
Family Allowances and National Insurance Act
Farm and Garden Chemicals Act
*Finance Act
Fishing Vessels Grants Act
Forestry Act
Fugitive Offenders Act
General Rate Act
Greenwich Hospital Act
Housing (Financial Provisions, &c.) (Scotland) Act
Housing Subsidies Act
Industrial and Provident Societies Act

Industrial Injuries and Diseases (Old Cases) Act
Irish Sailors and Soldiers Land Trust Act
Iron and Steel Act
Land Commission Act
Leasehold Reform Act
Legal Aid (Scotland) Act
Licensing (Amendment) Act
Licensing (Certificates in Suspense) (Scotland) Act
Llangollen International Musical Eisteddfod Act
Local Government (Termination of Reviews) Act
London Government Act
Marine, &c., Broadcasting (Offences) Act
Matrimonial Causes Act
Matrimonial Homes Act
Merchant Shipping Act
Merchant Shipping (Load Lines) Act
Misrepresentation Act
National Health Service (Family Planning) Act
National Insurance Act
National Insurance (Industrial Injuries) (Amendment) Act
Parliamentary Commissioner Act
Plant Health Act
Police (Scotland) Act
Post Office (Borowing Powers) Act
Post Office (Data Processing Service) Act
Prices and Incomes Act
Private Places of Entertainment (Licensing) Act
Protection of Birds Act
Public Records Act
Public Works Loans Act
Refreshment Houses Act
Remuneration of Teachers (Scotland) Act
Road Safety Act
Road Traffic Act
Road Traffic (Amendment) Act
Road Traffic (Driving Instruction) Act
Road Traffic Regulation Act

Road Transport Lighting Act
Royal Assent Act
Sea Fish (Conservation) Act
Sea Fisheries (Shellfish) Act
Sexual Offences Act
Shipbuilding Industry Act
Slaughter of Poultry Act
Superannuation (Miscellaneous Provisions) Act
Teachers of Nursing Act
Teachers' Superannuation Act
Tokyo Convention Act
Uniform Laws on International Sales Act
Vessels Protection Act
Water (Scotland) Act
Welsh Language Act
West Indies Act
Wireless Telegraphy Act

Local and Personal Acts

As their names imply, the operation of Local Acts is restricted to particular areas and that of Personal Acts to particular individuals. The list of Public General Acts above includes some statutes, such as the Llangollen International Musical Eisteddfod Act and the London Government Acts, whose application is clearly local: *they,* however, originated as Public Bills. Local Acts proper are distinguished by having originated as Private Bills. They can be grouped into six categories:

  (i) those relating to particular authorities;
 (ii) those creating bodies with local functions (water boards, harbour boards, etc.);
(iii) those authorizing local works by nationalized undertakings (electricity, gas, railways, canals, etc.);
(iv) those authorizing local works by national commercial concerns;
 (v) those concerning particular charitable institutions; and
(vi) those concerning particular educational institutions.

ELIZABETH II

1967 CHAPTER xl

An Act to confer further powers on the lord mayor, aldermen and citizens of the city of Manchester in relation to lands, water, highways, public health, local government, finance and pensions; and for other purposes.   [27th July 1967]

WHEREAS—

(1) The city of Manchester (in this Act called " the city ") is a county borough under the management and local government of the lord mayor, aldermen and citizens of the city (in this Act called " the Corporation "):

(2) It is expedient that further and better provision should be made with reference to lands and highways and the public health, local government and finances of the city and with respect to pensions:

(3) The Corporation are the owners of a public park and pleasure ground known as " Heaton Park " in the city:

FIG. 24. *Manchester Corporation Act 1967*

Figure 24 reproduces a page of an Act from the first category and shows part of the preamble — a feature of all Local Acts. The following list of Local Acts of 1967 illustrates the range of this kind of legislation and shows that it includes statutes confirming provisional orders.

Bath University of Technology Act
British Railways Act
British Transport Docks Act
Brunel University Act
Churches and Universities (Scotland) Widows' and Orphans' Fund (Amendment) Order Confirmation Act
City of London (Various Powers) Act
Dartford Tunnel Act
East Kilbride Burgh Act
Edinburgh Corporation Order Confirmation Act
Essex County Council (Canvey Island Approaches, etc.) Act
Forth Harbour Reorganisation Scheme Confirmation (Special Procedure) Act
Glasgow Corporation Order Confirmation Act
Greater London Council (General Powers) Act
Greater London Council (Money) Act
Greenock Corporation Order Confirmation Act
Guildford Corporation Act
Kingston upon Hull Corporation Act
London Bridge Act
London Transport Act
Manchester Corporation Act
Mersey Docks and Harbour Board Act
Metropolitan Water Board Act
Ministry of Housing and Local Government Provisional Orders Confirmation (Buxton, Stockport and York) Act
Ministry of Housing and Local Government Provisional Order Confirmation (Greater London Parks and Open Spaces) Act
Ministry of Housing and Local Government Provisional Order Confirmation (West Hertfordshire Main Drainage District) Act
Newcastle-under-Lyme Burgesses' Lands Act
Newquay Urban District Council Act

Pittenweem Harbour Order Confirmation Act
Port of London Act
Portsmouth Corporation Act
Rhymney Valley Sewerage Board Act
Royal Bank of Scotland Order Confirmation Act
St. Andrews Links Order Confirmation Act
Saint Barnabas, Lewisham Act
Saint Mary-le-Park, Battersea Act
Saint Stephen, South Lambeth Act
Somerset County Council Act
Tees Valley and Cleveland Water Act
The City University Act
University of Aston in Birmingham Act
University of Bradford Act
Wallasey Corporation Act

Personal Acts are extremely uncommon nowadays, and such instances
as do arise usually relate to private estates such as the Lucas Estate Act
1963. In earlier times they were concerned with such matters as change of
name, divorce and naturalization. Between 1798 and 1815 they were not
printed and could only be used as legal documents in the form of specially
authenticated copies. Now, however, most of them are printed and published by H.M.S.O., though even today some Private Acts of a very limited,
personal character are not printed.

PARTS OF AN ACT

A typical statute consists of a number of distinct parts. It is headed by
its *short title* which is normally the same as its *citation title* given at the
end of the text in the form "This Act may be cited as the [e.g.] Statutory
Instruments Act, 1946." An exception which can cause difficulty is the
sessional Consolidated Fund (Appropriation) Act which has the citation
title Appropriation Act and is so designated in the list of Acts on p. 112.
After the heading comes the *long title* which describes more fully the
purpose of the Act. There may or may not be a *preamble*, that is, a
statement of the reasons for the Act (the "mischief" it seeks to remedy)
and the effect it aims to achieve; it always begins with the word "Whereas

... " (see Fig. 24). While all Private Acts have preambles it must be said that this feature is generally coming to be much less used; only a small percentage of Public Acts now have them.

The actual provisions of the Acts are preceded by the *enacting formula* which reads: "Be it enacted by the Queen's most Excellent Majesty, by and with the advice and consent of the Lords Spiritual and Temporal, and Commons, in this present Parliament assembled, and by the authority of the same, as follows:" The real body of the Act is set out in numbered *sections* which may be divided into *subsections*, and these again, if necessary, subdivided into *paragraphs* and *sub-paragraphs*. For ease of reference sections are accompanied by brief marginal notes on their contents (see Fig. 23), and these are particularly useful in finding one's way about a long Act. Where necessary there are sections which define important words used in the Act; there may also be a section devoted to naming the date on which the Act will come into operation (or several dates on which different parts of the Act are to take effect), or responsibility for naming the date may be delegated to another authority. Finally there are often *schedules* containing details which would otherwise encumber the body of the Act — they may, for example, describe the functions of a board created by the Act or list the earlier statutes which it repeals.

CITATION OF ACTS

Under the provisions of the Acts of Parliament Numbering and Citation Act, 1962, all Acts from January 1963 onwards have been numbered serially each calendar year. The first Act to be numbered in this way was the Consolidated Fund Act 1963, whose proper mode of citation is 1963 c. 1; that is to say, chapter 1 of 1963. Use of the word "chapter" arises from the fact that at one time all the Acts passed in a parliamentary session were considered to be part of a continuous statute; each session had but one statute and the individual Acts of that session were its constituent chapters.

Prior to 1963 citation had been made by indicating the regnal year or years of the session in which the Act was passed. The first Public Libraries Act is thus cited as 13 & 14 Vict. c. 65; that is, the sixty-fifth Act of the parliamentary session occurring in the thirteenth and fourteenth years of the reign of Queen Victoria dating from her accession. Not infrequently it

happened that an Act was given two citations. The Consolidated Fund Act, 1962, for example, received the Royal Assent on 21 February 1962, that is, early in the tenth year of Elizabeth II's reign. At that time the Queen's Printer was obliged to use the citation 10 Eliz. 2 c. 7 since he could not be sure that the Queen would survive until her next Accession Day on 6 February the following year. But when in due course the Sovereign commenced her eleventh regnal year he was obliged to use the citation 10 & 11 Eliz. 2 c. 7 for the same Act. This latter citation in fact supersedes the first. Another occurrence which can cause confusion is when a session begins and ends within a single regnal year and another starts within that same year. This happened in 1950, and the result was that all Acts which received the Royal Assent during the 1950 session of Parliament which lasted from 1 March to 26 October 1950, and therefore came within the regnal year 11 December 1949 to 10 December 1950, were cited simply as 14 Geo. 6. This means that, for example, the Statute Law Revision Act, 1950, had the citation 14 Geo. 6 c. 6 and the Solicitors Act, 1950, the rather similar citation 14 & 15 Geo. 6 c. 6. On the other hand a session of Parliament can cover the end of one Sovereign's reign and part of the first regnal year of the next; and in this case both Sovereigns' names are included in the citation. There are no less than sixty-eight Acts with the citation 15 & 16 Geo. 6 & 1 Eliz. 2.

Clearly, this older method of citation can be very troublesome, as the equivalence between regnal and calendar years becomes a matter of familiarity only with constant use. The table on pages 120-25 shows the numbering of regnal years with their corresponding calendar dates.

Local Acts are differentiated by expressing the chapter number in small roman numerals whether preceded by the regnal year or the calendar year. Thus the Manchester Corporation Act 1967 is cited as 1967 c. xl. For Personal Acts the arabic chapter number is printed in italic type, e.g. the Lucas Estate Act 1963 is cited as 1963 c. *1*. General Synod (formerly Church Assembly) Measures have their numbers preceded by the abbreviation No., e.g. the Cathedrals Measure 1963 is cited as 1963 No. 2.

Finally it should be noted that in pre-1963 Acts the short title is separated from the year by a comma; whereas the comma is omitted in the titles of later Acts. Thus 11 & 12 Geo. 6 c. 38 is the Companies Act, 1948, but 1967 c. 81 is the Companies Act 1967.

In the present work citation title only are used.

Table of Regnal Years

JOHN
27 May 1199
19 Oct 1216

15	1213–14
16	1214–15
17	1215–16
18	May–Oct 1216

HENRY III
28 Oct 1216
16 Nov 1272

1	1216–17
2	1217–18
3	1218–19
4	1219–20
5	1220–21
6	1221–22
7	1222–23
8	1223–24
9	1224–25
10	1225–26
11	1226–27
12	1227–28
13	1228–29
14	1229–30
15	1230–31
16	1231–32
17	1232–33
18	1233–34
19	1234–35
20	1235–36
21	1236–37
22	1237–38
23	1238–39
24	1239–40
25	1240–41
26	1241–42
27	1242–43
28	1243–44
29	1244–45
30	1245–46
31	1246–47
32	1247–48
33	1248–49
34	1249–50
35	1250–51
36	1251–52
37	1252–53
38	1253–54
39	1254–55
40	1255–56
41	1256–57
42	1257–58
43	1258–59
44	1259–60
45	1260–61
46	1261–62
47	1262–63
48	1263–64
49	1264–65
50	1265–66
51	1266–67
52	1267–68
53	1268–69
54	1269–70
55	1270–71
56	1271–72
57	Oct–Nov 1272

EDWARD I
20 Nov 1272
7 July 1307

1	1272–73
2	1273–74
3	1274–75
4	1275–76
5	1276–77
6	1277–78
7	1278–79
8	1279–80
9	1280–81
10	1281–82
11	1282–83
12	1283–84
13	1284–85
14	1285–86
15	1286–87
16	1287–88
17	1288–89
18	1289–90
19	1290–91
20	1291–92
21	1292–93
22	1293–94
23	1294–95
24	1295–96
25	1296–97
26	1297–98
27	1298–99
28	1299–1300
29	1300–01
30	1301–02
31	1302–03
32	1303–04
33	1304–05
34	1305–06
35	Nov 1306–Jul 1307

EDWARD II
8 Jul 1307
20 Jan 1327

1	1307–08
2	1308–09
3	1309–10
4	1310–11
5	1311–12
6	1312–13
7	1313–14
8	1314–15
9	1315–16
10	1316–17
11	1317–18
12	1318–19
13	1319–20
14	1320–21
15	1321–22
16	1322–23
17	1323–24
18	1324–25
19	1325–26
20	Jul 1326–Jan 1327

EDWARD III
25 Jan 1327
21 Jun 1377

1	1327–28
2	1328–29
3	1329–30
4	1330–31
5	1331–32
6	1332–33
7	1333–34
8	1334–35
9	1335–36
10	1336–37
11	1337–38
12	1338–39
13	1339–40
14	1340–41
15	1341–42
16	1342–43
17	1343–44
18	1344–45
19	1345–46
20	1346–47
21	1347–48
22	1348–49
23	1349–50
24	1350–51
25	1351–52
26	1352–53
27	1353–54
28	1354–55
29	1355–56
30	1356–57
31	1357–58
32	1358–59
33	1359–60
34	1360–61
35	1361–62
36	1362–63
37	1363–64
38	1364–65
39	1365–66
40	1366–67
41	1367–68
42	1368–69
43	1369–70
44	1370–71
45	1371–72
46	1372–73
47	1373–74
48	1374–75
49	1375–76

50 1376–77	13 1411–12	25 1446–47	**EDWARD V**
51 Jan–Jun 1377	14 Sep 1412–	26 1447–48	9 Apr 1483
	Mar 1413	27 1448–49	25 Jun 1483
RICHARD II		28 1449–50	
22 Jun 1377	**HENRY V**	29 1450–51	**RICHARD III**
29 Sep 1399	21 Mar 1413	30 1451–52	26 Jun 1483
	31 Aug 1422	31 1452–53	22 Aug 1485
1 1377–78		32 1453–54	
2 1378–79	1 1413–14	33 1454–55	1 1483–84
3 1379–80	2 1414–15	34 1455–56	2 1484–85
4 1380–81	3 1415–16	35 1456–57	3 Jun–Aug 1485
5 1381–82	4 1416–17	36 1457–58	
6 1382–83	5 1417–18	37 1458–59	**HENRY VII**
7 1383–84	6 1418–19	38 1459–60	22 Aug 1485
8 1384–85	7 1419–20	39 Sep 1460–	21 Apr 1509
9 1385–86	8 1420–21	Mar 1461	
10 1386–87	9 1421–22		1 1485–86
11 1387–88	10 Mar–Aug 1422	**EDWARD IV**	2 1486–87
12 1388–89		4 Mar 1461	3 1487–88
13 1389–90	**HENRY VI**	9 Apr 1483	4 1488–89
14 1390–91	1 Sep 1422	(Henry VI re-	5 1489–90
15 1391–92	4 Mar 1461	stored 9 Oct	6 1490–91
16 1392–93		1470–c. Apr 1471)	7 1491–92
17 1393–94	1 1422–23		8 1492–93
18 1394–95	2 1423–24	1 1461–62	9 1493–94
19 1395–96	3 1424–25	2 1462–63	10 1494–95
20 1396–97	4 1425–26	3 1463–64	11 1495–96
21 1397–98	5 1426–27	4 1464–65	12 1496–97
22 1398–99	6 1427–28	5 1465–66	13 1497–98
23 Jun–Sep 1399	7 1428–29	6 1466–67	14 1498–99
	8 1429–30	7 1467–68	15 1499–1500
HENRY IV	9 1430–31	8 1468–69	16 1500–01
30 Sep 1399	10 1431–32	9 1469–70	17 1501–02
20 Mar 1413	11 1432–33	10 1470–71	18 1502–03
	12 1433–34	11 1471–72	19 1503–04
1 1399–1400	13 1434–35	12 1472–73	20 1504–05
2 1400–01	14 1435–36	13 1473–74	21 1505–06
3 1401–02	15 1436–37	14 1474–75	22 1506–07
4 1402–03	16 1437–38	15 1475–76	23 1507–08
5 1403–04	17 1438–39	16 1476–77	24 Aug 1508–
6 1404–05	18 1439–40	17 1477–78	Apr 1509
7 1405–06	19 1440–41	18 1478–79	
8 1406–07	20 1441–42	19 1479–80	**HENRY VIII**
9 1407–08	21 1442–43	20 1480–81	22 Apr 1509
10 1408–09	22 1443–44	21 1481–82	28 Jan 1547
11 1409–10	23 1444–45	22 1482–83	
12 1410–11	24 1445–46	23 Mar–Apr 1483	1 1509–10

2 1510–11	6 1552–53	11 1568–69	8 1610–11
3 1511–12	7 Jan–Jul 1553	12 1569–70	9 1611–12
4 1512–13	**MARY**	13 1570–71	10 1612–13
5 1513–14	6 Jul 1553	14 1571–72	11 1613–14
6 1514–15	24 Jul 1554	15 1572–73	12 1614–15
7 1515–16		16 1573–74	13 1615–16
8 1516–17	1 1553–54	17 1574–75	14 1616–17
9 1517–18	2 6–24 Jul 1554	18 1575–76	15 1617–18
10 1518–19		19 1576–77	16 1618–19
11 1519–20	**PHILIP and MARY**	20 1577–78	17 1619–20
12 1520–21	25 Jul 1554	21 1578–79	18 1620–21
13 1521–22	17 Nov 1558	22 1579–80	19 1621–22
14 1522–23		23 1580–81	20 1622–23
15 1523–24	1 & 2 1554–55	24 1581–82	21 1623–24
16 1524–25	2 & 3 1555–56	25 1582–83	22 1624–25
17 1525–26	3 & 4 1556–57	26 1583–84	23 24–27 Mar
18 1526–27	5 & 6 Jul–Nov	27 1584–85	1625
19 1527–28	1558	28 1585–86	
20 1528–29		29 1586–87	**CHARLES I**
21 1529–30	In each year after	30 1587–88	27 Mar 1625
22 1530–31	the Queen's	31 1588–89	30 Jan 1649
23 1531–32	marriage the	32 1589–90	
24 1532–33	period 6–24 July	33 1590–91	1 1625–26
25 1533–34	was indicated thus:	34 1591–92	2 1626–27
26 1534–35	1 & 3 6–24 Jul	35 1592–93	3 1627–28
27 1535–36	1555	36 1593–94	4 1628–29
28 1536–37	2 & 4 6–24 Jul	37 1594–95	5 1629–30
29 1537–38	1556	38 1595–96	6 1630–31
30 1538–39	3 & 5 6–24 Jul	39 1596–97	7 1631–32
31 1539–40	1557	40 1597–98	8 1632–33
32 1540–41	4 & 6 6–24 Jul	41 1598–99	9 1633–34
33 1541–42	1558	42 1599–1600	10 1634–35
34 1542–43		43 1600–01	11 1635–36
35 1543–44	**ELIZABETH I**	44 1601–02	12 1636–37
36 1544–45	17 Nov 1558	45 Nov 1602–	13 1637–38
37 1545–46	24 Mar 1603	Mar 1603	14 1638–39
38 Apr 1546–			15 1639–40
Jan 1547	1 1558–59	**JAMES I**	16 1640–41
EDWARD VI	2 1559–60	24 Mar 1603	17 1641–42
28 Jan 1547	3 1560–61	27 Mar 1625	18 1642–43
6 Jul 1553	4 1561–62		19 1643–44
	5 1562–63	1 1603–04	20 1644–45
1 1547–48	6 1563–64	2 1604–05	21 1645–46
2 1548–49	7 1564–65	3 1605–06	22 1646–47
3 1549–50	8 1565–66	4 1606–07	23 1647–48
4 1550–51	9 1566–67	5 1607–08	24 Mar 1648–
5 1551–52	10 1567–68	6 1608–09	Jan 1649
		7 1609–10	

COMMONWEALTH	JAMES II	7 1708−09	17 1743−44
From 30 Jan 1649	6 Feb 1685	8 1709−10	18 1744−45
to 29 May 1660	11 Dec 1688	9 1710−11	19 1745−46
public instruments		10 1711−12	20 1746−47
were simply dated	1 1685−86	11 1712−13	21 1747−48
with the day, the	2 1686−87	12 1713−14	22 1748−49
month and the year.	3 1687−88	13 Mar−Aug	23 1749−50
	4 Feb−Dec 1688	1714	24 1750−51
CHARLES II			25 1751−52
30 Jan 1649	WILLIAM and MARY	GEORGE I	26 1752−53
6 Feb 1685	13 Feb 1689	1 Aug 1714	27 1753−54
Charles II's regnal	8 Mar 1702	11 Jun 1727	28 1754−55
years are calculated	(Mary died		29 1755−56
from the death of	27 Dec 1694)	1 1714−15	30 1756−57
Charles I. The		2 1715−16	31 1757−58
restoration is	1 1689−90	3 1716−17	32 1758−59
therefore the twelfth	2 1690−91	4 1717−18	33 1759−60
year of his reign.	3 1691−92	5 1718−19	34 Jun−Oct
	4 1692−93	6 1719−20	1760
	5 1693−94	7 1720−21	
12 1660−61	6 Feb−Dec	8 1721−22	GEORGE III
13 1661−62	1694	9 1722−23	25 Oct 1760
14 1662−63		10 1723−24	29 Jan 1820
15 1663−64	WILLIAM III	11 1724−25	
16 1664−65	27 Dec 1694	12 Aug 1726−	
17 1665−66	8 Mar 1702	Jun 1727	1 1760−61
18 1666−67			2 1761−62
19 1667−68	7 1694−95	GEORGE II	3 1762−63
20 1668−69	8 1695−96	11 Jun 1727	4 1763−64
21 1669−70	9 1696−97	25 Oct 1760	5 1764−65
22 1670−71	10 1697−98		6 1765−66
23 1671−72	11 1698−99	1 1727−28	7 1766−67
24 1672−73	12 1699−1700	2 1728−29	8 1767−68
25 1673−74	13 1700−01	3 1729−30	9 1768−69
26 1674−75	14 Dec 1701−	4 1730−31	10 1769−70
27 1675−76	Mar 1702	5 1731−32	11 1770−71
28 1676−77		6 1732−33	12 1771−72
29 1677−78	ANNE	7 1733−34	13 1772−73
30 1678−79	8 Mar 1702	8 1734−35	14 1773−74
31 1679−80	1 Aug 1714	9 1735−36	15 1774−75
32 1680−81		10 1736−37	16 1775−76
33 1681−82	1 1702−03	11 1737−38	17 1776−77
34 1682−83	2 1703−04	12 1738−39	18 1777−78
35 1683−84	3 1704−05	13 1739−40	19 1778−79
36 1684−85	4 1705−06	14 1740−41	20 1779−80
37 Jan−Feb	5 1706−07	15 1741−42	21 1780−81
1685	6 1707−08	16 1742−43	22 1781−82
			23 1782−83

24 1783–84	1 1820–21	19 1855–56	**EDWARD VII**
25 1784–85	2 1821–22	20 1856–57	22 Jan 1901
26 1785–86	3 1822–23	21 1857–58	6 May 1910
27 1786–87	4 1823–24	22 1858–59	
28 1787–88	5 1824–25	23 1859–60	1 1901–02
29 1788–89	6 1825–26	24 1860–61	2 1902–03
30 1789–90	7 1826–27	25 1861–62	3 1903–04
31 1790–91	8 1827–28	26 1862–63	4 1904–05
32 1791–92	9 1828–29	27 1863–64	5 1905–06
33 1792–93	10 1829–30	28 1864–65	6 1906–07
34 1793–94	11 Jan–Jun	29 1865–66	7 1907–08
35 1794–95	1830	30 1866–67	8 1908–09
36 1795–96		31 1867–68	9 1909–10
37 1796–97	**WILLIAM IV**	32 1868–69	10 Jan–May
38 1797–98	26 Jun 1830	33 1869–70	1910
39 1798–99	20 Jun 1837	34 1870–71	
40 1799–1800		35 1871–72	**GEORGE V**
41 1800–01	1 1830–31	36 1872–73	6 May 1910
42 1801–02	2 1831–32	37 1873–74	20 Jan 1936
43 1802–03	3 1832–33	38 1874–75	
44 1803–04	4 1833–34	39 1875–76	1 1910–11
45 1804–05	5 1834–35	40 1876–77	2 1911–12
46 1805–06	6 1835–36	41 1877–78	3 1912–13
47 1806–07	7 1836–37	42 1878–79	4 1913–14
48 1807–08		43 1879–80	5 1914–15
49 1808–09	**VICTORIA**	44 1880–81	6 1915–16
50 1809–10	20 Jun 1837	45 1881–82	7 1916–17
	22 Jan 1901	46 1882–83	8 1917–18
REGENCY		47 1883–84	9 1918–19
Feb 1811–	1 1837–38	48 1884–85	10 1919–20
Jan 1820	2 1838–39	49 1885–86	11 1920–21
	3 1839–40	50 1886–87	12 1921–22
51 1810–11	4 1840–41	51 1887–88	13 1922–23
52 1811–12	5 1841–42	52 1888–89	14 1923–24
53 1812–13	6 1842–43	53 1889–90	15 1924–25
54 1813–14	7 1843–44	54 1890–91	16 1925–26
55 1814–15	8 1844–45	55 1891–92	17 1926–27
56 1815–16	9 1845–46	56 1892–93	18 1927–28
57 1816–17	10 1846–47	57 1893–94	19 1928–29
58 1817–18	11 1847–48	58 1894–95	20 1929–30
59 1818–19	12 1848–49	59 1895–96	21 1930–31
60 Oct 19–	13 1849–50	60 1896–97	22 1931–32
Jan 20	14 1850–51	61 1897–98	23 1932–33
	15 1851–52	62 1898–99	24 1933–34
GEORGE IV	16 1852–53	63 1899–1900	25 1934–35
29 Jan 1820	17 1853–54	64 Jun 1900–	26 May 35–
26 Jun 1830	18 1854–55	Jan 1901	Jan 36

EDWARD VIII	5 1940–41	ELIZABETH II	11 1962–63
20 Jan 1936	6 1941–42	6 Feb 1952	
11 Dec 1936	7 1942–43		From 1963, Acts
	8 1943–44	1 1952–53	cited by
GEORGE VI	9 1944–45	2 1953–54	calendar year
11 Dec 1936	10 1945–46	3 1954–55	
6 Feb 1952	11 1946–47	4 1955–56	
	12 1947–48	5 1956–57	
1 1936–37	13 1948–49	6 1957–58	
2 1937–38	14 1949–50	7 1958–59	
3 1938–39	15 1950–51	8 1959–60	
4 1939–40	16 Dec 1951–	9 1960–61	
	Feb 1952	10 1961–62	

EDITIONS OF THE ACTS

Acts are first published as single copies by H.M.S.O. Two prints are made on vellum, endorsed with the wording of the Royal Assent and signed by the Clerk of the Parliaments. Of these official copies one is preserved in the Public Record Office and the other in the House of Lords. The bulk of the printing on ordinary paper is put on sale to the public, and these single items are referred to as Queen's Printer's copies. Often they are available within a few days of receiving the Royal Assent. In libraries and lawyers' offices where files of Acts are needed for reference purposes it is usual for single copies to be discarded when the Acts issued during the year are republished in bound volumes.

Public General Acts and Measures

The annual bound volumes published by H.M.S.O. are entitled *Public General Acts and Measures;* nowadays there are usually two or three volumes per annum. They begin with four tables:

    I   Alphabetical List of the Public General Acts;
   II Chronological List of the Public General Acts;
  III Alphabetical List of the Local and Personal Acts;
  IV Chronological List of the General Synod Measures.

Then come the texts of the Acts themselves in chapter number order (see p. 118), and texts of the General Synod Measures. These are followed by two more tables:

    V   Tables of Derivations of the Consolidation Acts, and
    VI Effect of Legislation.

For each Act which consolidates related earlier enactments a table (V) is given showing against each section of the new Act the corresponding section or sections of the Acts they replace. In the table or effects (VI) earlier Acts and Measures which have been repealed or otherwise affected by the Acts, Measures and Statutory Instruments of the present year are listed in chronological order, and against each is indicated how it has been affected and by what part of the new legislation (Fig. 25). Concluding the bound volumes is an index to the Acts and Measures of the year in which titles of Acts and names of subjects are listed in one alphabetical sequence (Fig. 26). These annual volumes have been published since 1831, at first under the title *Public General Statutes*. Annotations to Acts are published annually.

Non-Official Editions

Several editions of the Acts, most of which are annotated, are issued by commercial publishers. *Current Law Statutes,* published by Sweet and Maxwell, appear first in paper parts which are eventually replaced by bound annual volumes. Each volume contains, in addition to chronological and alphabetical lists of the year's statutes, a Statute Citator which, in one chronological sequence comprises (i) statutes passed; (ii) statutory instruments issued under rule-making powers; (iii) cases on the construction of statutes; and (iv) statutes amended, applied, repealed or otherwise affected by legislation. In addition to including annotations this service also includes Scottish legislation.

While Halsbury's *Statutes of England* does not include Scottish legislation it offers other advantages. The third edition now in course of publication will consist of forty text volumes and a Consolidated Index Volume which will also contain the alphabetical and chronological lists of statutes printed in the work. Every important Public General Act and General Synod Measure in force will be included, together with a certain number of essential Private and Local Acts. The arrangement as in earlier editions will be under "titles", e.g. Admiralty, Banking, Companies, Elections,

Effect of Legislation

Session and Chap. or No. of Measure	Short title or Subject	How affected	Chapter of 1967 Act or number of Measure or Statutory Instrument
1967—*cont*:			
c. 4	West Indies Act 1967 ...	Apptd. days fixed for whole Act.	S.I. No. 222.
		S. 3(3) appl.	71, s. 2(3).
c. 8	Plant Health Act 1967 ...	S. 3(4)(*a*)(*b*) am. ...	80, s. 92, sch. 3 Pt. II.
c. 9	General Rate Act 1967 ...	Apptd. day for commencement of Act (1.4.1967).	S.I. No. 499.
		S. 47 rep. (saving) (1.4.1968).	9, s. 117(2).
		Sch. 8 am.	S.I. Nos. 406–413, 1336.
		Sch. 13 para. 2 am. ...	29, sch. 3 para. 12.
c. 10	Forestry Act 1967 ...	Restr. (S.)	86, s. 60.
		S. 1(2) ext. (S.)	86, s. 65(5)(*e*).
		S. 3 ext. (S.)	86, s. 58(1)–(4).
		S. 9(6) am. (" public open space ") (S.).	86, s. 58(5).
		S. 17(1) am.	69, s. 15(2).
		S. 30(5) am.	80, s. 92, sch. 3 Pt. I.
		S. 39 am. (S.)	86, s. 59.
		S. 41(3)(*b*), (4) am. (S.) ...	86, s. 58(6).
		S. 46 am. (S.)	86, s. 58(3).
		S. 46(5) am.	80, s. 92, sch. 3 Pt. I.
		S. 46(5)(*c*) am.	80, s. 103(1), sch. 6 para. 28.
		S. 48(3) am.	80, s. 92, sch. 3 Pt. I.
c. 12	Teachers Superannuation Act 1967.	Sch. 1 para. 3(1)(*d*) am....	28, s. 16(1)(*a*).
		Sch. 1 para. 4 rep.	28, s. 16(1)(*b*).
c. 13	Parliamentary Commissioner Act 1967.	Apptd. day for commencement of Act (1.4.1967).	S.I. No. 485.
		Sch. 3 para. 4 am. ...	68, s. 21(4).
c. 17	Iron and Steel Act 1967	S. 40(1) rep.	54, s. 45(8), sch. 16 Pt. VII.
c. 21	Road Traffic Act 1967 ...	Rep.	76, s. 110, schs. 7, 8.
c. 22	Agriculture Act 1967 ...	Apptd. day for commencement of Act exc. s. 22 (11.5.1967).	S.I. No. 733.
c. 25	National Insurance (Industrial Injuries) (Amendment) Act 1967.	Ss. 1(1)(2) rep. in pt., 1(3) rep., 1(4), 2, 3(3)(*b*) rep., 3(4) rep. in pt.	34, s. 15(1)–(3), sch.
c. 28	Superannuation (Miscellaneous Provisions) Act 1967.	S. 13(3) am.	77, ss. 52(1), 53, sch. 4.
c. 30	Road Safety Act 1967 ...	Apptd. day for s. 7 (15.6.1967).	S.I. No. 904.

FIG. 25. *Public General Acts and Measures: Effect of Legislation*

INDEX

TO THE

Public General Acts

AND

GENERAL SYNOD MEASURES 1972

A

ACCIDENTS. Road traffic provisions (c. 20, ss. 25–28) ...   I, pp. 195–197

ACTS OF PARLIAMENT.

Consolidation Acts. *See* BETTING AND GAMING DUTIES ACT (c. 25); CONTRACTS OF EMPLOYMENT ACT (c. 53); LAND CHARGES ACT (c. 61); LOCAL EMPLOYMENT ACT (c. 5); NATIONAL DEBT ACT (c. 65); POISONS ACT (c. 66); ROAD TRAFFIC ACT (c. 20); SUMMER TIME ACT (c. 6); TOWN AND COUNTRY PLANNING (SCOTLAND) ACT (c. 52).

ADMINISTRATION OF JUSTICE (SCOTLAND) ACT: c. 59 ...   ...   II, p. 1714

    § 1. Extended powers of courts to order inspection of documents and other property, . etc., II, p. 1714.
      2. Appeal to House of Lords from interlocutor of Court of Session on motion for new trial, II, p. 1715.
      3. Power of arbiter to state case to Court of Session, II, p. 1716.
      4. Rate of interest in sheriff court decrees or extracts, II, p. 1716.
      5. Short title, interpretation, commencement and extent, II, p. 1716.

ADMISSION TO HOLY COMMUNION MEASURE: No. 1 ...   ...   III, p. 2529

    § 1. Admission to Holy Communion, III, p. 2529.
      2. Short title, III, p. 2529.   •

AFFILIATION PROCEEDINGS (AMENDMENT) ACT: c. 49 ...   ...   II, p. 1157

    § 1. Powers of court on hearing complaint for affiliation order and on appeal, II, p. 1157.
      2. Time for application for summons, II, p. 1158.
      3. Procedure on application for, or for variation, revival or revocation of, affiliation order, II, p. 1158.
      4. Short title, extent and commencement, II, p. 1159.

AGENCY. Value added tax provisions (c. 41, s. 24) ...   ,..   I, p. 578

AGRICULTURE (MISCELLANEOUS PROVISIONS) ACT: c. 62 ...   ...   II, p. 1829

    § 1. Control of zoonoses, II, p. 1830.
      2. Application of provisions of Diseases of Animals Act 1950 to further animals, II, p. 1831.
      3. Seizure of milk etc. liable to spread disease, II, p. 1832.
      4. Furnishing by milk marketing boards of information derived from tests of milk, II, p. 1832.

FIG. 26. *Public General Acts and Measures: Index*

Housing, Insurance, Libel and Slander, Local Government, Negligence, Parliament, Real Property, Taxation, Town and Country Planning, etc. Each title is prefaced by a short introductory statement to that branch of the law, and annotations to the Acts given concisely the information necessary for understanding and applying them. The system of arranging Acts by subject does, however, mean that those dealing with more than one subject are split up, one part going under one heading, another part under a different heading. Updating is provided through a bound annual supplement of statutes, and a loose-leaf Current Statutes Service covering the most recent enactments.

From the same publisher comes *Butterworths Annotated Legislation Service* which is different again. It grew out of *Butterworths Emergency Legislation Service (Annotated): Statutes* of which there were two volumes plus a Complete Master Index. The present service is selective. Its slim numbered volumes come out irregularly; some contain several Acts, other just one. Detailed annotations are provided and this entails a certain delay in publication. A cumulative index volume is published containing both alphabetical and chronological lists keyed to the volume numbers.

The Law Reports Statutes are sent as unbound paper parts to subscribers to the Law Reports published by the Incorporated Council of Law Reporting.

Statutes at Large

When it is necessary to consult older statutes in the form in which they were originally promulgated there are several editions which may be used. First there are the various editions of the *Statutes at Large* of which the most frequently used are Runnington's new edition of Ruffhead's *Statutes at Large from Magna Charta to 25 George III (1784–5)* (10 vols., 1786), Tomlins and Raithby's *Statutes at Large, Magna Charta to the Union* (10 vols. quarto, 20 vols. octavo, 1811) and Danby Pickering's *Statutes at Large from Magna Charta to 1761* and its continuation volumes to 1806, totalling forty-six volumes (1762–1807). The two latter are continued by the officially published *Statutes of the United Kingdom of Great Britain and Ireland* which started with 1807 and came down to 1869.

The most accurate edition of the statutes for the early period is *Statutes of the Realm 1225–1713* which was prepared under the

authority of the Record Commissioners. It is in ten large volumes, with a separate Alphabetical Index and Chronological Index, and was published between 1810 and 1828. Texts are given in both modern English and in the language of the time where this was different. Each volume has its own index and in addition there are cumulative indexes by subject and by date. Useful information on the sources of early legislation is given in the introduction.

Acts and Ordinances of the Interregnum, 1642–1660 collected by C. H. Firth and R. S. Rait (H.M.S.O., 1911) apart from containing texts of these documents of the Commonwealth and indexes by date and subject also includes a study of the legislation of the period.

Further information on sources of early Statutes will be found in:

> HOLDSWORTH, W. S., *Sources and Literature of English Law* (1925).
> PRICE, M. O. and BITNER, H. *Effective Legal Research* (1953).
> SWEET and MAXWELL's *Guide to Law Reports and Statutes* (4th edn., 1962).
> WINFIELD, P. H. *The Chief Sources of English Legal History* (1925).

The Statutes Revised

All the statutes which were in force in whole or in part on the last day of 1948 are included in the latest edition of the *Statutes Revised* (32 vols, 1950). This is the third and last edition of this work; the first had comprised statutes in force at the end of 1878 (publication completed in 1885), and the second those in force at the end of 1920 (publication completed in 1929). Acts of a local or personal or private nature, and in some instances sections or parts of sections of a like nature, have been omitted. The Statute Law Revision Act, 1950, extended the categories of authorized omission by proving that:

> From any revised edition of the statutes published by authority there may be omitted enactments or words in respect of matters exclusively relating to territory within the jurisdiction of any one or more of the following, that is to say, Canada, Australia, New Zealand, the Union of South Africa, India, Pakistan, Ceylon, The Republic of Ireland, Burma and, so far as relates to matters within the powers of the Parliament thereof, Northern Ireland.

Repealed portions of Acts are omitted except where they are necessary for the construction of unrepealed parts, and in such cases they are printed in small type. Where a whole section is repealed a reference to the repealing enactment is usually inserted; otherwise the omission is indicated by asterisks. A Chronological Table of Statutes which is provided indicates the subject matter of the statute and, where appropriate, the reasons for total or partial omission. The text of this edition for statutes down to 1714 is, like that of the first and second edition, based on that of the *Statutes of the Realm*, giving parallel contemporary and modern English versions. Another table gives variances in citations between the *Statutes of the Realm* and Runnington's edition of *Ruffhead's Statutes at Large*.

Statutes in Force: Official Revised Edition

At present the Public General Statutes comprise the above edition of the *Statutes Revised* plus the annual volumes of the Public General Acts since 1949 and the single copies of Acts of the current year. Such, however, is the quantity of new legislation that it is estimated that by the end of 1965 over 9000 of the 26,000 pages of the *Statutes Revised* and over 4000 of the 21,000 pages of the *Public General Acts* for the period 1949–65 had been cancelled (Law Commission, *Third Annual Report, 1967–68*, H.M.S.O., 1968, para. 84). In view of this serious situation it has been decided to break with the old pattern of publication and to institute in its place a loose-leaf edition of the Statutes called *Statutes in Force: Official Revised Edition.* It is the responsibility of an editorial board working under the direction of the Statute Law Committee. Separate booklets each containing one statute are published in subject groups and in a form suitable for insertion into loose-leaf binders. This enables the statute book to be kept up to date by means of replacement booklets as necessary. Acts which relate to more than one subject are published in each appropriate subject group; though where this is felt to be unnecessary the editors supply adequate cross-references.

Complementing this new edition is the work of codification and consolidation of the statute law being carried out by the Law Commissions. The Law Commissioners in acknowledging this have undertaken to assist by pressing ahead with consolidation, thus ensuring that "clean" statutes are ready for the new edition; by preparing a series of statute law revision

Bills designed to eliminate ultimately all the obsolete and unnecessary enactments in the statute book; and by encouraging the use of methods of drafting designed to facilitate the "slotting in" to existing statutes of newly enacted amendments or additional material, thus reducing the need for periodical consolidations.

CODIFICATION

There is no better authority on the subject of codification in England than the Chairman of the Law Commission, Mr. Justice Scarman. Speaking on "Codification and Judge-Made Law" in the Faculty of Law of Birmingham University in October 1966, he said:

> Codification may well include amendment, statute law revision and consolidation: but each is a separate technique to which Parliament may have resort without going so far as to codify the law. Parliament may, and often does, amend without attempting a comprehensive restatement of the law: it leaves the general body of the law, whether statute or judge-made intact. Statute law revision and consolidation are techniques of law reform . . . which differ in material respects from codification. Statute law revision, as practised in England, is a process whereby obsolete and unnecessary enactments are removed from the statute book. Consolidation is the technique whereby existing statute law on a given topic is reduced into one without altering the substance of the law. Thus, codification will almost invariably include statute law revision and consolidation; but it is something more, for it purports not only to revise, re-arrange, and re-state existing statute law but to formulate comprehensively − with amendments, if necessary − all the law within its field, whether the law's historical source be statute, or custom in the shape of judicial decision.

In the last two decades of the last century and the first decade of this there were four codifying statutes, namely:

(i) Bills of Exchange Act, 1882

An Act to codify the law relating to Bills of Exchange, Cheques, and Promissory Notes;

(ii) Partnership Act, 1890

An Act to declare and amend the Law of Partnership;

(iii) Sale of Goods Act, 1893

An Act for codifying the Law relating to the Sale of Goods; and

(iv) Marine Insurance Act, 1906

The history of codification was next furthered by the Law Commissions

Act 1965 under whose provisions two Law Commissions were constituted, one for England and Wales and one for Scotland, with the duty

> to take and keep under review all the law with which they are respectively concerned with a view to its systematic development and reform, including in particular the codification of such law, the elimination of anomalies, the repeal of obsolete and unnecessary enactments, the reduction of the number of separate enactments and generally the simplification and modernisation of the law.

It remains, of course, for Parliament to pass, amend or reject such draft Bills as the commissions may think fit to introduce. Recent examples of consolidation Bills which have passed into law are the Capital Allowances Act 1968, the Criminal Appeal Act 1968 and the Rent Act 1968; and a statute law revision Bill which was recently enacted is the Statutue Law (Repeals) Act 1968.

OFFICIAL INDEXES

Monthly and Annual Catalogues

Acts of Parliament are first noted in the Daily Lists of government publications issued by H.M.S.O. (see pp. 19-21), and later appear in both the Monthly and Annual Catalogues. The information given consists simply of the title, chapter number and price; but the fact that the monthly and annual catalogues are indexed does mean that they provide subject access to the Acts. As already noted, the bound volumes of the Public General Acts and Measures also include chronological and alphabetical lists.

Index to the Statutes

The *Index to the Statutes* (Fig. 27) is produced by the Statutory Publications Office and published annually by H.M.S.O. in two volumes. It covers the legislation in force from 1235 (the date of the Statute of Merton) down to the present. Entries are grouped under subject headings and each item indexed is followed by a reference to relevant statutes in the form of a citation made up of the calendar year, chapter number, section, etc. At the beginning of each subject group there is a list of all the Acts

Index to the Statutes

on 31st December 1971

A

ABANDONMENT
　Of animals *See* ANIMALS, 1
　Of canals *See* CANAL, 3(*a*),(*d*)
　Of infants *See* INFANT, 1(*a*)
　Of mines *See* MINES AND QUARRIES, 3(*b*)(ii),(*n*)
　Of independent railways *See* NATIONAL TRANSPORT, 4(*e*)
　Of theatrical performers *See* THEATRE, 4
　Of tramways *See* TRAMWAY, 7

ABATEMENT, ENGLAND
　Of action, suit, indictment, proceeding, etc., by demise of Crown *See* CROWN, 3
　Application of certain repealed enactments to inferior cts. *See* INFERIOR COURT, E, 2
　Abated suit, revivor of, to enforce payment of costs *See* COSTS, 6
　　See also DAMAGES, 2, 3 (actions surviving death) *And see* PENSION, 3(*a*)

ABATEMENT, NORTHERN IRELAND
　Of indictment or information, by reason of dilatory plea *See* Criminal Law (Ireland) Act
　　1828 c.54 s.30
　Of proceedings in Landed Estates Court, now (in NI) Court of Chancery Judge *See* SUPREME
　　COURT, NI, 2(*h*),4(*b*)(viii)
　Abated suit, revivor of, to enforce payment of costs *See* COSTS, 6
　Reservation of matters relating to Supreme Ct., NI *See* SUPREME COURT, NI, 1

ABBEY LANDS *See* BISHOP, 3(*a*)

ABBREVIATE, SCOTLAND *See* BANKRUPTCY, S,2(*c*)(*e*)(*i*)

ABDICATION (King Edward VIII) *See* CROWN, 1,3

ABDUCTION
　1861 c.100　Offences against the person　　　　　1948 c.58　Crim. Justice
　1885 c.69　Crim. Law Amdt.

　　　　　　1 *Offences*　　　　　　　　　　　　　　　　2 *Procedure*

1 Offences

In England—
　of women and girls *See* SEXUAL OFFENCES, 1
　of child under 14, and receiving child so abducted: E 1861 c.100 s.56
　　　　　　　　　　　　　　　　　　　　　　1948 c.58 s.83, sch.10,Pt.I
In Scotland—
　of girl under 18, with intent of unlawful connexion: S 1885 c.69 s.7
Offences under s.56 of 1861 punishable more heavily where firearms carried *See* FIREARMS

FIG. 27. *Index to the Statutes*

indexed therein, giving the year and chapter number of each Act followed by its short title or, where none exists, an indicative title. Thus the short title of any Act cited in the text can easily be identified. There are numerous cross references both within headings and from one heading to another. At the beginning of the first volume each year is a Table of Statutes, on tinted paper, which lists in chronological order all the Acts and General Synod Measures and gives references to their location in the body of the work. Territorial limitations of the Acts are indicated by means of capital initials, e.g. E = England, S = Scotland; except that where there is an appreciable quantity of legislation relating to one part of Great Britain only (usually Scotland) a separate heading is included which incorporates the name of the part, e.g. Charities, Scotland. The effect of the Acts of the Scottish Parliaments 1424–1707 is shown throughout the text. No distinguishing mark is used in such instances to single them out, but in the lists at the beginning of headings these Acts are differentiated by an S within bold-face square brackets. As far as regards Northern Ireland the only headings to be retained are those whose subject matter is reserved for legislation by the Parliament at Westminster. To the extent to which legislative powers were handed over to the new Northern Ireland legislature in 1923, the relevant enactments were eliminated from the Index; for those which are still operative recourse should be had to the *Northern Ireland Index to the Statutes*. Groups of Acts are often given a collective title by which they may be cited – e.g. the Companies Acts 1948 to 1967 – and these are shown in a footnote to the heading under which such a group appears. All the Acts in a collective title need not necessarily have the same, or even a similar short title; their titles, can, however, be ascertained by selecting from the table of Acts at the top of the heading those Acts which have the same footnote letter against them as the collective title footnote itself. Powers to make regulations, etc., contained in the Acts are shown as ordinary entries in the various headings, but for any exercise of such powers reference should be made to the official *Index to Government Orders* (see pp. 155-6). Where an enactment is totally repealed, including cases of total repeal by Statute Law Revision Acts, references are moved. References to provisions effecting a partial repeal of one of the enactments cited in an entry are retained in the entry even when the Act of which they are part has been subsequently totally repealed or when they themselves have ben individually repealed

in the normal course of statute law revision. This is necessary to ensure that the fact of the partial repeal of the earlier Act is duly recorded and preserved in accordance with s. 38(2) of the Interpretation Act, 1889. There are a number of appendices relating to Acts which, though printed amongst Public Acts, are not indexed in detail, being of a local and personal or quasi-local and personal character; nor are their amendments (if any) shown. The headings used are: Canals; Cornwall, Duchy of; Crown Lands; Fortifications, Dockyards, etc.; Harbours; London; Marriages Confirmation; Public Buildings; and Public Works Loans. Nearly all the Acts listed in these appendices are omitted from the *Statutes Revised* as being local. In the case of Acts not included in the appendices reference should be made to the *Index to the Local and Personal Acts 1801–1947,* the *Supplementary Index to the Local and Personal Acts 1948–1966,* and the subsequent annual issues of the *Index of Local and Personal Acts* (see pp. 141-3). Finally there is a concordance of variant references to regnal years, statutes and chapters in the *Statutes of the Realm* and Ruffhead's edition of the statutes (see pp. 129-30).

Chronological Table of the Statutes

A statement of the history of each enactment is provided by the *Chronological Table of the Statutes* (Fig. 28) which, like the *Index to the Statutes* is prepared in the Statutory Publications Office and published annually by H.M.S.O. Again, it covers the period from 1235 down to the present. The first edition was published in 1870. The Table is based on the edition of the Record Commissioners, known as the *Statutes of the Realm,* as far as that edition extends, namely to the end of the reign of Queen Anne (13 Anne) in 1714. Thenceforth Ruffhead's edition (by Serjeant Runnington) has been followed, as far as it extends, namely to the end of the session of the twenty-fifth year of the reign of King George III (25 Geo. 3) in 1785. The variances between the *Statutes of the Realm* and Ruffhead's edition are partly shown in footnotes or in parentheses; and a full concordance of them precedes the body of the text. Later Acts are those printed by the Queen's (or King's) Printers as Public or Public General Acts. Where the subject matter is of restricted application – local personal or private – the fact is indicated. Ante-Union Acts of the Parliaments of Scotland and Ireland are not included in the general table, but a

chronological table of the Acts of the Scottish Parliaments before the Union of England and Scotland follows the table of the Westminister Acts and is prepared on similar lines.*

Below each calendar year (with, up to and including 1962, the appropriate regnal year following it in brackets) are set out the chapter numbers of the Acts in sequence and opposite them their short title or subject matter (with any necessary annotations), arranged as follows:

Repealed and Expired Acts. In the case of repealed Acts the short title of the Act (or in the absence of a short title, the general subject-matter) is printed in italic type with a reference to the repealing enactment. Short titles of expired Acts are also shown in italics but with the date of expiry and a reference to the relevant provisions.

Acts wholly or partly in force. The short title (or, in the absence of a short title, the general subject in square brackets) is printed in heavy type. References are added in ordinary type to subsequent enactments by which the operation of the Act has been amended, extended, restricted or otherwise affected. These subsequent enactments may include General Synod Measures, Statutory Rules and Orders or Statutory Instruments. The Orders in Council which adapted legislation in giving effect to constitutional changes in Ireland are not noted, but are mentioned in the *Index to the Statutes* under the headings "EIRE" and "NORTHERN IRELAND".

As regards repeals, annotations are made in accordance with the following general practice:

(a) in a few instances, Acts have been repealed in part after having been wholly repealed; in such cases the later partial repeal is disregarded;
(b) in other instances, Acts have been repealed more than once; in such cases a discretion has been exercised as to which repealing Act should be entered, and in some cases more than one is entered;
(c) a repeal made nugatory by an express or implied revival is not normally retained;

* A volume of the *Ante-Union Irish Acts (Revised)* was published by H.M.S.O. in 1885; that volume contains an index to such Acts arranged as in the *Index to the Statutes.* Information as to Ante-Union Irish Acts is given in the *Chronological Table of Statutes in Northern Ireland.* Poynings Act, extending English Statutes to Ireland, is printed in *Irish Statutes Revised,* p. 3. A second revised edition of *The Acts of the Parliaments of Scotland 1424–1707* was published by H.M.S.O. in 1966.

1962 (10 & 11 Eliz. 2)
        s. 7 ext.—Civil Aviation, 1968 (c. 61), s. 15 (4).
        am.—Civil Aviation, 1968 (c. 61), s. 15 (5).
  c. 9 .. **Local Govt. (Financial Provns. etc.) (S.).**
        s. 1 mod.—Local Govt. (Financial Provns.) (S.), 1963 (c. 12), s. 7 (5), sch. 1 para. 1.
        3 expld.—Gas, 1965 (c. 36), s. 3 (3) (12) (*a*).
        ext.—Gas, 1965 (c. 36), s. 3 (6) (12) (*a*).
        4 ext.—Local Govt. (S.), 1966 (c. 51), s. 25 (5).
        sch. 1 am.—S.I. 1964/2016 (1964 III, p. 5089); S.I. 1966/174; S.I. 1968/198.
        sch. 2 r. in pt.—Transport, 1962 (c. 46), ss. 66 (11), 95 (2), sch. 12 pt. II.
  c. 10 .. **Army Reserve.**
        s. 1, 2 r.—Reserve Forces, 1966 (c. 30), s. 23 (6) (7), schs. 1 para. 38, 2
        3 ext.—Reserve Forces, 1966 (c. 30), s. 8 (1) (2) (*b*).
        r. in pt. and superseded—Reserve Forces, 1966 (c. 30), ss. 4 (1) (2), 23 (7), sch. 2.
        4, 5, 6 r. in pt.—Reserve Forces, 1966 (c. 30), s. 23 (7), sch. 2.
        sch. am.—Reserve Forces, 1966 (c. 30), s. 23 (6), sch. 1 para. 39.
        r. in pt.—Reserve Forces, 1966 (c. 30), s. 23 (7), sch. 2.
  c. 11 .. *Consolidated Fund (No. 2).*—r., S.L.R., 1964.
  c. 12 .. **Education.**
        ext. (London)—London Govt., 1963 (c. 33), s. 30 (1).
        s. 1, 2 expld. (London)—London Govt., 1963 (c. 33), s. 33 (1).
        5, 6 r.—Education(S.), 1962 (c. 47), s. 147 sch. 8.
        9 saved—Family Allowances, 1965 (c. 53), s. 2 (2).
        10 r.—Education (S.), 1962 (c. 47), ss. 147, 148, schs. 8, 9.
        sch. 1 ext. (London)—London Govt., 1963 (c. 33), s. 33 (2).
  c. 13 .. **Vehicles (Excise).**
        excl.—Purchase Tax, 1963 (c. 9), s. 33 (3).
        am.—Wireless Telegraphy, 1967 (c. 72), s. 8 (1).
        s. 2 am.—S.I. 1968/439.
        5 am.—Finance (No. 2), 1964 (c. 92), s. 9 (6).
        excl.—Finance, 1966 (c. 18), s. 2 (13) (*a*).
        6 am.—Finance, 1965 (c. 25), s. 6 (1).
        7 expld.—Finance, 1962 (c. 44), s. 5 (1); Finance, 1967 (c. 54), s. 12.
        ext.—(E.) Finance, 1965 (c. 25), s. 7; Finance, 1967 (c. 54), s. 12.
        am.—Finance, 1967 (c. 54), s. 11 (1).
        8 am.—Purchase Tax, 1963 (c. 9), s. 28 (3); Transport, 1968 (c. 73), s. 147.
        power to ext.—Road Safety 1967 (c. 30), ss. 14 (9), 27.
        9 ext.—Finance, 1966 (c. 18), s. 8 (6).
        10 am.—Finance, 1967 (c. 54), s. 11 (1).
        12 expld.—Finance, 1962 (c. 44), s. 5 (1).
        am.—Finance, 1967 (c. 54), s. 11 (1); Finance, 1968 (c. 44), ss. 8 (2), 9.
        ext.—(E.) Finance, 1965 (c. 25), s. 7.
        15 mod.—Road Traffic (Amdt.), 1967 (c. 70), s. 4 (4).
        16 am.—Road Traffic, 1962 (c. 59), s. 46.
        ext.—Finance, 1964 (c. 49), s. 11 (1).
        17 am.—Finance, 1962 (c. 44), s. 5 (2).
        21 appl.—Road Traffic Regulation, 1967 (c. 76), s. 94 (2).
        24 am.—(E.) Hire-Purchase, 1965 (c. 66), s. 59, sch. 5; (S.) Hire-Purchase (S.), 1965 (c. 67), s. 55, sch. 5.
        sch. 1 r. in pt.—Finance, 1965 (c. 25), ss. 5 (3), 97 (5), schs. 5 pt. V para. 1, 22 pt. I.
        am.—Finance, 1965 (c. 25), s. 5 (3), sch. 5 pt. V para. 1; Finance, 1968 (c. 44), s. 8 (1), sch. 7 pt. I.
        sch. 2 mod.—Finance, 1968 (c. 44), s. 8 (3).
        sch. 3 expld.—Finance, 1965 (c. 25), s. 6 (3).

FIG. 28. *Chronological Table of the Statutes*

(d)where a temporary Act has been repealed by an Act also temporary but lasting longer than the original Act would have lasted if not repealed, the repeal is treated as final;

(e)where an Act has been partially repealed, and afterwards wholly repealed, the total repeal only is entered, except in the case of a partial repeal more extensive territorially than the total repeal;

(f)in like manner, partial repeals, covered by later partial repeals, are frequently omitted;

(g)the expiry in part of an Act which has not wholly ceased to be in force is not normally shown;

(h)repeals of Acts passed by the Parliament of England or of Great Britain after the date of Poynings Act which purport to extend beyond England or Great Britain are entered as unrestricted when effected by the Statute Law Revision Act, 1863 (ending with the reign of King James II); in the case of repeals of these Acts effected by Acts other than the Statute Law Revision Act 1963, where they are limited territorially the territorial limitation is noticed when the Act repealed had a more extensive operation territorially than the repeal: in other cases the repeal is entered as unrestricted.

As regards amendments there are two points to observe: the first is that in all cases an entry indicating an amendment should always be checked to see whether the amending enactment has itself been amended, and the second is that when the entry is in the form of "power to am." it is advisable to refer to the current *Index to Government Orders* to see whether the power has yet been exercised.

There are several observations to be made concerning Irish enactments. In 1923 it was decided that the *Chronological Table* should not attempt to show the effect of Acts of the newly established Northern Ireland legis-lature on the Acts contained in the Table. Where an Act in the Table extends to Northern Ireland and its subject matter is one on which the Northern Ireland Parliament can legislate, that Act is distinguished in the Table by an asterisk (*) inserted after its short title. The presence of such an asterisk against an Act is a warning that the Parliament of Northern Ireland has power to legislate, and may in fact have legislated, upon the subject of the Act or upon some aspect of it and that for details of any such legislation reference should be made to the *Northern Ireland Chrono-*

logical Table. Secondly, certain Acts are shown in the Table in brackets and italics preceded by the word "Irish". The enactments referred to are enactments which before 1920 applied only to Ireland and now apply only to Northern Ireland and are within their competence. The publication by Northern Ireland of their own *Chronological Table* made it possible to effect this change on the analogy of section 3 of the Statute Law Revision Act, 1950, which authorized (among other things) the omission from the *Statutes Revised* of enactments relating solely to Northern Ireland, the subject matter of which is within the powers of the Parliament thereof, and any enactments relating solely to the Republic of Ireland. Thirdly, certain Acts in italics in the Table are described as repealed and "Irish" or "residue Irish". These are Acts which originally related to Great Britain and Northern Ireland but have since been repealed except as to Northern Ireland and are within the competence of the Northern Ireland Parliament. Enactments not within the competence of the Northern Ireland legislature are treated in the normal manner.

Again, enactments relating solely to Commonwealth countries other than Independence Acts and enactments relating to customs and harbours in the Isle of Man are shown in italics (without annotations) and preceded by the words "Commonwealth" and "Isle of Man" respectively. For the transfer to Tynwald of the power to amend or repeal such Acts see the heading "Isle of Man" in the *Index to the Statutes in Force.*

Local and Personal Acts

In the *Index to Local and Personal Acts: consisting of classified lists of the Local and Personal and Private Acts and Special Orders and Special Procedure Orders 1801–1947* (H.M.S.O., 1949) items are grouped under the following headings:

    I   Bridges, Ferries, Road, Subways and Tunnels
    II   Transport (Rail, Road, Air)
    III   Canals, Rivers, Navigations
    IV   Harbours, Docks, Ports, Piers and Quays
    V   Local Government
    VI   Lighting
    VII   Water Supply

VIII Drainages and Drainage Embankments
 IX Inclosures, Open Spaces, etc.
  X Fisheries
 XI Charitable and Educational, etc., Foundations and Institutions
XII Ecclesiastical Affairs
XIII Personal and Private (including Estates)
XIV Trading and Other Companies
 XV Crown

In addition there are numerous cross-references in the text. Acts are classified by reference to their titles, and normally no attempt has been made to show the matter of each Act in detail (Fig. 29). The Local Government heading comprises the Acts of municipal corporations and other local authorities relating to their general functions, as contrasted with their special functions which are dealt with under the appropriate subject headings. Most of these acts are omnibus Acts and details of their contents are beyond the scope of the Index. Since 1947 such details have been given in the annual indexes to the Local and Personal Acts to which reference should be made.

The Index does not pretend to show whether all the Acts and Orders listed were still in force. In the preparation of previous editions no serious attempt was made to trace the subsequent history of all the Acts enumerated; repeals and amendments were only shown where they had appeared in earlier editions of the Index or were obvious from the titles of subsequent Acts. In this 1949 edition the Acts and Orders passed or made since 1900 have been examined for their effect on the earlier legislation, and where an earlier Act has been repealed, wholly or substantially by legislation subsequent to 1900, that fact has been noted. While, therefore, full effect has been given to the changes made by post-1900 legislation, the information given about pre-1901 repeals is not exhaustive.

For local Orders other than those included in this Index reference has to be made to the similarly classified lists at the end of the annual volumes of the statutory rules and orders and statutory instruments (see pp. 149-50).

In the *Supplementary Index to Local and Personal Acts 1948–1966* entries are arranged in similar groupings. Three kinds of cross-references are used:

INDEX TO LOCAL AND PERSONAL ACTS

CLASS I

BRIDGES, FERRIES, ROADS, SUBWAYS AND TUNNELS

(1)—*Bridges*

ABERDARE—
    Bridge works by U.D.C. - - - - - - - - - - 1–2G5.c.cix.
ABERDEEN—
    Bridge across Don at Persley, by Corporation   54–5V.c.cxxiv (*Rep.*3–4G6.c.iii.Sch.20).
    Maintenance of bridge at Persley by C.C. - - - - - 3–4G6.c.iii.s.224.
    Monymusk Bridge : construction of new bridge - - - - 6E7.c.xx.
    New bridge across Dee River at Allendale - - - {26G5.&1E8.c.lxxviii.Pt.IV.
                              {3–4G6.c.iii.Pt.vii.B.
    See also (3)—*Roads*, Aberdeen.
ABERGLASLYN RIVER - - - - - - - - - - {43G3.c.xxxviii ;
                                      {(*Rep.*5G4.c.cxvi).
ABERPERGWM ESTATE.   *See* Neath Canal.
ACTON (NORTHWICH)—
    Construction of swing bridge under Public Works Facilities Act, 1930 21–2G5.c.xxxiii.
ADUR RIVER.   *See* Shoreham (Sussex).
AFONRHYGORAD or DDWHRYD or MAENTWROG RIVER.   *See* Landecwyn.
AIRE RIVER—Hunslet-Leeds Road - - - - - {9G4.c.lxvii (*Rep.*22–3V.c.lxxxvi)
                                     {22–3V.c.lxxxvi.
    See also Leeds.
ALBERT BRIDGE over THAMES (Chelsea and Battersea)—
    Incorporation of Company - - - - - - - - 27–8V.c.ccxxxv.
                                 {32–3V.c.xliv ;
    Extension of time for completion and powers - - - - {34–5V.c.lxxiii ;
                                 {36–7V.c.xcvii.
    Abolition of toll - - - - - - - - - - - 40–1V.c.xcix.
ALLENDALE.   *See* Aberdeen.
ALMOND RIVER.   *See* Cramond.
ALVERSTOKE.   *See* Gosport and Alverstoke.
ARLINGHAM.   *See* Newnham.
ARUN RIVER.   *See* Littlehampton.
ASHTON-UNDER-LYNE AND DUKINFIELD—
    Bridge over Tame to Dukinfield - - - - - - 17–8V.c.xxxii.
    Alma Bridge purchased by Corporation - - - - - - 2E7.c.xliv.
AVON RIVER (Lanark) - - - - - - - - - - 54G3.c.cxcix.
    See also (3)—*Roads*, Avon River.
AVON RIVER (Warwick, Worcester, &c.).   *See* Evesham ; Stratford-on-Avon ; Tewkesbury.
AVON RIVER (Wilts., Somerset, &c.).   *See* Bathwick ; Bristol ; Stokeford.
AXE RIVER - - - - - - - - - - - - - 29–30V.c.ccxxviii.
AYR—
    Bridge over Water of Doon to Maybole - - 51G3.c.xxxviii (*Rep.*7–8G4.c.cix).
    Widening, &c., Ayr Bridge - - - - - - - - - 7–8V.c.ci.
    Rebuilding Ayr Bridge - - - - - 40–1V.c.lxvi (*Rep.*47–8V.c.xxxv).
    Cost of Bridge - - - - - - - - - - - 47–8V.c.xxxv.
    See also (3)—*Roads*, Ayr Bridge.
BACKWATER RIVER.   *See* Weymouth.
BALGOWNIE or POLGOWNIE in OLD MACHAR—
    Bridge over Don near - - - - - - - - - 6G4.c.lix.
BALLOCH AND BONHILL—
    Bridge over Leven - - - - - - 47G3.sess.2.c.xi (*Rep.*9G4.c.lxxxii).
BARKING.   *See* Essex.
BARKING ROAD—
    Bridge across Bow Creek - - - - - - - - - 54–5V.c.ccvi.
BARNES.   *See* Hammersmith.

FIG. 29. *Index to Local and Personal Acts 1801–1947*

(a) References within subdivisions· and in unsubdivided classes are shown thus:

FORTH ROAD BRIDGE *See* QUEENSFERRY

(b) References from one subdivision to another are shown thus:

CAERNARVON . . . .

See also (2) Ferries – CAERNARVON

(c) References from one class to another are shown thus:

BRITISH TRANSPORT COMMISSION *See* Cl. II (1)

There are two chronological lists, one for Local and one for Personal Acts to assist the inquirer in identifying references to Acts by calendar and regnal year, and a combined list in alphabetical order to assist in locating references to places, authorities and so forth. Attention is drawn in the preface to the fact that as the kind of typewriter used in producing the copy from which the Supplement was printed did not reproduce italics, references in the text to the chapter numbers of Personal Acts were unavoidably given in arabic figures; but as a separate list of these Acts is provided there is little risk of confusion on that account.

Each annual index, entitled *The Local and Personal Acts: tables and index to the Acts and certain Statutory Orders,* comprises four parts, as follows: Table 1 – Alphabetical List of the Local and Personal Acts; Table 2 – Chronological List of the Local and Personal Acts; Table 3 – Table of Orders which were subjected to special parliamentary procedure under the Statutory Orders (Special Procedure) Act, 1945; and Table 4 – Index to the Local and Personal Acts. In this last part, which is the main body of the text, the entries are listed in alphabetical order of subjects and places with ample cross-reference (Fig. 30). Table 3 includes a note to the effect that Orders which, though liable to Special Procedure were actually not so subjected are included in the Classified List of Local Statutory Instruments in the annual volume of Statutory Instruments.

NON-OFFICIAL INDEXES

Every legal textbook and treatise is to some extent an index to the statute law relating to its particular subject – Chitty on *Contracts,* Emmet on *Title,* Salmond on *Torts,* and so forth. In using them account must be taken of dates of publication. One way in which publishers try to keep

Table IV

Index to the Local and Personal Acts of 1968

A

Access. *See* Harbours, works; Roads; Streets.

Accounts. *See* Companies; Local Authorities.

Acquisition of land. *See* Lands.

Acquisition of Land (Authorisation Procedure) Act, 1946, application of:

Crosby	c. xxiv, s. 3
Ely Ouse-Essex ...	c. xxvi, s. 5
Medway	c. xxxiii, s. 4

Advocates' Widows' and Orphans' Fund Order Confirmation Act ... ... c. xliv

Airdrie Court House Commissioners (Dissolution) Order Confirmation Act ... ... c. i

Airport, regulation of ... ... Newcastle-on-Tyne ... ... c. xlii, s. 80

Allotments:
huts, etc., purchase of, for cultivators Leicester ... c. xl, s. 111
lands held for ... ... Epping Forest ... c. iii, s. 7

All Saints, Streatham, Act ... ... c. vii

Amenities, preservation of:

Medway	c. xxxiii, s. 52
Mid-Glamorgan	c. xxxi, s. 30

Appeals:

G.L.C. (General)	c. xxxix, s. 17
Hounslow ...	c. xxviii, s. 62
Lancashire ...	c. xxix, s. 59
Leicester ...	c. xl, s. 129
Newcastle-on-Tyne	c. xlii, s. 84

Appointed Days:
fixing of:

Durham	c. xxxviii, s. 101
Leicester ...	c. xl, s. 130

FIG. 30. *The Local and Personal Acts* (Annual catalogue)

pace with new legislation is to produce works in loose-leaf format. Sweet and Maxwell publish volumes of this kind in their Local Government Library series including, for example, an *Encyclopedia of Road Traffic Law and Practice* and an *Encyclopedia of Public Health Law and Practice* among its titles.

The most complete non-official index is Halsbury's *Laws of England* (3rd edn. 1952–64) which has forty-three volumes, plus a Cumulative Supplement in two bound volumes, and a loose-leaf Current Service. This work, as its sub-title states, is a complete statement of the whole law of England. Its text is arranged alphabetically under "titles", from Action to Wills. In each volume every paragraph is numbered so as to enable very specific references to be given in the detailed indexes (which occupy volumes 41 and 42) and to form a precise link with the corresponding numbered updating services. Cases as well as statutes are covered. Publication of a fourth edition began in 1973.

GENERAL SYNOD MEASURES

General Synod Measures are passed by the General Synod of the Church of England and, like Bills, they receive the Royal Assent to acquire the same authority as Acts of Parliament. In content they relate only to matters affecting the Church of England. They do not pass through Parliament in the same way as Bills; each one passed by General Synod is examined by the Ecclesiastical Committee which, as stipulated by the Church of England Assembly (Powers) Act, 1919, consists of fifteen Members of the House of Lords and the same number of Members of the House of Commons. The Committee then reports to Parliament on the nature, effect and expediency of the measure. Parliament, in fact, does not have the opportunity to amend it; its only means of expressing disapproval of a measure is to fail to pass the resolution required for it to be presented for Royal Assent.

G.S.M.'s are first published as separates and are later bound into the volumes of *Public General Acts and General Synod Measures* already described.

CHAPTER 10

Delegated Legislation and Administrative Tribunals

DELEGATED LEGISLATION

Purpose and Nature

Delegated legislation arises when Parliament specifically empowers another authority, usually a Minister, to make rules and regulations which have the effect of law. This is necessary because it is impractical to include sufficient detail within the body of each Act of Parliament to cover every contingency the legislation might involve. An examination of some of the older Acts will reveal the degree of detail which was at one time incorporated. By comparison, the terms of recent Acts are much broader; and at the same time the volume of delegated legislation in the form of statutory instruments has increased considerably.

The practice of delegation is particularly prevalent during wartime when the normal processes of Parliament are quite incapable of producing the necessary volume of legislation. As long ago as 1539 the Statute of Proclamations gave to the King power to legislate by proclamation in cases of national emergency. There was a substantial increase in the practice of delegating legislative powers towards the middle of the last century when a number of Acts were passed in the train of the 1832 Reform Bill. More recently both the First and Second World Wars occasioned further upsurges. The Emergency Powers (Defence) Act, 1945 continued a similar Act of 1939 which provided that "His Majesty may make by Order in Council ... such Regulations as appear to him to be necessary or expedient for securing the public safety, the defence of the realm, the maintenance of public order and the efficient prosecution of any war in which His Majesty may be engaged, and for maintaining supplies and services

essential to the life of the community." As a result a vast number of orders and regulations necessary for the defence of the country and the prosecution of the war were issued. The publishing firm of Butterworth provided an excellent service in documenting this paperwork, and the evidence can be seen in the multi-volume set of *Butterworth's Emergency Legislation.* There are now more than 2000 Statutory Instruments made each year.

Discussion of delegated legislation is hampered by difficulties of nomenclature: there are regulations, rules, orders, warrants, minutes, schemes, and byelaws — among others. In 1932 the Committee on Ministers' Powers made the following recommendation:

> The expressions "regulation" "rule" and "order" should not be used indiscriminately in statutes to describe the instruments by which law-making power conferred on Ministers by Parliament is exercised. The expression "regulation" should be used to describe the instrument by which the power to make substantive law is exercised, and the expression "rule" to describe the instrument by which the power to make law about procedure is exercised. The expression "order" should be used to describe the instrument of the exercise of (A) executive power, (B) the power to take judicial and quasi-judicial decisions. [Cmd. 4060, para. 15(I)].

Under the Statutory Instruments Act, 1946, where Parliament confers by Act power to make, confirm or approve orders, rules, regulations or other subordinate legislation, the document by which that power is exercised is known as a "statutory instrument".

Though technically Orders in Council are a form of legislation by royal decree and therefore original rather than delegated legislation there are Orders in Council which are the exercise of a power conferred on Her Majesty in Council — and these, according to the Statutory Instruments Act, 1946, are to be classed as statutory instruments. Prerogative Orders in Council are now only made in the case of laws for overseas territories. The tests of certain instruments made under prerogative powers — and these include Proclamations, Warrants and Letters Patent as well as Orders in Council — are given in the annual volumes of statutory instruments, and particulars of them are included in the *Index to Government Orders* described below. Others appear in the *London Gazette,* while some are not published at all. It might be noted here that Orders in Council are approved by the Sovereign at a meeting of the Privy Council, whereas Orders of Council are made by the Privy Council in the Sovereign's absence.

Further reading on the subject of delegated or subsidiary legislation

includes C. K. Allen's *Law and Orders: an enquiry into the nature and scope of delegated legislation and executive powers in English law* (3rd edn. 1965); J. E. Kersell's *Parliamentary Supervision of Delegated Legislation: the United Kingdom, Australia, New Zealand and Canada* (1960); and the *Handbook on Statutory Instrument Procedure* published by the Statutory Publications Office (2nd edn. 1968).

Numbering and Classification

Normally, statutory instruments produced by government departments are passed to the Statutory Publications Office where they are first scrutinized for errors, then entered in the register, allocated their serial numbers and forwarded to H.M.S.O. When registering these documents the Editor of Statutory Instruments is acting on behalf of the Queen's Printer of Acts of Parliament. A fresh sequence of numbers is begun each year, and this means that the proper citation of a particular instrument is made in the form "S.I. number/year". In the case of commencement orders, certain legal and all Scottish orders, this is followed by a further serial number in brackets. Some departments have their own numbering series in addition, and their numbers are usually printed at the foot of the first page of their instruments. Such codes are not used in citations and are not given in the annual volumes.

There are certain exceptions to the official numbering procedures just outlined. Where an instrument has to be approved by Parliament (or by the House of Commons) before it can come into operation, it will not be numbered until it has been so approved. Secondly, where, under the provisions of any enactment, a statutory instrument is subject to Special Parliamentary Procedure the responsible department has to notify the Editor when the instrument has come into operation and send him a copy for registration. Numbering dates from the Rules Publication Act, 1893, and its continuation was assured by the Statutory Instruments Act, 1946.

Instruments are classified as either local or general as indicated in the Statutory Instruments Regulations 1947, reg. 4: " . . . a statutory instrument which is in the nature of a local and personal or private Act shall be classified as local, and [one] which is in the nature of a Public General Act shall be classified as general." Responsibility for classification rests with the department concerned, with the proviso that the Statutory Instru-

ments Reference Committee could direct otherwise. It is usual for instruments classified as *general* to be printed and sold, and for *local* instruments not to be printed and sold, but there are exceptions to this general principle. Instruments of short duration, for instance, may not be printed, and documents such as Army Orders will be published in their own regular series. There are exceptions, too, for bulky schedules. On the other hand, the Reference Committee may direct that a particular local instrument should be printed and sold. Local instruments are normally distributed in duplicated form to interested parties.

Annual Volumes

As regards older instruments it may fairly be said that up to 1890 the situation over publication was not at all satisfactory. Though many appeared in the *London Gazette* there were many more which were never published. In 1891 it was decided to collect them together and publish them in annual volumes. Two years later the Rules Publication Act, 1893, was promulgated and provided that all statutory rules (as they were then called) should be sent to the Queen's Printer of Acts of Parliament and be numbered, printed and sold by him. The 1893 Act also regularized the method of publication by providing that "Where any statutory rules are required by any Act to be published or notified in the London, Edinburgh, or Dublin Gazette, a notice in the Gazette of the rules having been made, and of the place where copies of them can be purchased, shall be sufficient compliance with the said requirement" (s. 3(3)).

So, from 1891 onwards first statutory rules and orders and then statutory instruments (with the exception of local instruments and certain other categories noted above) have been published both singly and in annual volumes.

Up to 1961 they were arranged in the volumes in classified order, and only those instruments which were still in force at the end of the year were reprinted in the bound volumes. Since 1961 they have appeared in numerical order and as there is no need under this system to wait until all the instruments for one year have been published before establishing their order in the annual volumes, these bound sets are now produced much more expeditiously.

Each annual set of bound volumes at present contains some 900 docu-

ments. To take an example, *Statutory Instruments 1967* consists of three parts, each in two volumes, making six volumes in all for the year; they comprise some 5500 pages excluding prefatory material and indexes. There is a complete numerical list (Fig. 31) and a classified list of local instruments (Fig. 32). Included in an appendix are certain instruments not registered as statutory instruments: Royal Proclamations, Orders in Council, Letters Patent and Royal Instructions relating to the Constitutions and so forth of Overseas Territories or to appeals to the Judicial Committee, etc.

Revised Editions

There have so far been three revised editions of statutory rules and orders and statutory instruments. The first covered those in force in 1889, the second those in force in 1904 and the third those in force at 31 December 1948. The title of this latter publication is *The Statutory Rules and Orders and Statutory Instruments Revised to December 31, 1948,* and it was published in twenty-five volumes between 1949 and 1952. Instruments of a temporary character are omitted, as are certain Rules of Court and departmental legislation of the Governments of Eire and Northern Ireland. Instruments relating to Northern Ireland for affecting the transfer of administration, adaptation of enactments, etc., are, however, included. The system of arrangement is similar to that adopted for the previous editions, wherein the instruments were grouped under subject headings arranged alphabetically. The last volume contains an Alphabetical List of the subject headings used, a Numerical Table of instruments and a Table of Effects. The Numerical Table is in fact in two parts: Part I gives those instruments issued in the years covered by the parent work, and Part II includes all general instruments made between 1 January 1949 and 31 December 1951 which were still in operation at the latter date. The Table of Effects is also brought up to 1951. It shows for each instrument in the parent work and in Part II of the Numerical Table anything which has occurred between 1 January 1949 and 31 December 1951 to modify its operative effect. The annual *Table of Government Orders* described below provides updating information.

NUMERICAL LIST

of those Statutory Instruments of 1967 which were printed and sold under the Statutory Instruments Act 1946

[*Note.*—With respect to each instrument listed, two dates are shown; the first is the date on which it was made, and the second, which is in square brackets, is the date on which it was first issued by Her Majesty's Stationery Office.]

No.	Subject	Part	Page
2	West Shropshire Water Bd., 4 Jan. [10 Jan.] ...	(n) III,	5484
3	West Somerset Water, 4 Jan. [10 Jan.]	(n) III,	5484
5	Sheffield–Grimsby Trunk Road (Bigby Street and Bigby Road, Brigg), 4 Jan. [23 Jan.]	(n) III,	5463
6	Essex River Authority (Alteration of Boundaries of the Dengey Internal Drainage District), 25 July 1966 [12 Jan.]	(n) III,	5476
7	County of Northumberland (Electoral Divisions), 4 Jan. [10 Jan.]	(n) III,	5478
10	Dog Racecourse Totalisator, 4 Jan. [13 Jan.] ...	I,	1
11	East Surrey Water, 6 Jan. [12 Jan.]	(n) III,	5484
14	Leeds–Scarborough Trunk Road (West Heslerton Diversion), 5 Jan. [24 Jan.]	(n) III,	5464
15	Truro Relief Road (Boscawen and Kenwyn Bridges), 3 Jan. [17 Jan.]	(n) III,	5463
17	Southern Rhodesia (Carriage of Petroleum) (Overseas Territories), 11 Jan. [17 Jan.]	I,	9
18	Southern Rhodesia (Prohibited Trade and Dealings) (Overseas Territories), 11 Jan. [17 Jan.]	I,	10
19	Southern Rhodesia (Prohibited Trade and Dealings) (Channel Islands), 11 Jan. [17 Jan.]	I,	25
20	Southern Rhodesia (Prohibited Trade and Dealings) (Isle of Man), 11 Jan. [17 Jan.]	I,	39
24	Bahrain, 11 Jan. [17 Jan.]	I,	53
25	Double Taxation Relief (Taxes on Income) (Federal Republic of Germany), 11 Jan. [19 Jan.] ...	I,	55
26	Double Taxation Relief (Taxes on Income) (Switzerland), 11 Jan. [19 Jan.]	I,	68
27	Pensions Appeal Tribunals (S.), 10 Jan. [19 Jan.]...	I,	78
28	Bucks Water Undertaking (Valuation), 11 Jan. [18 Jan.]	(n) III,	5481
29	Teachers (Colleges of Education) (S.), 10 Jan. [20 Jan.]	I,	79

(n) Instrument classified as local, noted in the Classified List of Local S.I. at the page shown above, but not set out in full.

FIG. 31. *Statutory Instruments* (Annual catalogue): *Numerical List*

CLASS 1.—ROADS, BRIDGES, ROAD TRAFFIC   5463
AND RIGHTS OF WAY

(1) *Bridges and tunnels.*
(2) *Establishment as highways.*
(3) *Parking places.*

(4) *Rights of way (extinguishment, stopping up, diversion, re-opening, retention of pipes in highways, etc.).*
(5) *Traffic regulation.*

(1) Bridges and tunnels

*TYNE TUNNEL TOLLS O. 1967 CONFIRMATION INSRT., made by Minister of Transport under Tyne Tunnel Act 1960 (c. xxxix), s. 30; 2 Oct. (1454).

TRURO RELIEF ROAD (BOSCAWEN AND KENWYN BRIDGES) SCHEME 1966 CONFIRMA-TION INSRT., made by Minister of Transport under Highways (Miscellaneous Provisions) Act 1961 (c. 63), s. 3; 3 Jan. (15).

(2) Establishment as highways

(a) TRUNK ROADS

Restriction of traffic on trunk roads—*see* (5) below.

Trunk roads in built-up areas—*see* (5) below.

(i) *England and Wales*

Minister of Transport—Orders under Highways Act 1959 (c. 25), s. 7.

Bradford–Kendal Trunk Road (Tearnside Hall Diversion); 7 Feb. (151).
Exeter–Leeds Trunk Road (Lichfield Eastern By-pass) (Connecting Roads No. 2); 28 Nov. (1801).
Folkestone–Honiton Trunk Road (Firle Diversion); 9 June (893).
Levens Bridge–Carlisle Trunk Road—
    (Barrow Banks Diversions); 24 Nov. (1775).
    (Harecroft Diversion); 13 Feb. (192).
Liverpool–Hull Trunk Road (Gelderd Road Diversion); 24 July (1158).
Liverpool–Skegness Trunk Road (Worksop); 23 May (798).
London–Bristol Trunk Road (Hick's Gate, Near Keynsham) Extension; 18 Oct. (1552).
London–Thurso Trunk Road (Wideopen and Seaton Burn Diversion); 19 May (796).
London–Great Yarmouth Trunk Road—
    (Brentwood By-Pass) (Slip Roads); 16 Nov. (1720).
    (Hatfield Peverel By-Pass Slip Roads); 1 Feb. (120).
London–Penzance Trunk Road (Station Road and Other Roads, Penzance); 20 Oct. (1554).
Newcastle upon Tyne–Edinburgh Trunk Road (Improvement at Bagraw Bridge); 25 Jan. (100).
Newport–Shewsbury Trunk Road (Diversion near Stock Farm); 19 May (834).
North-West of Doncaster–Kendal Trunk Road (Bradford Road, Tingley Diversion); 7 Dec. (1843).
Sheffield–Grimsby Trunk Road (Bigby Street and Bigby Road, Brigg); 4 Jan. (5).
West of Maidenhead–Oxford Trunk Road (Crowmarsh Gifford, Trunking); 17 July (1086).

FIG. 32. *Statutory Instruments* (Annual catalogue): *Classified List of Local Instruments*

Official Indexes

Regulation 9 of the Statutory Instruments Regulations, 1947 (S.I. 1/1948) brought into effect Section 3 of the Statutory Instruments Act, 1946, by specifying that "... His Majesty's Stationery Office shall from time to time publish a list to be known as the 'Statutory Instrument Issue List', showing the serial number and short title of each statutory instrument which has been issued for the first time by that Office during the period to which that list relates, and the date on which each such instrument was so issued". This first listing is made in the H.M.S.O. *Daily List*.

Next comes the "Monthly List of Statutory Instruments"; Fig. 33 reproduces a page from the *List of Statutory Instruments for the Month of November 1969*. It has three parts – a List of Statutory Instruments by Subject, an Index, and a Numerical List of Statutory Instruments by Subject Headings. In the first list, as illustrated, instruments issued during the month are grouped under broad subject headings such as agriculture, civil aviation, education, housing, local government, road traffic, social security. Where appropriate, reference is made to the statutes or instruments under which the listed items have been made; and local S.I.s which have not been printed and published by H.M.S.O. are indicated by an asterisk. An important characteristic of the index is the fact that it cumulates during the year. To find a particular instrument issued during the course of a year, therefore, one has only to consult the latest monthly list and, if necessary, the subsequent daily lists. The numerical list, on the other hand, refers only to the month concerned. Again each serial number is given the subject heading under which it appears in the principal list. Certain numbers are designated by capital letters as:

C. Commencement Orders (bringing an Act or part of an Act into operation),

L. Instruments relating to fees or procedure in courts in England and Wales,

S. Instruments which apply to Scotland only.

These symbols are also used in the *List of Statutory Instruments [year]*, in which the instruments of the past twelve months are grouped under subject headings. Subject and numerical indexes are provided. In the case of instruments resulting from an enactment a reference to the enact-

LIST OF STATUTORY INSTRUMENTS BY SUBJECT

November 1969

Statutes, S.R. & O. and S.I. under which Instruments are made are shown in square brackets or cross-headings
***Indicates local Instruments which were **not** printed and published by Her Majesty's Stationery Office*

Number

ACQUISITION OF LAND

1570   Compulsory Purchase of Land (General Vesting Declaration) (S.) Regs.
(S.128)   [*Town and Country Planning (S.) Acts 1949 s. 107; 1969 ss. 31, 103, sch. 2 paras. 1, 2, 4*]

AGRICULTURE

Instrts. made under the *Agriculture and Horticulture Act 1964 s. 1(2)(4)–(7)*, unless otherwise stated

Price Stability of Imported Products—
1564   (Levy Arrangement) (Amdt. No. 2) O. [*S. 1(2)–(4)(6)(7)*]
1550   (Rates of Levy No. 23) O.—Revoking 1969/1518; *Revoked by 1969/1677*
1677   (Rates of Levy No. 24) O.—Revoking 1969/1550

BETTING AND GAMING

1605   Dog Racecourse Totalisator (Percentage) O. [*Betting, Gaming and Lotteries Act 1963 sch. 5 para. 3*]

BUILDING SOCIETIES

1587   Building Societies (Accounts and Annual Return etc.) (Amdt.) Regs. [*Building Societies Act 1962 ss. 78(2), 88(3), 91(2)*]

CHILDREN AND YOUNG PERSONS

Instrts. made under the *Children and Young Persons Act 1969 s. 73*

Children and Young Persons Act 1969—
1552   (Commencement No. 1) O.
(C.43)
1565   (Commencement No. 2) O.
(C.44)

CINEMATOGRAPHS AND CINEMATOGRAPH FILMS

1575   Cinematograph (Safety) (S.) (Amdt.) Regs. [*Cinematograph Act 1909 s.1*]
(S.129)

FIG. 33. *Monthly List of Statutory Instruments*

ment is given; also indicated are any earlier instruments which listed items revoked. The following is a sample entry showing these features, taken from the 1968 list:

PLANT HEALTH

165 Importation of Potatoes (Health) (G.B.) (Amdt.) O. *Plant Health Act 1967* Revoking 1964/1979

The letter O indicates that this was an Order, as distinct from, say, an Order in Council.

Also published annually (since 1966) is a *Table of Government Orders* which is a cumulative list of general statutory rules and orders and statutory instruments, certain instruments made under the Royal Prerogative and other instruments which are not registrable, dating from 1671 onwards. It replaces *S.I. Effects* and the *Numerical Table of S.R. & O. and S.I.,* and records all revocations to date of the instruments which it lists and the amendments, modifications, etc., effected since 1 January 1949 of those still in force. The arrangement is chronological. Instruments which have been revoked or are regarded as spent, etc., or which have become part of the law of certain overseas territories are shown in italic type and a reference is given to the revoking enactment, if any. Instruments which are wholly or partly in force are shown in bold type, and where any such instrument has been amended, extended, modified or otherwise affected references are added in ordinary type. The title of each instrument made before 1961 is followed by a reference to the volume and page of the annual volume of S.R. & O. or S.I. where its text may be found. This is necessary because up to 1961 entries in the annual volumes were in classified, not numerical, order. A half-yearly *Noter-up* is issued to supplement the *Table.*

An *Index to Government Orders* is published biennially. It was first published in 1891 under the title *Index to the Statutory Rules and Orders in Force;* then between 1951 and 1960 it was called *Guide to Government Orders.* The *Index* contains summaries of all statutory powers to enact subordinate legislation and of the current exercise of those powers. These are grouped under subject headings, and below each summary is set out the S.R. & O. or S.I. number, the title and the annual volume or other reference of every general instrument made under the power and still in force. Local instruments are not, as a rule, listed (they are listed in the

annual bound volumes), but particulars are given of certain instruments made under prerogative powers.

Halsbury's Statutory Instruments

A complete reference service is provided by *Halsbury's Statutory Instruments* published by Butterworths. The work comprises twenty-three basic volumes, plus a bound index and a loose-leaf updating volume. Every current statutory instrument is included: some are quoted in full, others summarized, the rest simply listed — treatment being decided to accord with the editors' assessment of the lawyer's requirements. Arrangement is by subject, the instruments being classified and grouped under "titles". Each title begins with notes on the subject matter dealt with and references to other parts of the work. The texts of the S.I.s which then follow incorporate all the amendments, up to the date of their publication in this compendium, and are annotated and cross-referenced. Individual volumes are consolidated and replaced whenever the sheer bulk or importance of new material necessitates such a course. This also applies to the index volume which meanwhile is kept up to date by quarterly issues of a cumulative supplement designed to fit into a pocket at the back of the parent volume. The loose-leaf material is divided into three: (i) a Chronological List of Instruments, kept up to date by the addition of pages each quarter; (ii) an Annual Cumulative Supplement (arranged under titles corresponding to those in the main volumes and keyed to the relevant pages) which is entirely replaced each year; and (iii) a Quarterly Survey which contains material subsequent to the issue of the last annual supplement. There are three issues of this survey during the year, and the second and third are cumulative. At the end of the fourth quarter all this material is replaced entirely and absorbed into the new Annual Cumulative Supplement.

ADMINISTRATIVE TRIBUNALS

An administrative tribunal is an independent body set up by statute to take decisions which would otherwise have to be taken either administratively by a government department or by the ordinary courts. The

constitution and working of most of these tribunals was placed under the general supervision of the Council on Tribunals by the Tribunals and Inquiries Act, 1958. The Council's annual report made to the Lord Chancellor and the Secretary of State for Scotland is published as a House of Commons Paper. It includes figures of the numbers of tribunals and of the cases dealt with by each class of tribunal during the year.

Following is a review of the publishing activities of the more active tribunals:

Agricultural Arbitrators
Agricultural Land Tribunals
Decisions are not published. They are, however, reported from time to time in legal and farming periodicals.

Civil Aviation Authority
> Decisions are recorded in *Civil Aviation Authority Official Record Series 2: Air Transport Licensing Notices* usually issued weekly and obtainable from the Civil Aviation Authority, 129 Kingsway, London, W.C.2. (These Notices should be read in conjunction with *Civil Aviation Official Record, Air Transport Licensing Series 1*), issued in March and April 1972 and subsequent amendments).

Commons Commissioners
> Decisions are not published by H.M.S.O. A booklet *Decisions of the Commons Commissioners: Official Texts* (containing 25 such texts) is obtainable from the Commons, Open Spaces and Footpaths Preservation Society, 166 Shaftesbury Avenue, London, W.C.2. Further selected decisions are reported in the Society's Journal.

Immigration Appeal Tribunal and Immigration Adjudicators
> Selected determinations are published at intervals by H.M.S.O.

Industrial Tribunals
> Selected decisions are published by H.M.S.O. – see under Labour, Ministry of (now Department of Employment and Productivity) on p. 212. Also useful are *Knight's Industrial and Commercial Reports* (Charles Knight & Co., 1966–).

Lands Tribunal
> Decisions are not published officially, but they are extensively covered in the *Estates Gazette* and the *Journal of Planning and Property Law*. Reports of decisions relating to compensation are

published by Sweet & Maxwell in their quarterly *Property and Compensation Reports.* Reports of decisions relating to rating cases are published in the journal *Rating and Valuation Reporter* and are also obtainable on subscription from the publishers, Rating Publications Ltd.

Local Valuation Courts

Decisions are not published, but as regards rating cases see previous entry.

Mental Health Review Tribunals

Decisions are not published.

National Health Service Tribunals

Decisions are not published but are mentioned from time to time in *The Executive Council,* the journal of the Society of Clerks of N.H.S. Executive Councils, 42 West Cliff, Preston, Lancs.

National Insurance Tribunals

Selected decisions of the National Insurance Commissioners are published by H.M.S.O. – see under Social Security, Ministry of (now Department of Health and Social Security) on p. 221. They are issued first in loose-leaf form and then in bound volumes.

Comptroller-General of Patents, Designs and Trade Marks

Selected reports are available on subscription from the Patent Office.

Pensions Appeal Tribunals

Decisions are not published.

Rent Assessment Committees

Selected decisions (duplicated) are issued several times a year and are available from the Greater London Rent Assessment Panel, Waverley House, Noel Street, London W.1.

Rent Tribunals

Decisions are not published, but reports of some of the more noteworthy appear in the Press.

Revenue Tribunals

Appeals to the courts arising from decisions by these tribunals are reported in *Tax Cases* obtainable on subscription from H.M.S.O.

Road Traffic Licensing Authorities

Each authority issues a printed record of *Applications and Decisions.*

Supplementary Benefit Appeal Tribunals

Decisions are not published.

Traffic Commissioners

The commissioners for each area print decisions in their *Notices and Proceedings.*

Transport Tribunal

Decisions are obtainable on subscription through H.M.S.O.

Value Added Tax Tribunals

Selected decisions published from time to time by H.M.S.O.

An important document on this subject is the Report of the Committee on Administrative Tribunals and Enquiries (Chairman: Sir Oliver Franks), 1957 (Cmnd. 218). Secondary sources include:

ALLEN, Sir C. K., *Administrative Jurisdiction* (1956).

BELL, K., *Tribunals in the Social Services* (1969).

ELCOCK, H. J., *Administrative Justice* (1969).

POLLARD, R. S. W. (Editor), *Administrative Tribunals at Work: a symposium* (1950).

ROBSON, W. A., *Justice and Administrative Law* (3rd edn. 1951).

STREET, H., *Justice in the Welfare State* (The Hamlyn Lectures, 20th series, 1968).

VANDYK, N. D., *Tribunals and Inquiries: a guide to procedure* (1965).

Some articles are included in D. C. M. Yardley's *A Source Book of English Administrative Law* (1963), and more recent references occur in the Administrative Law section of *Current Law.*

CHAPTER 11

Committees and Tribunals of Inquiry

INVESTIGATING committees are set up for a variety of purposes and take different names to distinguish their functions. The very important class of Royal Commissions has already been considered, and it is the purpose of this chapter to describe and list some other *ad hoc* bodies.

DEPARTMENTAL COMMITTEES

Ministers are empowered to set up departmental committees to carry out investigations into matters of public concern. Frequently they rank in importance with Royal Commissions and may similarly constitute a significant part of the pre-legislative process. The Minister concerned may decide whether or not he will present a committee's report to Parliament; if he does so he uses the device of presenting "By Command of Her Majesty". It is usual to do this when legislation is anticipated so as to ensure that Parliament is made aware of the report and that Members may easily acquire copies in order to prepare themselves for the debate which will in all probability ensue. This explains why, for example, the Roberts Report on the Structure of the Public Library service in England and Wales was issued as a Command Paper whereas the Parry Report on University Libraries was a Non-Parliamentary Publication.

Like Royal Commissions these departmental committees receive evidence from interested institutions and associations, and from individuals. Publication of evidence is again at the discretion of the responsible Minister. Aside from the opportunity it affords of examining the validity of the committee's conclusions, this evidence along with any published reports of sponsored research frequently has its own independent value to

students of the subject under investigation. As an example, one may take the volumes of evidence to the Radcliffe Report on the Working of the Monetary System, 1959.

Use of the chairman's name as the popular designation of a committee or its report is common practice. Thus one refers to the Wheare Report (on Children and the Cinema), the Fulton Report (on the Civil Service), the Swann Report (on Manpower Resources for Science and Technology), and so forth. Useful in this connection is *British Government Publications: an index to chairmen and authors, 1941–1966,* edited by A. Mary Morgan and published by the Library Association in 1969, which consists of an alphabetical listing (with some unfortunate omissions) *under chairmen of departmental committees, working parties, etc., and authors of other official publications (see Fig. 12). It is intended eventually to produce a companion volume covering the preceding years. The H.M.S.O. annual *Catalogue of Government Publications* also includes authors and chairmen in its index; so, too, do the Fords' *Breviates* described on pp. 34-37. Nor should it be overlooked that the present work which includes lists of different kinds of official reports provides name references in its index. The list of reports which follows gives the titles, dates, chairmen and Command numbers, where appropriate, of the more important reports published between 1900 and 1972.

WORKING PARTIES

A working party may be set up to examine in more detail some point raised in the report of a main committee, or it may be asked to investigate the implications of putting a certain recommendation into practice. It has not been thought necessary for the purpose of the following list to distinguish them from the reports of departmental committees.

TRIBUNALS OF INQUIRY

Tribunals of inquiry are quite distinct from the statutory inquiries described in Chapter 10. The Tribunals of Inquiry (Evidence) Act, 1921, provides that if both Houses of Parliament resolve that it is expedient that a tribunal should be established to inquire into a definite matter described

*A seven-page list of amendments was issued in 1972.

in the resolution as of urgent public importance, and in pursuance of such resolution a tribunal is appointed either by the Crown or by a Secretary of State, then such a tribunal for certain purposes shall have all the powers, rights, and privileges that are vested in the High Court. Unlike a Royal Commission it can enforce the attendance of witnesses whom it may examine under oath, and it may compel the production of documents.

The Royal Commission on Tribunals of Inquiry 1966 (Cmnd. 3121) expressed themselves as strongly of the opinion that the inquisitorial machinery set up under the Act of 1921 should never be used for matters of local or minor public importance but should always be confined to matters of vital public importance concerning which there is "something in the nature of a nation-wide crisis of confidence". In such cases they considered that no other method of investigation would be adequate. By way of example they instanced the Budget Leak Tribunal (1936), the Lynskey Tribunal (1948), the Bank Rate Tribunal (1957), the Vassall Tribunal (1962) and the inquiry by Lord Denning into the Profumo Case (1963). In an appendix they listed all the inquiries which had in fact been held under the Act. Other appendices reproduced the texts of both the 1921 Act and the Special Commission Act, 1888.

SELECT ALPHABETICAL LIST OF DEPARTMENTAL COMMITTEES, WORKING PARTIES, TRIBUNALS OF INQUIRY, ETC., 1900–72

Dates given are the years in which reports were published. Chairmen are included in the index at the end of the volume.

Cd., Cmd., Cmnd. = Command Paper

M/E = Minutes of Evidence

Abortion   1939
    (Sir N. Birkett) Non-Parliamentary
Administrative Tribunals and Enquiries   1957
    (Sir O. Franks) Cmnd. 218
Adolescent — Education   1926
    (Sir W. H. Hadow) Non-Parliamentary
Adoption of Children   1954
    (Sir G. Hurst) Cmd. 9248

Adoption of Children   1972
    (Judge F. A. Stockdale & Sir William Houghton) Cmnd. 5107
Adoption Societies and Agencies   1937
    (F. Horsburgh) Cmd. 5499
Adult Education in England and Wales — Organisation and Finance
    1954   (E. Ashby) Non-Parliamentary
After-Care and Supervision of Discharged Prisoners   1958
    (B. J. Hartwell) Non-Parliamentary
After-Care — Organisation   1967
    (Mr. Justice Barry) Non-Parliamentary
After-Care: *see also* Voluntary Service in After-Care
Agricultural Graduates — Demand   1964
    (C. I. C. Bosanquet) Cmnd. 2419
Agriculture's Import Saving Role   1968
    (Sir E. Bacon) Non-Parliamentary
Air Pollution   1954
    (Sir H. Beaver) Cmd. 9322
Aircraft — Landing and Take-Off in Bad Weather   1951
    (Lord Brabazon) Cmd. 8147
Aircraft Industry   1965
    (Lord Plowden) Cmnd. 2853
Aircraft: *see also* National Aircraft Effort
Alcoholics   1965
    (A. K. M. Macrae) Non-Parliamentary
Allotments   1949
    (G. Brown) Non-Parliamentary
Allotments   1969
    (H. Thorpe) Cmnd. 4166
Alternatives to Short Terms of Imprisonment   1957
    (Earl of Drogheda) Non-Parliamentary
Amphetamines and LSD   1970
    (Sir Edward Wayne) Non-Parliamentary
Animals: *see* Welfare of Animals
Antibiotics in Animal Husbandry, etc.   1969
    (M. M. Swann) Cmnd. 4190
Army Cadet Force   1957
    (J. Amery) Cmnd. 268

Art and Design Education – Structure   1970
    (Sir William Coldstream) Non-Parliamentary
Audio-Visual Aids in Higher Scientific Education   1965
    (B. Jones) Non-Parliamentary
Bankruptcy Law Amendment   1957
    (Judge L. B. Blagden) Cmnd. 221
Before Five   1971
    (Isabel McHaffie) Non-Parliamentary
Betting on Horse Races: *see* Levy on Betting on Horse Races
Bilingual Traffic Signs   1972
    (Roderic Bowen) Cmnd. 5110
Biological Manpower   1971
    (R. D. Keynes) Cmnd. 4737
Blind Persons: *see* Welfare of the Blind
Borstals – Work and Vocational Training in Borstals (England and Wales)
    1963
    (Sir W. Anson) Non-Parliamentary
Boy Entrants and Young Servicemen   1970
    (Lord Donaldson) Cmnd. 4509
British Air Transport in the Seventies   1969
    (Sir R. Edwards) Cmnd. 4018
British Railways – Reshaping   1963
    (R. Beeching) Non-Parliamentary
Broadcasting   1950
    (Lord Beveridge) Cmd. 8116
Broadcasting   1962
    (Sir H. Pilkington) Cmnd. 1753
Cabs and Private Hire Vehicles   1939
    (Sir C. Hindley) Cmd. 5938
    See also Taxicab Service
Cannabis   1969
    (Sir E. Wayne) Non-Parliamentary
Capital Projects Overseas   1968
    (Earl of Cromer) Cmnd. 3516
Caravans as Homes   1959
    (Sir Arton Wilson) Cmnd. 872

Care of Children   1946
    (M. Curtis) Cmd. 6922
Carriers' Licensing   1965
    (Lord Geddes) Non-Parliamentary
Cars for Cities   1967
    (Lord Kings Norton; J. Garlick) Non-Parliamentary
Casual Poor — Relief   1930
    (L. R. Phelps) Cmd. 3640
Cement Production   1941
    (G. Balfour) Cmd. 6282
Census of Production   1945
    (Sir G. H. Nelson) Cmd. 6687
Census of Production and Distribution   1954
    (Sir W. R. Verdon Smith) Cmd. 9276
Central Training Council   1970
    (F. Cousins) Cmnd. 4335
Charitable Trusts — Law and Practice Relating to   1952
    (Lord Nathan) Cmd. 8710
Cheque Endorsement   1956
    (A. A. Mocatta) Cmnd. 3
Child Welfare Centres   1967
    (Sir W. Sheldon) Non-Parliamentary
Children and the Cinema   1950
    (K. C. Wheare) Cmd. 7945
Children and Young Persons   1960
    (Visc. Ingleby) Cmnd. 1191
Children and Young Persons (Scotland)   1964
    (Lord Kilbrandon) Cmnd. 2306
Children in their Primary Schools (2v.)   1967
    (Lady Plowden) Non-Parliamentary
Children with Specific Reading Difficulties   1972
    (J. Tizard) Non-Parliamentary
Children: *see also* Adoption of Children; Care of Children; Child Welfare
    Centres; Neglect of Children; Welfare of Children in Hospital
Civil Aeroplanes   1939
    (H. G. Brown) Cmd. 6038

Computers for Research   1966
    (B. H. Flowers) Cmnd. 2883
Computing in Universities – Teaching   1970
    (G. A. Barnard) Non-Parliamentary
Constituencies – Abnormally large   1945
    (D. C. Brown) Cmd. 6634
Constitution   1969–
    (Lord Crowther)
Consumer Credit   1971
    (Lord Crowther) Cmnd. 4596
Consumer Protection   1962
    (J. T. Molony) Cmnd. 1781
Contempt – Law of (as it affects Tribunals of Inquiry)   1969
    (Lord Justice Salmon) Cmnd. 4078
Contract Farming   1972
    (Sir James Barker) Cmnd. 5099
Co-operative Selling in the Coal Mining Industry   1926
    (Sir F. W. Lewis) Cmd. 2770
Copyright   1952
    (H. S. Gregory) Cmd. 8662
Coroners   1936
    (Lord Wright) Cmd. 5070
Corporal Punishment   1938
    (E. Cadogan) Cmd. 5684
Corporal Punishment   1960
    (Mr. Justice Barry) Cmnd. 1213
Cost of Living   1968
    (A. S. Marre) Cmnd. 3677
    (See also Working Classes Cost of Living
Costs at Statutory Inquiries – Award of   1964
    (D. B. Bogle) Cmnd. 2471
Cotton Imports   1952
    (R. V. N. Hopkins) Cmd. 8510
Countryside – Preservation   1938
    (Sir J. Maud) Non-Parliamentary
County Court Procedure   1949
    (Mr. Justice Austin Jones) Cmd. 7668

Court of Criminal Appeal   1965
     (Lord Donovan) Cmnd. 2755
Court Proceedings — Mechanical Recording   1966
     (Mr. Justice Baker) Cmnd. 3096
Court Proceedings — Recording   1972
     (S. P. Osmond) Non-Parliamentary
Courts of Summary Jurisdiction   1933
     (Sir W. F. K. Taylor) Cmd. 4296
Courts of Summary Jurisdiction in the Metropolitan Area   1937
     (Sir A. Maxwell) Non-Parliamentary
Credit: *see* Consumer Credit
Crichel Down — Disposal of Land   1954
     (Sir A. E. J. Clark) Cmd. 9176
Crime Recording: the Scottish Criminal Statistics   1968
     (A. Thomson) Cmnd. 3705
Criminal Courts — Business   1960
     (Mr. Justice Streatfield) Cmnd. 1289
Criminal Procedure (Indictable Offences) — Alterations   1921 (1923)
     (Sir A. Bodkin) Cmd. 1813
Criminal Statistics   1967
     (M. Perks) Cmnd. 3448
Crowd Safety at Sports Grounds   1972
     (Lord Wheatley) Cmnd. 4952
CS Gas   1971
     (Sir Harold Himsworth) Pt. I. Cmnd. 4173; Pt. II Cmnd. 4775
Curriculum and Examinations in Secondary Schools   1943
     (Sir C. Norwood) Non-Parliamentary
Curriculum of the Senior Secondary School   1959
     (J. S. Brunton) Non-Parliamentary
'D' Notice Matters   1967
     (Lord Radcliffe) Cmnd. 3309
Dairy Effluents   1969
     (R. J. MacWalter) Non-Parliamentary
Day Release   1964
     (C. Henniker-Heaton) Non-Parliamentary
Deaf Children — Education   1968
     (M. M. Lewis) Non-Parliamentary

Decimal Currency   1963
    (Earl of Halsbury) Cmnd. 2145
Defamation – Law   1948
    (Lord Porter) Cmd. 7536
Denning: Lord Denning's Report   1963
    (Lord Denning) Cmnd. 2152
Dental Services in Health Centres   1969
    (J. B. Hardie) Non-Parliamentary
Departmental Records   1954
    (Sir J. Grigg) Cmd. 9163
Depopulation in Mid-Wales   1964
    (W. M. Ogden; A. Beacham) Non-Parliamentary
Depositions   1949
    (Mr. Justice Byrne) Cmd. 7639
Detention Barracks   1943
    (Mr. Justice Oliver) Cmd. 6484
Detention Centres   1970
    (K. Younger) Non-Parliamentary
Detention of Girls in a Detention Centre   1968
    (K. Younger) Non-Parliamentary
Diligence   1958
    (Sheriff H. McKechnie) Cmnd. 456
Disablement – Assessment   1965
    (Lord McCorquodale) Cmnd. 2847
Discharged Offenders – Residential Homes for Homeless   1966
    (Marchioness of Reading) Non-Parliamentary
Discharged Prisoners' Aid Societies   1953
    (Sir A. Maxwell) Cmd. 8879
Dismissal Procedures   1967
    (N. Singleton) Non-Parliamentary
District General Hospital – Functions   1969
    (Sir D. Bonham-Carter) Non-Parliamentary
District Nurses – Training   1955
    (Sir F. Armer) Non-Parliamentary
Doctors' and Dentists' Remuneration 9th Report   1968
    (Lord Kindersley) Cmnd. 3600
Doctors in an Integrated Health Service   1971
    (J. H. F. Brotherston) Non-Parliamentary

Empire Migration   1932
 (Visc. Astor) Cmd. 4075
Employers and Employed — Relations   1918
 (J. H. Whitley) Cd. 9001; Cd. 9099; Cd. 9153
English Language — Examining of   1964
 (Sir J. Lockwood) Non-Parliamentary
 see also Teaching of English in England
Epilepsy   1969
 (J. J. A. Reid) Non-Parliamentary
Epilepsy in Scotland — Medical Care   1968
 (J. H. Hutchison) Non-Parliamentary
Epileptics — Medical Care   1956
 (Sir H. Cohen) Non-Parliamentary
Evacuation   1938
 (Sir J. Anderson) Cmd. 5837
Examinations in Secondary Schools   1947
 (Sir M. Holmes) Non-Parliamentary
Exchequer Equalisation Grants (England and Wales)   1953
 (F. L. Edwards) Non-Parliamentary
Exchequer Equalisation Grants (Scotland)   1953
 (Sir C. C. Cunningham) Non-Parliamentary
Explosives: *see* Precautions Necessary to Secure Safety in the Use of Ex-
 plosives in Coal Mines
Fair Wages   1908
 (Sir G. H. Murray) Cd. 4422
Farming: *see* Contract Farming
Ferries in Great Britain   1947
 (N. S. Beaton) Non-Parliamentary
Field Monuments — Protection   1969
 (Sir D. Walsh) Cmnd. 3904
15 to 18 (2v.)   1959–60
 (Sir G. Crowther) Non-Parliamentary
Finance and Industry   1931
 (Lord Macmillan) Cmd. 3897
Fines, etc. — Imprisonment by Courts of Summary Jurisdiction in Default
 of Payment   1934
 (Sir J. F. Williams) Cmd. 4649

Fire Service   1970
    (Sir Ronald Holroyd) Cmnd. 4371
Fire Service   1971
    (Sir Charles Cunningham) Cmnd. 4807
Fish Toxicity Tests   1970
    (A. Key) Non-Parliamentary
Fishing Industry   1961
    (Sir A. Fleck) Cmnd. 1266
Flow of Candidates in Science and Technology into Higher
    Education   1968
    (F. S. Dainton) Cmnd. 3541
Flying – Control   1939
    (Lord Gorell) Cmd. 5961
Foot-and-Mouth Disease   1969
    (Duke of Northumberland) Cmnd. 3999; 4225
Football   1968
    (D. N. Chester) Non-Parliamentary
Footpaths   1968
    (Sir A. Gosling) Non-Parliamentary
Forensic Psychiatry   1969
    (J. Harper) Non-Parliamentary
From School to Further Education   1963
    (J. S. Brunton) Non-Parliamentary
Fuel and Power Resources – National Policy for Use   1952
    (Visc. Ridley) Cmd. 8647
Funds in Court   1959
    (Mr. Justice Pearson) Cmnd. 818
Gas Industry   1945
    (G. Heyworth) Cmd. 6699
Gatwick Airport   1954
    (Sir C. Campbell) Cmd. 9215
General Medical Services in the Highlands and Islands   1967
    (Lord Birsay) Cmnd. 3257
General Nursing Councils for England and Wales and Scotland   1954
    (Miss J. K. Aitken) Non-Parliamentary
German Outrages – Alleged   1915
    (Visc. Bryce) Cd. 7894

Government: *see* Machinery of Government
Government Accounts – Form of   1950
    (W. F. Crick) Cmd. 7969
Government Industrial Establishments   1971
    (Sir John Mallabar) Cmnd. 4713
Government Research Departments: *see* Liaison between Universities and
  Government Research Departments
Graduates for Secondary Education – Training   1972
    (J. S. Brunton) Non-Parliamentary
Grant-Aided Schools: *see* Tuition Fees in Grant-Aided Schools
Grants to Students   1960
    (Sir C. Anderson) Cmnd. 1051
Grassland Utilisation   1958
    (Sir S. Caine) Cmnd. 547
Grit and Dust Emissions   1967
    (D. Hicks) Non-Parliamentary
Group Practice – Organisation   1971
    (R. H. Davis) Non-Parliamentary
Habitual Drunken Offenders   1971
    (T. G. Weiler) Non-Parliamentary
Half our Future   1963
    (J. H. Newsom) Non-Parliamentary
Halls of Residence   1957
    (W. R. Niblett) Non-Parliamentary
Handicapped Children in the Care of Local Authorities and Voluntary
  Organisations   1970
    (R. G. Mitchell) Non-Parliamentary
Heroin: *see* Morphine and Heroin Addiction
Higher Appointments   1944
    (Lord Hankey) Cmd. 6576
Higher Education   1963
    (Lord Robbins) Cmnd. 2154
Higher Technical Education – Future Development   1950
    (Sir R. M. Weeks) Non-Parliamentary
Higher Technological Education   1945
    (Lord E. Percy) Non-Parliamentary

Local Government Officers – Qualifications, Recruitment, Training and
    Promotion   1934
        (Sir H. Hadow) Non-Parliamentary
Local Land Charges   1951
        (Sir J. Stainton) Cmd. 8440
London Airport: *see* Third London Airport
London County Council Remand Homes   1945
        (G. R. Vick) Cmd. 6594
London Taxicab Trade   1970
        (A. M. Stamp) Cmnd. 4483
London Transport   1955
        (S. P. Chambers) Non-Parliamentary
Londonderry – Events of Jan 30   1972
        (Lord Widgery) 1971–72 HC 220
LSD: *see* Amphetamines and LSD
Machinery of Government   1918
        (Lord Haldane) Cd. 9230
Magistrates' Courts in London   1961
        (C. D. Aarvold) Cmnd. 1606
Maintenance Engineering   1970
        (I. Maddock) Non-Parliamentary
Major Ports of Great Britain   1962
        (Visc. Rochdale) Cmnd. 1824
Majority – Age   1967
        (Mr. Justice Latey) Cmnd. 3342
Management Studies in Technical Colleges   1962
        (J. W. Platt) Non-Parliamentary
Managers – Training and Development   1969
        (Sir J. Hunt) Non-Parliamentary
Manpower Resources for Science and Technology   1966
        (Sir W. Jackson) Cmnd. 3103
Manpower Resources for Science and Technology   1968
        (M. Swann) Cmnd. 3760
        See also Scientific Manpower
Marriage Guidance   1948
        (Sir S. Harris) Cmd. 7566
Marriage Law of Scotland   1969
        (Lord Kilbrandon) Cmnd. 4011

Maternity Services 1958
(Earl of Cranbrook) Non-Parliamentary
Matrimonial Causes 1947
(Mr. Justice Denning) Cmd. 7024
Matrimonial Proceedings in Magistrates' Courts 1959
(Mr. Justice Davies) Cmnd. 638
Mau Mau — Historical Survey of the Origins and Growth 1960
(E. D. Corfield) Cmnd. 1030
Medical Administrators 1972
(R. B. Hunter) Non-Parliamentary
Medical Rehabilitation 1972
(A. Mair) Non-Parliamentary
Medical Work in Hospitals — Organisation 1967
(Sir G. Godber) Non-Parliamentary
Medicines in Hospital Wards and Departments — Control 1972
(A. Roxburgh) Non-Parliamentary
Metrication 1968
(A. H. A. Wynn) Non-Parliamentary
Midges — Control 1946
(F. A. E. Crew) Non-Parliamentary
Midwives 1948
(Mrs. M. D. Stocks) Non-Parliamentary
Milk Distribution 1948
(W. D. A. Williams) Cmd. 7414
Mineral Development 1949
(Lord Westwood) Cmd. 7732
Ministers and Members of Parliament — Remuneration 1964
(Sir G. Lawrence) Cmnd. 2516
Ministers of the Crown and other Public Servants — Allegations reflecting
on Official Conduct 1949
(Sir G. J. Lynskey) Cmd. 7616
Ministers' Powers 1932
(Lord Donoughmore) Cmd. 4060
Misuse of Drugs in Scotland 1972
(J. A. Ward) 2nd Rept. Non-Parliamentary
Modern Languages — Research and Development 1967
(L. Farrer-Brown) Non-Parliamentary

New Forest   1947
    (H. T. Baker) Cmd. 7245
New Industrial Development   1932
    (J. H. Thomas) Non-Parliamentary
New Local Authorities — Management and Structure   1972
    (M. A. Bains) Non-Parliamentary
New Roads in Towns   1972
    (W. Burns) Non-Parliamentary
New Towns   1946
    (Lord Reith of Stonehaven) Cmd. 6876
New Trials in Criminal Cases   1954
    (Lord Tucker) Cmd. 9150
Night Baking   1937
    (Lord Alness) Cmd. 5525
Night Baking   1951
    (Sir F. Rees) Cmd. 8378
Night Employment of Male Young Persons in Factories and Workshops   1913
    (Lord Ashton) M/E Cd. 6711
Noise   1963
    (Sir Alan Wilson) Cmnd. 2056
Noise from Motor Vehicles   1962
    (Sir Alan Wilson) Cmnd. 1780
Noise: *see also* Neighbourhood Noise
Non-Custodial and Semi-Custodial Penalties   1970
    (K. Younger) Non-Parliamentary
Non-Recurrent Grants (Students)   1968
    (J. F. Wolfenden) Non-Parliamentary
Non-Residential Treatment of Offenders under 21   1962
    (Mr. Justice Barry) Non-Parliamentary
Northern Ireland: *see* Interrogation of Prisoners Suspected of Terrorism; Physical Brutality in Northern Ireland; Terrorist Activities in Northern Ireland
Nuclear Explosions — Effect of High Altitude Nuclear Explosions on Scientific Experiments   1963
    (J. A. Ratcliffe) Cmnd. 2029

Nuclear Power for Ship Propulsion   1964
(Sir J. Dunnett) Cmnd. 2358
Nuclear-Powered Merchant Ships — Safety   1960
(P. Faulkner) Cmnd. 958
Nuclear Ships   1971
(S. W. Spain) Non-Parliamentary
Nurses in an Integrated Health Service   1972
(Dame Muriel Powell) Non-Parliamentary
Nursing   1972
(A. Briggs) Cmnd. 5115
Nursing Services   1938
(Earl of Athlone) Non-Parliamentary *See also* Senior Nursing Staff
Structure
Official Facilities for the Circulation of Documents — Allegation of
Misuse   1958
(Sir N. Brook) Cmnd. 583
Official Secrets Act 1911   1972
(Lord Franks) Cmnd. 5104
Old Age   1954
(Sir T. Phillips) Cmd. 9333
Open University   1969
(Sir P. Venables) Non-Parliamentary
Oriental, Slavonic, East European and African Studies   1946
(Earl of Scarbrough) Non-Parliamentary
Out of School   1948
(Sir F. Clarke) Non-Parliamentary
Oxygen Therapy — Uses and Dangers   1969
(K. W. Donald) Non-Parliamentary
Pedestrian Crossings: *see* Road Safety (Pedestrian Crossings)
People and Planning   1961
(A. M. Skeffington) Non-Parliamentary
Persistent Offenders   1932
(Sir J. C. Dove-Wilson) Cmd. 4090
Personal Injuries Litigation   1968
(Lord Justice Winn) Cmnd. 3691
Personal Injury — Limitation of Action in Cases of   1962
(Mr. Justice Davies) Cmnd. 1829

Physical Brutality in Northern Ireland   1971
    (Sir Edmund Compton) Cmnd. 4823
Plastics   1944
    (H. V. Potter) Non-Parliamentary
Police Duties — Employment of Women   1920
    (J. L. Baird) Cmd. 877 (M/E Cmd. 1133)
Police Extraneous Duties   1953
    (J. H. Burrell) Non-Parliamentary
Police Manpower, Equipment and Efficiency   1967
    (D. Taverne) Non-Parliamentary
Police Service — Recruitment of People with Higher Educational Qualifications   1967
    (D. Taverne) Non-Parliamentary
Police Service of England, Wales and Scotland   1920
    (Lord Desborough) Cmd. 253; 574
Police Uniform   1947
    (Sir F. Brook) Non-Parliamentary
Policewomen — Employment   1924
    (W. C. Bridgeman) Cmd. 2224
Pollution: Nuisance or Nemesis?   1972
    (Sir Eric Ashby) Non-Parliamentary
Poor Law in Scotland   1938
    (J. Keith) Cmd. 5803
Poor Persons' Rules   1925
    (Mr. Justice Lawrence) Cmd. 2358
Port Transport Industry   1956
    (Mr. Justice Devlin) Cmd. 9813
Port Transport Industry   1965
    (Lord Devlin) Cmnd. 2734
Ports Efficiency   1952
    (Lord Llewellin) Non-Parliamentary
Ports: *see also* Major Ports of Great Britain; South Wales Ports
Power Stations — Economy in Construction   1953
    (Sir H. Beaver) Non-Parliamentary
Precautions Necessary to Secure Safety in the Use of Explosives in Coal Mines   1950
    (A. M. Bryan) Non-Parliamentary

Road Safety (Pedestrian Crossings)   1941
    (J. Callaghan) Non-Parliamentary
Roads: *see* New Roads in Towns
Ronan Point — Collapse of Flats   1968
    (H. Griffiths) Non-Parliamentary
Royal Commissions — Procedure   1910
    (Lord Balfour of Burleigh) Cd. 5235
Russian — Teaching of   1962
    (N. G. Annan) Non-Parliamentary
Safety and Health at Work   1972
    (Lord Robens) Cmnd. 5034
Schools Curricula and Examinations   1964
    (Sir J. Lockwood) Non-Parliamentary
Science in Education in Wales Today   1965
    (F. Llewellyn-Jones) Non-Parliamentary
Science Policy   1966
    (Sir H. Massey) Cmnd. 3007
Scientific Civil Service — Organisation   1965
    (Sir M. Tennant) Non-Parliamentary
Scientific Interchange   1972
    (Sir Harold Thompson) Cmnd. 4843
Scientific Manpower   1946
    (Sir A. Barlow) Cmd. 6824
    See also Manpower Resources for Science and Technology
Scientific Research in the Universities   1971
    (Sir Harrie Massey) Cmnd. 4798
Scottish Administration   1937
    (Sir J. Gilmour) Cmd. 5563
Scottish Prison System   1949
    (C. W. G. Taylor) Non-Parliamentary
Scottish Prisons   1900
    (Earl of Elgin and Kincardine) Cd. 218
Scottish Teachers' Salaries Memorandum   1968
    (Lord Robertson) Non-Parliamentary
Secondary Education   1938
    (W. Spens) Non-Parliamentary
Secondary School Examinations other than the G.C.E.   1958
    (R. Beloe) Non-Parliamentary

Security Procedures in the Public Service   1962
  (Lord Radcliffe) Cmnd. 1681
Senior Nursing Staff Structure   1965
  (B. Salmon) Non-Parliamentary
Service by Youth   1966
  (G. S. Bessey) Non-Parliamentary
Sewage Disposal: *see* Taken for Granted
Sexual Offences against Young Persons   1925
  (Sir R. Adkins) Cmd. 2561
Share-pushing   1937
  (Sir A. H. Bodkin) Cmd. 5539
Shares of No Par Value   1954
  (M. L. Gedge) Cmd. 9112
Sheriff Court, The   1967
  (Lord Grant) Cmnd. 3248
Shipbuilding   1966
  (R. M. Geddes) Cmnd. 2937
Shipping   1969
  (Visc. Rochdale) Cmnd. 4337
Ships: *see* Nuclear Ships
Sick Pay Schemes   1964
  (A. S. Marre) Non-Parliamentary
Sinews for Survival   1972
  (R. B. Verney) Non-Parliamentary
Small Firms   1971
  (J. E. Bolton) Cmnd. 4811
Smallholdings: *see* Statutory Smallholdings
Smokeless Fuels: *see* Solid Smokeless Fuels
Social and Economic Research — Provision for   1946
  (Sir J. Clapham) Cmd. 6868
Social Insurance and Allied Services   1943
  (Sir W. Beveridge) Cmd. 6404/5
Social Services in Courts of Summary Jurisdiction   1936
  (S. W. Harris) Cmd. 5122
Social Services: *see also* Local Authority and Allied Social Services
Social Studies   1965
  (Lord Heyworth) Cmnd. 2660

Taken for Granted   1970
    (Lena M. Jeger) Non-Parliamentary
Tax-Paid Stocks   1953
    (Sir M. Hutton) Cmd. 8784
Taxation of Trading Profits   1951
    (J. M. Tucker) Cmd. 8189
Taxation Treatment of Provisions for Retirement   1953
    (J. M. Tucker) Cmd. 9063
Taxicab Service   1953
    (Visc. Runciman) Cmd. 8804
    (See also Cab and Private Hire Vehicles; London Taxicab Trade
Teacher Education and Training   1972
    (Lord James of Rusholme) Non-Parliamentary
Teachers — Conditions of Service in Further Education in
  Scotland   1965
    (A. G. Rodger) Non-Parliamentary
Teachers — Demand for and Supply of   1963—66
    (A. L. C. Bullock) Non-Parliamentary
Teachers — Future Demand for   1958
    (Sir G. Crowther) Non-Parliamentary
Teachers for Training Colleges — Supply and Training   1957
    (Sir W. Jackson) Non-Parliamentary
Teachers in Scotland   1958
    (T. M. Knox) Cmnd. 644
Teachers in Scotland — Supply   1951—62
    (T. Grainger-Stewart) 1st Cmd. 8123; 2nd Cmd. 8721; 3rd Cmnd. 196; 4th Cmnd. 1601
Teachers' Salaries (Training Colleges)   1945
    (Sir H. Pelham) Non-Parliamentary
Teaching Council for England and Wales   1970
    (T. R. Weaver) Non-Parliamentary
Teaching of English in England   1924
    (Sir H. Newbolt) Non-Parliamentary
Teaching Profession in Scotland   1963
    (Lord Wheatley) Cmnd. 2066
Technical College Resources — Use   1968/69
    (Sir H. Pilkington; Sir J. Hunt) Non-Parliamentary

Vassal Case   1963
      (Lord Radcliffe) Cmnd. 2009
Veterinary Practice by Unregistered Persons   1945
      (Sir J. R. Chancellor) Cmd. 6611
Visually Handicapped in Education   1972
      (M. D. Vernon) Non-Parliamentary
Voluntary Service in After-Care   1967
      (Marchioness of Reading) Non-Parliamentary
Water in England and Wales —*Future Management   1971
      (Sir Alan Wilson) Non-Parliamentary
Water Service in Scotland   1972
      (W. L. Taylor) Non-Parliamentary
Welfare of Animals kept under Intensive Livestock Husbandry Systems   1965
      (F. W. R. Brambell) Cmnd. 2836
Welfare of Children in Hospital   1958
      (Sir H. Platt) Non-Parliamentary
Welfare of the Blind   1937
      (Lord Blanesburgh) Non-Parliamentary
Welsh Language — Legal Status   1965
      (Sir D. H. Parry) Cmnd. 2785
Welsh Language Publishing   1952
      (A. W. Ready) Cmd. 8661
Welsh Language Today   1963
      (R. I. Aaron) Cmnd. 2198
Women and Young Persons — Hours of Employment in Factories   1969
      (C. J. Maston) Non-Parliamentary
Women in the Civil Service — Employment   1971
      (E. M. Kemp-Jones) Non-Parliamentary
Working Classes Cost of Living   1918
      (Lord Sumner) Cd. 8980
Works of Art — Sale by Public Bodies   1964
      (Lord Cottesloe) Non-Parliamentary
Young Offenders — Custodial Training   1962
      (Sheriff W. J. Bryden) Non-Parliamentary
Young Offenders — Treatment   1927
      (Sir E. Cecil) Cmd. 2831

CHAPTER 12

Non-Parliamentary Publications

INTRODUCTION

As has already been noted, documents originating in government departments and not in pursuance of a statutory requirement may be presented to Parliament at the discretion of the responsible Minister. Those which are *not* so presented are normally published by Her Majesty's Stationery Office as Non-Parliamentary Publications. Some "Act papers" — that is to say reports required to be produced by the provisions of Acts of Parliament — are also classed as Non-Parliamentary, the largest group of this type being statutory instruments. Figure 3 shows how Non-Parliamentary Publications are announced in H.M.S.O.'s daily list. Sometimes it is difficult to understand why one department rather than another should have issued a particular item. What, for instance, has the Animals (Restriction of Importation) Act 1964 to do with the Department of Education and Science? Some of the answers can only come from a study of the various government departments, and particularly useful in this connection is the New Whitehall Series published by George Allen & Unwin Ltd. Titles currently available are:

BRIDGES, LORD, *The Treasury* (2nd edn. 1967).

CLARKE, Sir FIFE, *The Central Office of Information* (1970)

CROMBIE, Sir JAMES, *Her Majesty's Customs and Excise* (1962).

EMMERSON, Sir HAROLD, *The Ministry of Works* (1956).

INCE, Sir GODFREY, *The Ministry of Labour and National Service* (1960)

JEFFRIES, Sir CHARLES, *The Colonial Office* (1955).

JENKINS, Sir GILMOUR, *The Ministry of Transport and Civil Aviation* (1959).

JOHNSTON, Sir ALEXANDER, *The Inland Revenue* (1965).

KING, Sir GEOFFREY, *The Ministry of Pensions and National Insurance* (1958).

MILNE, Sir DAVID, *The Scottish Office* (1958).

NEWSAM, Sir FRANK, *The Home Office* (2nd edn. 1955).

SHARP, Lady EVELYN, *The Ministry of Housing and Local Government* (1969).

STRANG, LORD, *The Foreign Office* (1955).

WINNIFRITH, Sir JOHN, *The Ministry of Agriculture, Fisheries and Food* (1962).

Even these, however, are no substitute for a file of a department's own annual report, which are authoritative factual statements of activities and achievements, backed up by statistical data.

The considerable growth in the volume of government publishing over the past years is a direct result of the increasing involvement of the central administration in the day-to-day conduct of the nation's affairs. Non-Parliamentary Publications have an immense subject coverage: they range from the highly technical report on the pressure drag of aerofoils at super-sonic speeds to the practical leaflet on how to deal with ants indoors. Reference works like *Britain: an official handbook* and popular guides to ancient monuments and historic buildings rub covers with factory forms and surveys of the regional economic planning councils. An 8-page Civil Service Pay Research Unit report costing 4p is listed next to a 640-page history of the Office and College of Arms at £21. There are statistics on everything from family expenditure to overseas trade; studies on man-power in the chemical industry and roads in the landscape; advice on planning a farm business and on painting metalwork; and all manner of reports on topics as diverse as university libraries and highland transport services.

These examples, taken from H.M.S.O.'s 1967 catalogue, are included in the following list of all the Non-Parliamentary Publications (except statutory instruments) published in that year. Only by reproducing in full a representative annual list of titles in this way can the extent of depart-mental publishing by conveyed accurately. Only brief titles are given so as to keep the list within reasonable limits, and for the same reason where a number of documents were issued in the same series — Ministry of Agricul-

ture leaflets, for example — only selected items are listed. So as to illustrate the fuller descriptions given in the official indexes a specimen page from the H.M.S.O. annual *Catalogue of Government Publications* is reproduced in Fig. 5.

ABSTRACT FROM 1967 OFFICIAL CATALOGUE

AGRICULTURE AND FISHERIES, DEPARTMENT OF, FOR SCOTLAND
Agricultural Statistics, Scotland, 1966.
Crofters Commission. Annual Report for 1966.
Freshwater and Salmon Fisheries Research 38. The food, growth and population structure of salmon and trout in two streams in the Scottish Highlands.
Highland Transport Services. Report of the Highland Transport Board.
Key to Potato Trials and Collections at East Craigs, 1967.
Marine Research, 1967. *5 items, e.g.*
   1. The food of cod in the North Sea and on West of Scotland Grounds
   3. Plaice investigations in Scottish waters.
Planning the Farm Business.
Red Deer Commission. Annual Report for 1966.
Register of Potato Crops Certified, 1967.
Residual Values of Fertilizers and Feeding Stuffs. 19th Report (1967).
Scottish Agricultural Economics. Vol. XVII.
Scottish Agriculture. Vol. XLVI.
Scottish Sea Fisheries. Statistical Tables, 1966.
Soils of the country round Haddington and Eyemouth.

AGRICULTURE, FISHERIES AND FOOD, MINISTRY OF
Advisory Leaflets. *20 items, e.g.*
   169 The House-Sparrow. Revised.
   283 Advice to Intending Beekeepers. Revised.
   366 Ants Indoors. Revised.
   534 The Rabbit.
   540 Lighting for Egg Production. Revised.
Agricultural Statistics, 1964–65:
   England and Wales. United Kingdom.
Agriculture. Vol. 74.
Aspects of Dairy Economics, 1962–65.

Bulletins. *9 items, e.g.*

  5 Fruit Spraying Machines. 6th edn.

  136 Watercress Growing. 3rd edn.

  197 Flowers from Bulbs and Corms.

Cereals Deficiency Payments Scheme. 5th edn.

Chemicals for the Gardener. Supplement No. 1

Circulars FSH. *100 items relating to e.g.*

  (England and Wales) Public Health (Imported Food) Regulations, 1937 and 1948.

  (England and Wales) The Cheese (Amendment) Regulations, 1966.

  (England and Wales) The Meat Pie and Sausage Roll Regulations, 1967.

  (England and Wales) The Canned Meat Product Regulations, 1967.

Costs and Efficiency in Milk Production, 1965—66.

Covent Garden Market Authority. 5th Report, 1965—66

Dairy Floors.

Experimental Horticulture. *2 issues.*

Experimental Husbandry. *2 issues.*

Experimental Husbandry Farms and Experimental Horticulture Stations. 8th Progress Report, 1967.

Farm as a Business. No. 8. Aids to Management Dairying. 2nd edn.

Farm Buildings Pocket Book. New edn.

Farm Classification in England and Wales, 1964—65.

Farm Incomes in England and Wales, 1965.

Fatstock Guarantee Scheme, 1967—68.

Fishery Investigations:

  A Study of the Oystercatcher in Relation to the Fishery for Cockles in the Burry Inlet, South Wales.

  An Introductory Account of the Smaller Algae of British Coastal Waters Part IV: Cryptophyceae.

Fixed Equipment of the Farm. Leaflets:

  38 Floor and Roof Construction. Revised.

  40 Wall Construction. Revised.

  51 Housing the Sow and Litter.

Food Additives and Contaminants Committee:

  Report on Aldrin and Dieldrin Residues in Food.

  Second Report on Cyclamates.

Food Standards Committee. Report on Cream.

Fumigation with the Liquid Fumigants Carbon Tetrachloride, etc.

Horticulture in Britain. Part 1. Vegetables.

Mechanisation Leaflet for Farmers and Growers. *5 items, e.g.*

16 Bale Handling Equipment and Systems.

17 Potato Harvesting with Diggers.

N.A.A.S. Quarterly Review. *5 issues.*

Output and Utilisation of Farm Produce in the United Kingdom 1962–63 to 1965–66. New edn.

Plant Pathology. *5 issues.*

Plant Varieties and Seeds Gazette. *13 issues.*

Report on the Animal Health Services in Great Britain, 1965.

Report on Safety, Health, Welfare and Wages in Agriculture, Oct. 1, 1965 to Sept. 30, 1966.

Return of Proceedings under the Diseases of Animals Act, 1950, for the year 1966.

Sea Fisheries Statistical Tables: 1965, 1966.

Smallholdings Organised on the Basis of Centralised Services. Report and accounts for the year 1965–66.

Technical Bulletin No. 14. Soil potassium and magnesium.

ARTS COUNCIL OF GREAT BRITAIN

22nd Annual Report and Accounts. Year ended March 31, 1967. A new Charter.

CENTRAL STATISTICAL OFFICE

Abstract of Regional Statistics. No. 3, 1967.

Economic Report on 1966.

Economic Trends. *11 issues.*

Statistics:

Annual Abstract of Statistics. No. 104, 1967.

Financial. *12 issues, 1 supplement.*

Monthly Digest. *12 issues, 1 supplement.*

National Income and Expenditure, 1967.

Studies in Official Statistics No. 12. Fourth Series. New contributions to economic statistics.

United Kingdom Balance of Payments, 1967.

CIVIL SERVICE COMMISSION

Annual Report, 1966.

Question Papers.
Clerical Class. *11 items.*
Customs and Excise. *2 items.*
Executive Class. *1 item.*
Her Majesty's Stationery Office. *1 item.*
Home Office. *2 items.*
Post Office. *4 items.*

CIVIL SERVICE PAY RESEARCH UNIT
Report for the years 1964–65 and 1965–66.

COLLEGE OF ARMS
Heralds of England. A history of the Office and College of Arms.

COMMONWEALTH AGRICULTURAL BUREAUX
37th Annual Report of the Executive Council, 1965–66.

COMMONWEALTH ECONOMIC COMMITTEE
Commonwealth Trade, 1965.
Non-Ferrous Metals, 1966.
Vegetable Oils and Oilseeds. No. 16.

COMMONWEALTH EDUCATION LIAISON COMMITTEE
Commonwealth Scholarship and Fellowship Plan. 7th Annual Report.
Education and Training of Technicians.

COMMONWEALTH OFFICE
Arms. Granted by Royal Warrant.
    Antigua.
    St. Christopher-Nevis-Anguilla.
Colonial Reports, 1961 to 1965.
    Cayman Islands.
    St. Lucia.
    Dominica.
    Bahama Islands.
    Falkland Islands and Dependencies.
    St. Helena.
    British Solomon Islands.
    Gibraltar.
    Mauritius.
    Swaziland.

Commonwealth Development Corporation. Annual Report and Statement
of Accounts.
Commonwealth No. 3. Mauritius General Election, 1967.
Commonwealth Office Yearbook, 1967.
Electoral Registration in Mauritius.
Flags.
  Antigua.
  Barbados.
  Governor-General of Barbados.
  Governor-General of Guyana.
  St. Christopher-Nevis-Anguilla.
  St. Lucia.
Guide to the India Office Library with a note on the India Office Records.
2nd edn.
Hong Kong. Report for the year 1966.
Seychelles. Proposals for Constitutional Advance.

COMMONWEALTH WAR GRAVES COMMISSION
48th Annual Report

CONSUMER COUNCIL
Annual Report, 1966–67.
Living in a Caravan.

COURT OF SESSIONS SCOTLAND
Rules of Court. *8 items.*

CROWN ESTATE COMMISSIONERS
Report of the Crown Estate Commissioners.

CUSTOMS AND EXCISE
Annual Statement of the Trade of the United Kingdom.
  1964 Vols. I, III-V.
  1965 Vols. I-V.
  1966 Vols. II-III.
Classification of Chemicals in the Brussels Nomenclature, 1967.
Classification Opinions Adopted by the Customs Co-operation Council.
Export List, 1968.
H.M. Customs and Excise Tariff Amendments. *14 items.*

H.M. Customs and Excise Warehousing Manual. Amending Supplement No. 7.

List of Bonded Warehouses.

Protective Duties, 1965.

Statistical Classification for Imported Goods and for Re-exported Goods, 1968.

DEFENCE, MINISTRY OF

Air Force Department:

    Air Almanac. *3 items.*

    Air Force List. Spring 1967.

    Air Publication 826. Regulations for Civilian Industrial Employees Amendment List. *2 items.*

    Manual of Air Force Law. Amendment List.

    Queen's Regulations for the Royal Air Force. Amendments Lists.

    Sight Reduction Tables for Air Navigation. Vols. II & III

Army Department:

    Allowance Regulations Amendments. *19 items.*

    Army List, 1967.

    Army Orders. *12 items.*

    Manual of Military Law. *2 items.*

    Physical Training in the Army, 1958. Amendment.

    Queen's Regulations for the Army, 1961. Amendments. *15 items.*

    Regulations for the Territorial Army Volunteer Reserve, 1967. *5 items.*

    Royal Warrants (Pay, Pensions). *3 items.*

    Soldier Magazine. Vol. 23, 1967.

    Special Army Orders, 1967. *11 items.*

    Defence Guides. *3 items.*

    Defence Lists. *5 items.*

    Defence Specifications. *90 items.*

Navy Department:

    Admiralty Hydrographic Service, 1795—1919.

    Admiralty Manual of Navigation. Vol. I. Change No. 2.

    Admiralty Manual of Seamanship. Vol. II. New edn. 1967.

    Admiralty Memorandum on Navy Court Martial Procedure. Charges. *2 items.*

    Naval Marine Engineering Practice. Vol. I.

Navy List, Spring 1967.

Appendix to the Navy List. Rates of Pay, etc.

Queen's Regulations for the Royal Navy. Revised Jan. 2, 1967.

DIPLOMATIC SERVICE ADMINISTRATION OFFICE

Diplomatic Service List, 1967.

ECONOMIC AFFAIRS, DEPARTMENT OF

Britain and the E.E.C.

Development Areas.

Region With a Future. A Draft Strategy for the South West.

Strategy for the South East.

West Midlands: Patterns of Growth.

EDUCATION AND SCIENCE, DEPARTMENT OF

Animals (Restriction of Importation) Act, 1964:

 Report of the Advisory Committee, 1965.

 Summary of Statistics, 1968.

Building Bulletins. *4 items.*

Children and their Primary Schools. A Report of the Central Advisory
 Council for Education (England). *2 vols.*

Circulars and Administrative Memoranda, 1966.

Circular 18/66. Addendum I. Training of Teachers.

Commonwealth Collections of Micro-Organisms.

 Australia, 1966.

 Canada, 1967.

Compendium of Teacher Training Courses in England and Wales,
 1968–69.

Computer Education. A Report of an Interdepartmental Working Group.

Education Pamphlet No. 52. Towards world history.

Education Survey 1. Units for partially hearing children.

Examination in Art (National Diploma in Design).

 Question Papers. *2 items.*

Form 207 Pen. Allocation of Pension. New edn.

Further Education of the General Student.

Immigrants and the Youth Service. Report of a Committee of the Youth
 Service Development Council.

Inside the Primary School.

Lists:

 10 Index to Department of Education and Science Circulars and

Administrative Memoranda.

42 (1966). List of Special Schools for Handicapped Pupils in England and Wales.

National Film School.

National Lending Library for Science and Technology. Current Serials received.

NLL Translations Bulletin. Vol. 9, 1967. *12 items.*

Pamphlet No. 21. The School Library. New edn.

Project Magazine. *3 items.*

Report of the Arbitral Body on Salaries of Teachers in Primary and Secondary Schools.

Report of the Committee on Scales of Salaries for the Teaching Staff of Colleges of Education.

Review of the Present Safety Arrangements for the Use of Toxic Chemicals in Agriculture and Food Storage. Report by the Advisory Committee on Pesticides and other Toxic Chemicals.

Scales of Salaries for Teachers in Primary and Secondary Schools.

Schools Council:

Curriculum Bulletin No. 2. A School Approach to Technology.

The New Curriculum.

Examinations Bulletins. *3 items.*

Humanities for the Young School Leaver.

Welsh Committee:

Another Year — to endure or enjoy?

Welsh. A Programme of Research and Development.

Working Papers:

9 Standards in C.S.E. and G.C.E. English and Mathematics.

10 Curriculum Development.

11 Society and the Young School Leaver.

12 The Education Implications of Social and Economic Change.

13 English for the Children of Immigrants.

14 Mathematics for the Majority.

15 Counselling in Schools.

Science Policy Studies No. 1. The sophistication factor in science expenditure.

Science Research Council. Report of the Council for the year 1966—67.

Scientific Research in British Universities and Colleges, 1966—67:

Vol. I. Physical Sciences.
Vol. II. Biological Sciences.
Vol. III. Social Sciences.
Statistics of Education. *3 items.*
Statistics of Science and Technology.
Trends in Education. *4 items.*

FOREIGN OFFICE
Bahrain Notices. *7 items*
British and Foreign State Papers 1959–60. Vol. 164.
Documents on British Foreign Policy 1919–1939. 1st Series. Vol. XV.
 International Conferences and Conversations, 1921.
European Atomic Energy Community:
 Regulations. *14 items.*
 Treaty Setting up the European Atomic Committee (Euratom). Rome,
  Mar. 25, 1957. New edn.
European Economic Community:
 Agreement Setting up an Association between the E.E.C. and Greece.
  Brussels, 25 Sept. 1961.
 Regulations. *438 items.*
 Treaty Setting up the European Economic Community. Rome, March
  25, 1957. New edn.
London Diplomatic List, 1967. *6 items.*
Persian Gulf Gazette. *6 items.*
Qatar Notices. *2 items.*
Trucial States Notices. *9 items, e.g.*
 7 of 1966. The Dubai Air Traffic Regulation, 1966.

FORESTRY COMMISSION
Argyll Forest Park Guide. 4th edn.
Booklets:
 16 Forest Management Tables. Supplement.
 17 Thinning Control in British Woodlands.
 19 Timber Extraction by Light Agricultural Tractor.
Bulletins:
 40 Rooting and Stability in Sitka Spruce.
 41 Forest Management, etc., of Wood in Sweden.
Forest Records. *5 items, e.g.*

52 Home Grown Roundwood.

63 Forestry Quarantine and its Biological Background.

Leaflets. *4 items, e.g.*

12 Taxation of Woodlands. Revised 1966.

Report on Forest Research.

Year ended March 1966.

Year ended March 1967.

FRIENDLY SOCIETIES, REGISTRY OF

Annual Return Forms. *20 items.*

Report of the Chief Registrar of Friendly Societies for the year 1966:

Part 1. General.

Part 2. Friendly Societies.

Part 3. Industrial and Provident Societies.

Part 4. Trade Unions.

Part 5. Building Societies.

Report of the Industrial Assurance Commissioner for the year 1966.

GENERAL REGISTER OFFICE

International Classification of Diseases.

Official List. *2 items, e.g.*

List of Registration Officers, etc. Corrected to Jan. 1, 1967.

Registrar General's Annual Estimates of the Population of England and Wales and of Local Authority Areas, 1966.

Registrar General's Statistical Review of England and Wales for the year:

1961. Supplement on Cancer. New edn.

1964. Part III. Commentary.

1965. Part I. Tables, Medical.

1965. Part II. Tables, Population.

Report on Hospital In-Patient Enquiry:

For the two years 1960 and 1961. Part III. Commentary.

For the year 1963. Part I. Tables.

Returns:

Births, Deaths, Infectious Diseases and Weather (Weekly) *52 items.*

Births, Deaths and Marriages, Infectious Diseases, Weather, Population Estimates (Quarterly). *4 items.*

Sample Census, 1966:

England and Wales County Reports. *58 items.*

Great Britain. Summary Tables.

Studies on Medical and Population Subjects. No. 21. Population Projections for the South East.

GENERAL REGISTER OFFICE, SCOTLAND

Annual Estimates of the Population of Scotland, 1966.

Annual Report of the Registrar General for Scotland, 1965.

Place Names and Population, Scotland.

Returns:

    Births, Deaths and Marriages (Quarterly). *4 items.*

    Births, Deaths and Marriages. Infectious Diseases, New Claims for Sickness Benefits. Weather Report (Weekly). *52 items.*

Sample Census, 1966. Scotland. County Reports. *10 items.*

HEALTH, MINISTRY OF

Abstracts of Efficiency Studies in the Hospital Service. *12 items, e.g.*

    101 Catering Department. Patients Choice Menu System.

    104 Linen Services

    111 Out-Patients Arrangements.

Central Health Services Council:

    Child Welfare Centres. Report of the Sub-Committee of the Standing Medical Advisory Committee.

    Standing Medical and Dental Advisory Committees. Dental Anaesthesia.

Central and Scottish Health Services Councils. Standing Joint Committee on the Classification of Proprietary Preparations. Report on the Definition of Drugs (Borderline Substances).

Committee on Safety of Drugs. Report of the year ended Dec. 13, 1966.

First Report of the Joint Working Party on the Organisation of Medical Work in Hospitals.

Food Hygiene Codes of Practice. 7. Hygiene in the operation of coin operated food vending machines.

Hospital Abstracts:

    Vol. 6, 1966. Index.

    Vol. 7, 1967. *12 items.*

Hospital Building Note No. 26. Operating Department.

Hospital Design Note No. 4. Noise Control.

Hospital Technical Memoranda. *3 items, e.g.*

    19 Facsimile Telegraphy: The transmission of pathology reports within a hospital.

Local Authority Building Note. No. 6. Residential Hostels for the Mentally Disordered.

Memorandum of Vaccination against Smallpox.

National Health Service.

Hospital Costing Returns. *3 items.*

Supplementary Ophthalmic Services. Statement specifying the fees and charges for the testing of sight and the supply or repair of glasses.

National Health Service Superannuation Scheme.

On the State of the Public Health. The Annual Report of the Chief Medical Officer of the Ministry of Health for the year 1966.

Report by the Working Party on Ambulance Training and Equipment. Part 2. Equipment and Vehicles.

Reports on Public Health and Medical Subjects. No. 116. A census of patients in psychiatric beds, 1963.

Statement of Fees and Charges for the Testing of Sight, etc. Amendments, *2 items.*

Statistical Report Series. No. 2. Report on the Census of Children and adolescents in non-psychiatric wards of National Health Service hospitals. June 1964 and March 1965.

HISTORICAL MANUSCRIPTS COMMISSION

Calendar of White and Black Books of the Cinque Ports, 1432–1955.

The Cartulary of Dale Abbey.

De L'isle and Dudley Manuscripts. Vol. VI. Sidney Papers.

National Register of Archives.

Index to Lists of Accessions to Repositories from 1954 to 1958.

List of accessions to repositories in 1966.

HOME OFFICE

Civil Defence Corps Training Syllabuses.

Vol. I. Training During a Four Year Engagement.

Vol. II. First Aid and Home Nursing.

Civil Defence Instructors' Notes. Vol. I. General and Supplementary Notes, 1967.

European Agreement concerning the International Carriage of Dangerous Goods by Road (A.D.R.) Annexes.

Explosives Acts 1875 and 1923. List of authorised Explosives.

Parliamentary Elections, England and Wales. The Electoral Registration Officers and Returning Officers Order, 1967.

Place of Voluntary Service in After-Care. Second Report of the Working Party.

Police Manpower, Equipment and Efficiency. Reports of three Working Parties.

Probation and After-Care Directory 1967 and Amendment Lists.
10 items.

Recruitment of People with Higher Education Qualifications into the Police Service.

Reports on a Fatal Accident in an Explosives Factory at Stevenston, Ayrshire on May 20, 1965.

Studies in the Causes of Delinquency and the Treatment of Offenders:
10 Types of Delinquency and Home Background.
11 Studies of Female Offenders.
12 The use of the Jesness Inventory on a Sample of British Probationers.

HOUSING AND LOCAL GOVERNMENT, MINISTRY OF
Alkali, &c. Works. 103rd Annual Report.

Ashford Study. Consultants' proposals for designation.

Betterment Levy. An explanatory memorandum of Part III of the Land Commission Act, 1967.

Central Lancashire. Study for a city. Consultant's proposals for designation.

Chimney Heights.
2nd edn. of the 1956 Clean Air Act Memorandum.
Chimney Heights Charts.

Circulars. *59 items, e.g.*
6/67 The Building Regulations 1965. Use of Self Extinguishing Grades of P.V.C. Sheeting.
16/67 The Land Commission.
20/67 Minister's Awards for good Design in Housing, 1967.
22/67 Noise: Industrial Noise.
25/67 Clean Air Act, 1956. Supplies of solid smokeless fuels.
32/67 Telephone Facilities on new Housing Estates.
73/67 Subsidies for Housing Associations.

Committee on the Management of Local Government.

Vol. 1. Report of the Committee.

Vol. 2. The Local Government Councillor.

Vol. 3. The Local Government Elector.

Vol. 4. The Local Government Administration Abroad.

Vol. 5. Local Government Administration in England and Wales.

Main points of the report of the Committee.

Committee on the Staffing of Local Government. Report.

Dee Crossing Study. Phase 1. A report to the technical working party.

Design Bulletins:

3 Part 7. Service Cores in High Flats. Protection against lightning.

5 Landscaping for Flats.

12 Cars in Housing.

13 Safety in the Home.

Form H.20. Return of Income and Expenditure. Year ended March 31, 1967.

General Rate Act, 1967. Tables of Comparison.

Grit and Dust. The measurement of emissions from boiler and furnace chimneys. Standard levels of emission.

Gypsies and Other Travellers.

Handbook of Statistics, 1966.

Historic Towns. Preservation and Change.

Houses Held on Ground Lease: Some Rights. 3rd edn.

Housing Role of the Greater London Council within London. Standing Working Party on London Housing.

Housing Statistics. Great Britain, 1967. *4 items.*

Housing Subsidies Manual.

Local Government Act, 1933. Local Government Financial Statistics England and Wales, 1964–65.

Local Government Superannuation Act, 1953. Local Government Superannuation (Benefits) Regulations, 1954. Tables.

Local Housing Statistics. England and Wales, 1967. *4 items.*

Management Study on Development Control.

Memorandum of Advice on the Preparation of Charging Schemes under Section 58 of the Water Resources Act 1963.

Needs of New Communities. A report prepared by a Sub-Committee of the Central Housing Advisory Committee.

Planning Bulletin No. 8. Settlement in the Countryside.

9th Progress Report of the Standing Technical Committee on Synthetic Detergents.

Public Cleansing. Refuse Collection and Disposal; Street Cleansing. Costing Returns, 1964–65.

Public Health Act, 1961. The Building Regulations, 1965. Selected Decisions.

Radioactivity in Drinking Water in the United Kingdom 1966 results.

Rates and Rateable Values in England and Wales, 1967–68.

Refuse Storage and Collection. Report of the Working party on refuse collection.

Report of the Inquiry into Local Objections to the Proposed Development of Land at Stansted as the Third Airport for London. Dec. 6, 1965 to Feb. 11, 1966.

Report of a Public Inquiry into the Future Use or Uses of the Broad Sanctuary Site, City of Westminster.

Report of the Working Party on Grit and Dust Emissions, 1967.

Safeguard to be Adopted in the Operation and Management of Waterworks. New edn.

Statistics of Decisions on Planning Applications. England and Wales, 1966.

Water Resources Act 1963. 4th Annual Report of the Water Resources Board for the year ending Sept. 30, 1967.

Wessex Rivers. Hydrological Survey.

Working Party on the Design and Construction of Underground Pipe Sewers. Notes on guidance on practical considerations in structural design. Second Report.

INDUSTRIAL DESIGN, COUNCIL OF

22nd Annual Report of the Council of Industrial Design and of its Scottish Committee, 1966–67.

Design Magazine, 1967. *12 items.*

INFORMATION, CENTRAL OFFICE OF

Britain in Brief. 9th edn.

Britain: An Official Handbook, 1967.

Commonwealth in Brief. 3rd edn.

Commonwealth Survey. Vol. 12, No. 26.

Commonwealth Today, 1967. *4 items.*

50 Facts about Britain's Economy. Revised.

1968 International Year for Human Rights.

Reference Pamphlets:

    7 Education in Britain. New edn.

    31 Labour relations and conditions of work in Britain. New edn.

    33 The British Parliament. New edn.

    34 Children in Britain. New edn.

    40 The Central Government of Britain. New edn.

    43 Agriculture in Britain. New edn.

    Britain and the Developing Countries. *3 items.*

Survey of British and Commonwealth Affairs (formerly Commonwealth Survey). *29 items.*

INLAND REVENUE

Case Commentary on the Income Tax Acts. 11th Supplement, 1966.

Harrison's Index to Tax Cases. 6th edn. 14th Supplement, 1966.

Income Tax Acts. 18th Supplement to the 1952 edn.

Profits Tax. Provisions of the Finance Acts, etc. 9th Supplement.

Tax Cases Reported under the Direction of the Board of Inland Revenue. *3 items.*

LABOUR, MINISTRY OF

Accidents at Factories, Offices, Shops, Docks and Construction Sites. *4 items.*

Accidents in the Construction Industry.

Central Training Council.

    An Approach to the Training and Development of Managers.

    Training of Training Officers.

Changes in Rates of Wages and Hours of Work. *10 items.*

Choice of Careers Booklets. *7 items.*

Civil Service Arbitration Tribunal Awards. *4 items.*

Code of Practice for the protection of persons exposed to ionising radiations in research and teaching. 4th impression.

Conciliation Act, 1896.

    [Reports of inquiries] . *2 items.*

Dismissal Procedures.

Efficient Use of Manpower.

Factories Act, 1961. Forms. *16 items.*

Family Expenditure Survey. Report for 1966.

Glossary of Training Terms.

H.M. Factory Inspectorate. Chromic Acid Mist.

Industrial Court Awards. *35 items.*

Industrial Training Research Register, 1967.

Industrial Tribunals. Reports and decisions. *14 items.*

Manpower Studies. No. 5. Electronics.

O.S.R. 19. The Offices, Shops and Railway Premises First Aid Order. 1964. Training Organisations. Certificates of Approval. *2 items.*

Power Press and Drop Stamping Problems in the Cutlery and Silverware Trades in Sheffield and District.

Report by Mr. A. J. Scamp of an Inquiry into the Employment of Coal Trimmers in the Ports of Blyth, etc.

Report of a Commission of Inquiry on the Hair, Bass and Fibre Wages Council (Great Britain), etc.

Report of Inquiry into the Locally Determined Aspects of the System of Payment, etc., of Registered Dock Workers in the Port of Liverpool.

Safety, Health and Welfare.

    Booklets. *2 items.*

    Form S.H.W. 395. Dangers from gassing, etc.

    Wall Sheet. Do's and Don'ts of lifting and carrying.

Studies in Official Statistics No. 6. Index of Retail Prices. 4th edn., 1966.

Time Rates of Wages and Hours of Work, 1967.

LAND REGISTRY

Land Registration Acts, 1925–1966.

    Forms. *4 items.*

    Practice Leaflets for Solicitors. *2 items.*

Report to the Lord Chancellor on H.M. Land Registry for the Year 1966.

LONDON MUSEUM

St. Pancras Hotel and Station from Pentonville Road: Sunset. Painted in 1888 by John O'Connor (1830–89). Large Colour Reproduction.

LORD CHANCELLOR'S OFFICE

Accounts of Receipts and Expenditure of the High Court and Court of Appeal, 1966–67.

Annual Report of the Council on Tribunals, 1966.

8th Annual Report of the Keeper of Public Records, 1966.
County Courts Branch. The London County Courts Directory. 8th edn.
Law Commission:
  2nd Annual Report, 1966—67.
  Imputed Criminal Intent.
  Transfer of Land. Interim Report on Root of Title to Freehold Land.
  Transfer of Land. Report on Restrictive Covenants.
  Law Com. No. 13. Civil liability for animals.
Legal Aid and Advice. Report of the Law Society, etc., 1965—66.
Legal Aid Booklet. Supplement.
Legal Aid Handbook. Supplement.
Rules of the Supreme Court, 1965. Supplements.

MEDICAL RESEARCH COUNCIL
Current Medical Research.
Memorandum No. 23 (3rd edn. 1967). Nomenclature of fungi.
Monitoring Report No. 14. Assay of strontium-90 in human bone.
Special Report Series. 265. Observations on the pathology of Hydro-
  cephalus. 3rd Impression.

METEOROLOGICAL OFFICE
Annual Report, 1966.
Daily Aerological Cross-Sections.
Handbook of Weather Messages. *2 items.*
Met Forms. *2 items.*
Meteorology for Mariners. 2nd edn. 1967.
Quarterly Surface Current Charts of the South Pacific Ocean. 2nd edn.
  1967.
Scientific Papers. *2 items.*
Ships' Code and Decode Book.
Tables of Temperature, Relative Humidity and Precipitation for the World.
  2 items.

MUSEUMS AND GALLERIES, STANDING COMMITTEE ON
Report on the Area Museum Services, 1963—1966.

NATIONAL ECONOMIC DEVELOPMENT OFFICE
Action on the Banwell Report.

Economic Development Committee for Hotels and Catering. Your Manpower.

Exports by Air.

Hotel and Catering EDC. Visitors to Britain.

Investment Appraisal. 2nd edn. 1967.

Manpower in the Chemical Industry.

Productivity, A Handbook of Advisory Services.

Productivity, Prices and Incomes. A general review, 1966.

Second Report on Efficiency in Road Construction.

NATIONAL GALLERIES OF SCOTLAND
60th Report of the Board of Trustess, 1966.

NATIONAL MARITIME MUSEUM
A Barque Running Before a Gale. By Thomas J. Somerscales, 1842–1927. Large Print.

The Second Dutch War. Described in pictures and manuscripts of the time.

NATIONAL MUSEUM OF ANTIQUITIES OF SCOTLAND
13th Report by the Board of Trustees, 1966–67

NATIONAL PARKS COMMISSION
Coastal Preservation and Development.
  The Coasts of Kent and Sussex.
  The Coasts of Hampshire and the Isle of Wight.
  The Coasts of South-West England.
National Park Guide. No. 5. Brecon Beacons.

NATIONAL PORTRAIT GALLERY
Annual Report of the Trustees, 1965–66.
Illustrated Booklets, Kings and Queens Series.
  House of Tudor.
  House of Windsor.
Poster. Kings and Queens of Britain.

NATIONAL SAVINGS COMMITTEE
Annual Report, 1967.

NATURAL ENVIRONMENT RESEARCH COUNCIL
Institute of Geological Sciences. Annual Report for 1966.

Institute of Geological Sciences, etc.

　British Regional Geology. The Grampian Highlands. 3rd edn.

　Bulletins of the Geological Survey of Great Britain. *2 issues.*

　Memoirs of the Geological Survey of Great Britain. England and Wales.

　　Geology of the Country Around:

　　　Canterbury and Folkestone.

　　　Chesterfield, Matlock and Mansfield.

　　　Nantwich and Whitchurch.

Overseas Geology and Mineral Resources:

　Vol. 10, No. 1.

　Statistical Summary of the Mineral Industry. World production, exports
　　and imports, 1960–65.

Ordnance Survey Annual Report, 1965–66.

OVERSEAS DEVELOPMENT, MINISTRY OF

British Aid. June 1967.

Directorate of Overseas (Geodetic and Topographical) Surveys. Annual
　　Report.

Guide to the Overseas Service (Pensions Supplement) Regulations 1966
　　and the Pensions Increase Act 1965. New edn.

Journal of Administration Overseas. *4 issues.*

Overseas Research Publication. 15: Economic Survey of the New Hebrides.

Report of the Tripartite Economic Survey of the East Caribbean. Jan.–
　　April 1966.

Tropical Products Institute:

　Report, 1966.

　Tropical Science. *4 issues.*

POST OFFICE

Cable and Wireless Ltd. Report and Accounts, 1967.

Fifth Report of the Mobile Radio Committee, 1967.

Post Office Guide. July 1967 edn.

Postal Addresses.

Radio for Merchant Ships. Performance Specifications, *2 items.*

POWER, MINISTRY OF

Digest of Pneumoconiosis Statistics, 1966.

Fuel for the Future.

Gas Council. Annual Report and Accounts, 1966–67.

Report of the Minister of Power, 1967.

Gas Act, 1948. Gas Examiner's Working Note Book (Fairweather Recording Calorimeter).

Mines and Quarries Act, 1954. M. & Q. Forms. *12 items.*

Mining Examinations (Surveyors) (Amendment) Rules, 1967.

Report of H.M. Chief Inspector of Mines and Quarries, 1966.

Reports of H.M. Inspectors of Mines and Quarries. *7 items.*

Safety Circulars. *5 items.*

Safety in Mines Research, 1966.

Statistical Digest, 1966.

Thermal Insulation (Industrial Buildings) Act, 1957. Explanatory Memorandum. New edn.

PRIVY COUNCIL
Prerogative Orders in Council. *24 items.*

PUBLIC BUILDING AND WORKS, MINISTRY OF
Advisory Leaflets. *20 items, e.g.*
    11 Painting Metalwork. 3rd edn. 1967.
    35 Prestressed Concrete. 2nd edn. 1967.
    69 Reducing Noise in Buildings.
Ancient Monuments and Historic Buildings. Guides. *18 items, e.g.*
    Appuldurcombe House, Isle of Wight.
    Hampton Court Palace.
    Upnor Castle, Kent.
List of Ancient Monuments in England and Wales.
List of Ancient Monuments in Scotland.
Building Research Station:
    Building Research, 1966.
    Building Research Station Digests. *15 items, e.g.*
        92 Pulverised Fuel Ash in Building Materials. Revised May 1966.
        84 Accuracy in Building.
    Building Science Abstracts. *13 issues.*
    Changing Appearance of Buildings.
    National Research Station. National Building Studies. *4 items.*
Dimensional Co-ordination for Building. *4 items.*
Excavations Annual Report, 1966.

Going Metric in the Construction Industry.
Research and Development:
  R. & D. Building Management Handbook.
  R. & D. Bulletin: Serial Tendering.
Sand and Gravel Production, 1965–66.
Schedule of Rates for Building Works, 1965. Amendment No. 1.
Maps and Plans in the Public Record Office. I. British Isles.
Privy Council Registers. Reproduced in facsimile. *2 vols.*

PUBLIC TRUSTEE OFFICE
59th Annual Report of the Public Trustee, 1966–67.

QUEEN'S AND LORD TREASURER'S REMEMBRANCER
Edinburgh Gazette. *106 issues.*

ROYAL BOTANIC GARDEN, EDINBURGH
Notes fom the Royal Botanic Garden, Edinburgh. *3 issues.*

ROYAL BOTANIC GARDENS, KEW
Kew Bulletin. *4 issues.*

ROYAL COMMISSIONS
Royal Commission on Ancient Monuments, Scotland:
  Inventory of Peebleshire.
Royal Commission on Local Government in England:
  Minutes of Evidence. *12 items.*
  Written Evidence. *11 items.*
Royal Commission on Local Government in Scotland:
  Minutes of Evidence. *3 items.*
  Written Evidence. *4 items.*
Royal Commission on the Penal System in England and Wales:
  Minutes of Evidence.
  Written Evidence. *4 items.*
Royal Commission on Trade Unions and Employers' Associations:
  Minutes of Evidence. *30 items, e.g.*
      45 Tuesday, July 26, 1966. Witness: Sir Roy Wilson, Q.C.
      52 Tuesday, Oct. 4, 1966. Witness: The Law Society.
      61 Tuesday, Nov. 29, 1966 and 65 Tuesday Jan. 31, 1967. Witness:
      Trades Union Congress.

Research Papers:
1 Productivity Bargaining. 2 Restrictive Labour Practices.
5 (Part I). Trade Unions Structure and Government.
6 Trade Union Growth and Recognition.

ROYAL GREENWICH OBSERVATORY
Bulletins. *7 items.*
Nautical Almanac Office:
Astronomical Ephemeris, 1968.
Nautical Almanac, 1968.
The Star Almanac for Land Surveyors for the year 1968.

ROYAL MINT
97th Annual Report of the Deputy Master and Comptroller, 1966.
The Royal Mint. An Outline History. 4th edn.

ROYAL OBSERVATORY, EDINBURGH
Publications. *3 items.*

SCIENCE MUSEUM
Illustrated Booklets:
Agriculture. Hand Tools to Mechanization.
Lighting. 2: Gas, mineral oil, electricity.
Leonardo da Vinci's Aeronautics.
Talking Machines, 1877–1914.
Time Measurement. Descriptive catalogue of the collection.
Weights and Measures: Their Ancient Origins, etc.

SCOTTISH DEVELOPMENT DEPARTMENT
Annual Report of the Scottish Valuation Advisory Council, 1966.
Betterment Levy (Scotland). An explanatory memorandum on Part III of
the Land Commission Act 1967.
Cairngorm Area. Report of the Technical Group.
Housing Management in Scotland.
Housing Returns for Scotland. *3 items.*
Housing (Scotland) Act 1966. Tables of Comparison.
Irvine New Town.
Local Government (Scotland) Act, 1947. Local Financial Returns
(Scotland), 1965–66.

Memorandum on the Building Standards (Scotland).
Model Water Byelaws (Scotland).
Rates and Rateable Values in Scotland, 1966–67.
Scotland's Older Houses.
Scottish Housing Advisory Committee. Allocating Council Houses.
Scottish Statistical Office:
    Digest of Scottish Statistics. *2 issues.*

SCOTTISH EDUCATION DEPARTMENT

Administration of Schemes for the Award of National Certificates and
    Diplomas in Scotland. Rules 1.
Ascertainment of Children with Hearing Defects.
Bulletin No. 1. English in the secondary school – early stages.
Circulars. *4 items.*
Consultative Committee on the Curriculum. Curriculum Papers. *2 items.*
Education (Scotland) Act, 1962. *11 items.*
Memorandum on Entry Requirements and Courses, 1967.
Public Education in Scotland. 6th edn.
Scottish Certificate of Education. Examination Board Report for 1966.
Scottish Educational Statistics, 1966.
Teaching of Classics in Schools.

SCOTTISH HOME AND HEALTH DEPARTMENT

Handbook on Scottish Administration. Revised edn. 1967.
Hospital Planning Note No. 6.
Local Authority Records.
Local Government Superannuation Act, 1953. Tables prepared by the
    Government Actuary.
National Health Service, Scotland. Analysis of Running Costs of Scottish
    Hospitals, 1966.
National Health Service (Scotland) Act, 1947. Superannuation Scheme for
    Scotland, 1955–62.
Organisation of Medical Work in the Hospital Service in Scotland.
Police (Discipline) (Scotland) Regulations, 1967.
    Discipline Form.
    Investigation Form.
Police (Scotland) Examinations Board. Question Papers.
Probation Service – Scotland. Record of Supervision Forms.

Scottish Health Services Council:
  Hospital medical records in Scotland.
  Report for 1966.
  Rheumatic Fever in Scotland.
Scottish Health Statistics, 1965.
Sheriff Court Records. Report of a Committee.
Scottish Law Commission:
  2nd Annual Report, 1966–67.
  Divorce.
  Law Commissions Act 1965.
    Proposals for Reform of the Law of Evidence relating to Corroboration.

SCOTTISH LAND COURT
Appendices to Report by the Scottish Land Court.

SCOTTISH OFFICE
Private Legislation (Scotland) Procedure. *6 items.*
Ultimus Haeres (Scotland) (Account and List of Estates), 1966.

SCOTTISH RECORD OFFICE
Descriptive List of Plans in the Scottish Record Office. Vol. I.
Indexes:
  62 Index to Register of Deeds.
  63 Index to Particular Register of Sasines.
Register of the Privy Seal of Scotland. Vol. VII.

SOCIAL SECURITY, MINISTRY OF
Administration of the Wage Stop.
Circumstances of Families.
Everybody's Guide to Social Security.
Index and Digest of Decisions given by the Commissioner under the
  National Insurance Acts, etc. *2 Supplements.*
Law Relating to Family Allowances and National Insurance. *3 Supplements.*
Law Relating to National Insurance (Industrial Injuries). *2 Supplements.*
National Insurance Act, 1965. Decisions.
  Unemployment Benefit.
National Insurance Acts, 1965 and 1966. Decisions.

Maternity Benefit.
Sickness Benefit.
National Insurance (Industrial Injuries) Acts.
Decisions of the Commissioner. *11 items.*
Preliminary Drafts of the National Insurance Regulations *7 items.*
Order in Council concerning pensions and other grants.
Pneumoconiosis and allied occupational chest diseases.
Reported Decisions of the Commissioner under the National Insurance:
Family Allowances Acts. Vol. IV.
(Industrial Injuries) Acts. Vol. IV.

STATIONERY OFFICE
Catalogue of Government Publications, 1966.
Consolidated Index to Government Publications, 1961–1965.
International Organisations and Overseas Agencies Publications, 1965 and
1966.
London Gazette. *276 issues.*

STATUTORY PUBLICATIONS OFFICE
Annotations to Acts.
Chronological Table of the Statutes, 1235–1966.
Index of Short Titles of the Current Acts of the Parliament of Scotland,
1425–1707.
Index to Government Orders in Force, 1966.
Index to the Statutes in Force, 1966.
List of Statutory Instruments:
1966: *4 issues.*
1967: *10 issues.*
Statutory Instruments:
1966: Part III.
1967: Parts I and II.
Supplementary Index to the Local and Personal Acts, 1948–1966.
Table of Government Orders, 1671–1966.
Table of Government Orders, 1966. A "noter-up".

TATE GALLERY
* Reports: 1965–66 and 1966–67.

TECHNOLOGY, MINISTRY OF
Aeronautical Research Council:
   Current Papers. *88 items, e.g.*
   850 List of current papers, Nos. 801–850.
   921 The pressure drag of an aerofoil with six different round leading
      edges, at transonic and low supersonic speeds.
   Reports and Memoranda. *61 items, e.g.*
      3440 Design of a Supersonic Nozzle.
      3450 Published Reports and Memoranda of the Aeronautical Re-
         search Council. Sept. 1967.
   Technical Report for the year 1955: Vols. I and II.
Aerospace Material Specifications. D.T.D. *39 items, e.g.*
   901F Cleaning and Preparation of Metal Surfaces.
   904C Cadmium Plating.
Aircraft Material and Process Specifications. D.T.D. Series:
   Numerical and Classified List. Jan. 1967.
   Supplement No. 1. July 1967.
Committee on Common Standards for Electronic Parts. Second Report.
Fire Research Station.
   Fire Research, 1966.
   Fire Research Technical Papers:
      17 A Study of the Performance of Automatic Sprinkler Systems.
      18 Fully-developed Compartment Fires – two kinds of behaviour.
   Symposium No. 1. Major aircraft fires.
   United Kingdom Fire Statistics, 1965.
Forest Products Research Laboratory:
   Bulletins. *3 items.*
   Home Grown Timbers. Larch.
   Insect and Marine Borer Damage to Timber and Woodwork.
   Leaflets. *3 items.*
   Special Reports. *2 items.*
Hydraulics Research, 1966.
National Engineering Laboratory:
   Annual Report, 1966.
* Now published by the Gallery itself.

Heat Bibliography, 1966.
Pump Design, Testing and Operation.
National Physical Laboratory:
    Changing to the Metric System.
    Notes on Applied Science No. 5. Gauge making and measuring. 3rd edn.
    Ocean Wave Statistics.
    Report for the Year 1966.
    Units and Standards of Measurement.
Report of the Government Chemist, 1966.
Staff Titles and Job Description in Commercial Data Processing.
Survey of Professional Engineers, 1966.
Torry Research Station.
    Annual Report, 1966.
    The National Collection of Industrial Bacteria. Catalogue of Strains.
        2nd edn.
Warren Spring Laboratory. The Investigation of Atmospheric Pollution,
    1958–66. 32nd Report.
Water Pollution Research Laboratory:
    Water Pollution Abstracts. *12 issues and index.*
    Water Pollution Research, 1966.

TRADE, BOARD OF

Accidents to Aircraft on the British Register, 1966.
Air Navigation. The Order and Regulations (Loose Leaf). Supplements. *6
    items.*
Aircraft Noise. Report of an international conference.
Aviation Law for Applicants for the Private Pilot's Licence.
Bankruptcy. General Annual Report for the year 1966.
Board of Trade Aircraft Radio Maintenance Engineers' Licences. 1965
    edn. Amendment List No. 1.
Boiler Explosions, 1965.
Boiler Explosions Acts, 1882 and 1890. Reports of Preliminary Inquiries.
    4 items.
British European Airways Corporation. Annual Report and Statement of
    Accounts, 1967.
Business Monitor. Production Series. *Over 400 items.*
Census of Production for 1963:

Part 105. Cement.

Part 106. Abrasives.

Cinematograph Films Council. 29th Annual Report. 1967.

Civil Aircraft Accidents. C.A.P. Series. *21 items.*

Civil Aviation Act, 1949. The Civil Aviation (Customs Airports) Order, 1967.

Commonwealth and the Sterling Area. Statistical Abstract No. 87, 1966.

Companies Act, 1948. Investigation into the affairs of Copestake, Crampton & Co. Limited.

Companies General Annual Report by the Board of Trade, 1966.

European Free Trade Association. A Compendium for the use of Exporters. Amendment 3.

Examination for Certificates of Competency in the Merchant Navy. *6 items.*

Fees for Marine Surveys and Other Marine Services. Revised Dec. 1, 1967.

Flight and Pilot's Licences. *4 items.*

Fuelling of Landplanes and Helicopters.

Import Licences. *5 items.*

Insurance Business. Summary of Accounts and Statements.

Journal. *52 issues.*

Manual of Air Traffic Control.

Amendments. *4 items.*

Mercantile Navy List.

1965. Part II. Motor Vessels.

1966. Part I. Steam and Sailing Vessels.

Merchant Shipping Act, 1894. Reports of Court. *8 items.*

Overseas Trade Accounts of the United Kingdom. *12 issues.*

Papers Set at Examination for the Senior Commercial Airline Transport Pilot's and Flight Navigator's Licences. *3 items.*

Particulars of Dealers in Securities and of Unit Trusts, 1967.

Registry of Ships. Monthly Supplement to the Mercantile Navy List. *12 issues.*

Report on Overseas Trade. *12 items.*

Ship Captain's Medical Guide, 1967.

Shipping Casualties and Deaths. Return for 1965.

Signal Letters of United Kingdom and Commonwealth Ships. *13 items.*

Weights and Measures Act 1963. Notice of Examination of Patterns. *19 items.*

TRANSPORT, MINISTRY OF

Agreement between The Steamship Mutual Underwriting Association Ltd., and the Minister of Transport for the Re-insurance of British Ships against War Risks.

Better Use of Town Roads.

Bituminous Materials in Road Construction.

Goods Vehicle Testers' Manual.

Highway Statistics, 1966.

Memorandum No. 785. Permissible working stresses in concrete and reinforcing bars for highway bridges and structures.

Passenger Transport in Great Britain, 1965.

Railway Accidents:

> Report to the Minister of Transport on the Safety Record of the Railways in Great Britain during the year 1966.
>
> Reports. *11 items.*

Road Accidents, 1965 and 1966.

Road Research, 1965–66.

Road Research Laboratory:

> Road Abstracts, 1964 and 1965.
>
> Road Note No. 10. Rapid methods of analysis for bituminous road materials. 2nd edn.
>
> R.R.L. Special Report No. 6. Report on the 70 m.p.h. Speed Limit trial.
>
> Technical Papers:
>
>> 56 Traffic Signals.
>>
>> 76 Vehicle operating costs on bituminous, gravel and earth roads in East and Central Africa.

Road Traffic Acts, 1930 to 1962. Annual Reports of the Traffic Commissioners to the Minister of Transport, 1966–1967.

Road Traffic Act, 1960. Annual Reports of the Licensing Authorities, 1965–1966.

Roads in England. Report by the Minister of Transport, 1967.

Roads in the Landscape.

Traffic Cases, Vol. 32, Part 9.

Traffic Signs Manual.

> Chapter 11. Illumination of Signs.
>
> Chapter 13. Sign Construction and Mounting.

United Kingdom Railway Advisory Service. Technical Bulletin. No. 2. Use of Headlamps.

TREASURY
Bank of England Report, 1967.
British Imperial Calendar and Civil Service List, 1967.
Civil Service Training and Education. A second specimen set of audio, shorthand and typewriting tests.
Crown's Nominee Account, 1966.
Crown Proceedings Act, 1947. List of authorised Government Departments.
Glossary of Management Techniques.
Greek Loan of 1898. Account.
H.M. Ministers and Heads of Public Departments. *5 issues.*
Post Office Savings Banks. Account of all deposits received and paid, 1966.
Public Works Loan Board. 92nd Annual Report.
Revocation of General Consent under the Control of Borrowing Order, 1958.
Savings Banks Funds: Post Office Savings Banks Fund. Account for the Year 1966.
Treasury Centre for Administration Studies. C.A.S. Occasional Papers. *6 items, e.g.*
  1 The design of information-processing systems for government.
  6 The elementary ideas of game theory.
Trustee Savings Banks:
  Account.
  75th Annual Report.

UNIVERSITY GRANTS COMMITTEE
First Employment of University Graduates, 1965—66.
Report of the Committee on Libraries.
University Building Notes. Student Residence.

VICTORIA AND ALBERT MUSEUM
Ballet Designs and Illustrations, 1581—1940.
Bulletin. *4 issues.*
German Wood Statuettes, 1500—1800.

Large Picture Books:

33 Persian Miniature Painting from Collections in the British Isles.

34 The Engravings of S. W. Hayter.

35 Edward Gordon Craig, 1872—1966.

Monograph No. 19. Sketches by Thornhill.

Small Picture Books:

63 Toys.

64 German Domestic Silver, 1618—1700.

WATER RESOURCES BOARD

Publications:

2 Morecambe Bay Barrage.

3 Solway Barrage.

4 Morecambe Bay and Solway Barrages.

5 Interim Report on Water Resources in the North.

WELSH OFFICE

Circulars. *4 items, e.g.*

29/67 Awards for good design in housing, 1967.

Digest of Welsh Statistics No. 13, 1966.

GREEN PAPERS

In 1967 the Department of Economic Affairs and H.M. Treasury issued a document entitled *The Development Areas: a proposal for a regional employment premium,* and at a press conference on 5 April when it was publicly announced it was referred to as the "Green Paper" — simply because that happened to be the colour of its cover. It was, however, a rather special publication, for it gave substance to the Government's acceptance of the view frequently expressed by such bodies as the Confederation of British Industry and the Trades Union Congress that the opinion of interested parties should be sought and considered while official policy was still in the formative stage (see *H.C.Deb.* vol. 744, 5 April 1967, col. 245). Journalists, politicians, lobbyists and others accustomed to statements of firm government policy in the form of White Papers quickly accepted the term Green Paper as a convenient shorthand for this new concept of announcing tentative proposals. The Secretary of State for

Economic Affairs was soon defining the Green Paper to the House of Commons as "a statement by the Government not of policy already determined, but of propositions put before the whole nation for discussion" (*H.C.Deb.* vol. 747, 5 June 1967, col. 651).

Other ministries adopted the style: July 1968 saw the publication of the Ministry of Transport's *How Fast? a paper for discussion,* and the Ministry of Health's *National Health Service* which was in fact the first to call itself a Green Paper. These were followed in December by *Administrative Reorganisation of the Scottish Health Services* (Scottish Home and Health Department), in February 1969 by *The Task Ahead* (Department of Economic Affairs) and in March 1969 by *Roads for the Future* (Ministry of Transport).

All of the first six Green Papers were issued as Non-Parliamentary publications. First to be published in the Parliamentary category was *Public Expenditure: a new presentation* which appeared in April 1969 as a Command Paper (Cmnd. 4017).

Further information is given in John E. Pemberton's "Government Green Papers", *Library World,* vol. lxxi, no. 830, pp. 46ff, August 1969).

CHAPTER 13

Reference Books

AMONGST its output H.M.S.O. publishes a number of reference works, often updated annually, which may be treated separately in order to give them due prominence. Nearly every government publication has some reference value, but the following have been selected as being works whose primary aim is to be a source of ready reference. It must be emphasized that this *is* only a selection, and that many other works described more appropriately in other chapters of this guide also have a reference function.

Air Almanac

Produced jointly by H.M. Nautical Almanac Office (Royal Greenwich Observatory) and the Nautical Almanac Office (United States Naval Observatory), and published annually by H.M.S.O. Its object is to provide, in a convenient form, the astronomical data required for air navigation. Following the detailed calendar showing the position of the Sun, Aries, Mars, Jupiter, Saturn and the Moon at ten-minute intervals come a navigational star chart, an explanation, a table of standard times, tables of sunrise, sunset, twilight, etc.

Air Force List

Prepared in the Ministry of Defence and published annually by H.M.S.O. A directory of officers in all branches of the service with various other data including orders and medals, associations, and prizewinners. After a comprehensive name index comes a List of Retired Officers of the R.A.F. (arranged by branches) with its own index.

First published in 1949; previously the *Monthly Air Force List* (1919–1939).

Ancient Monuments in England and Wales

A list prepared by the Department of the Environment and published from time to time (latest edition 1972) with annual supplements. Its object is to register the fact that the preservation of a monument is in the national interest and thereby to enlist the support of the owner and others in its protection. The arrangement is by county, within each of which the individual entries are grouped by type of monument, e.g. burial mounts, camps and settlements, Roman remains, linear earthwork, ecclesiastical buildings, crosses, castles, bridges, etc.

Ancient Monuments in Scotland

As previous item, but covering the counties of Scotland.

Army List

Prepared in the Ministry of Defence and published annually by H.M.S.O. in two parts. Part I is a directory of officers by corps, etc., with subject and name indexes. Prefatory information includes a list of regiments and corps, precedence of corps and of infantry regiments. Part II is a list of officers in receipt of retired pay, the "Retired List".

Astronomical Ephemeris

Produced jointly by H.M. Nautical Almanac Office (Royal Greenwich Observatory) and the Nautical Almanac Office (United States Naval Observatory) and published annually by H.M.S.O. An Explanatory Supplement to the volume for 1960 (H.M.S.O., 1961, repr. 1962) contains detailed explanations of the data together with a derivation and numerical illustrations, as well as useful permanent tables omitted from the later volumes. An explanation appears at the end of each annual volume.

Formed in 1960 of a union of the *American Ephemeris and Nautical Almanac* and the (British) *Astronomical Ephemeris.*

Britain: an official handbook

Prepared in the Central Office of Information and published annually by H.M.S.O. According to its introduction it is the mainstay of reference facilities provided by the British Information Services in many countries. At first only available overseas in a limited free edition, it was placed on sale in 1954 and has since become an established work of reference on the United Kindom. Its chapters cover the Land and the People; Government; Law and Order; Defence; Social Welfare; Education; Planning and Housing; the Churches; Promotion of the Sciences and the Arts; the National Economy; Industry; Agriculture, Fisheries and Forestry; Transport and Communications; Finance; Trade and Payments; Labour; Sound and Television Broadcasting; the Press; and Sport. There are many statistical tables, an extensive guide to further reading on the subject of each chapter, and an appendix giving notes for visitors to the United Kingdom. The volume is equipped with a comprehensive index.

British and Foreign State Papers

Compiled and edited in the Librarian's Department of the Foreign and Commonwealth Office, and published by H.M.S.O. Volume 1 covered the years 1812–14. Contains the texts of Acts, agreements, charters, communiqués, constitutions, conventions, pacts, protocols, etc. Some examples taken from vol. 166, 1961–62, are:

Act of Parliament establishing the Department of Technical Co-operation;

Statement by the Prime Minister on the policy of Her Majesty's Government towards the European Economic Community;

Exchange of Notes between the United Kingdom and the United States of America on the setting up of a Missile Defence Alarm System Station in the United Kingdom;

Executive Order No. 10924 providing for the establishment of a
United States Peace Corps;

The Queen's Speeches on the Opening and Closing of Parliament;

United Nations Resolution on the problem of apartheid in South
Africa;

Treaty of Commerce, Establishment and Navigation between the
United Kingdom and Japan.

The volume concludes with a detailed index.

A list of volumes available is given in Sectional List No. 69: *Overseas
Affairs;* and it should be noted that vol. 165 of the papers is a *General
Index* to vols. 139–64 (1935–60).

British Documents on the Origins of the War

Edited in the Foreign Office by G. P. Gooch and Harold Temperley and
published by H.M.S.O. between 1927 and 1938, this multi-volume work is
now available from the Johnson Reprint Corporation.

British Imperial Calendar and Civil Service List

Prepared in the Civil Service Department and published annually by
H.M.S.O. The directory proper is preceded by details of the Royal Households, a list of Representatives in Britain of other Commonwealth
Countries and of the Republic of Ireland, members of the Cabinet, and
staff of the Cabinet Office. There is also an Index to Departments and
Sub-departments which form the main body of the work. There are in fact
three directories of public departments, one for England and Wales, one
for Scotland and a third for Northern Ireland. Names of the principal
officers in each section of each department are given as well as the relevant
addresses and telephone numbers (Fig. 34). There follow salary tables for
Ministers and for the various grades of civil servants; and the volume
concludes with a name index.

The work was first published in 1809.

205

DEPARTMENT OF EDUCATION AND SCIENCE

Curzon Street, London W1
Telephone: 01–493 7070
Telegrams: (Inland) Aristides Audley London
(Overseas) Aristides London W1
Telex: 264329 DES London

Secretary of State for Education and Science
The Rt Hon Edward Short, MP

Private Secretary (Principal)
D. W. Tanner

Assistant Private Secretary (Higher Executive Officer)
W. Gamble

Parliamentary Private Secretary
W. Price, MP

Minister of State
The Rt Hon Alice Bacon, CBE, MP

Private Secretary (Higher Executive Officer)
Miss J. Y. Alexander

Parliamentary Private Secretary
G. J. Oakes, MP

Minister of State
Mrs Shirley Williams, MP

Private Secretary (Assistant Principal)
Mrs M. K. Tait

Minister of State
The Rt Hon Jennie Lee, MP

Private Secretary (Assistant Principal)
N. W. Stuart

Parliamentary Under-Secretary of State
D. H. Howell, MP

Private Secretary (Assistant Principal)
Miss K. H. Quick

Permanent Under-Secretary of State
Sir Herbert Andrew, KCMG, CB

Private Secretary
Miss D. M. Allen

Deputy Under-Secretaries of State
J. F. Embling, CB   T. R. Weaver, CB
H. F. Rossetti, CB

Secretary for Welsh Education (Under-Secretary)
E. Davies

Chief Medical Officer (at Ministry of Health)
Sir George Godber, KCB

206

DEPARTMENT OF EDUCATION AND SCIENCE

Chief Dental Officer (at Ministry of Health)
Surgeon Rear-Admiral W. Holgate, CB, OBE

FINANCE BRANCH

Curzon Street, W1
Telephone: 01–493 7070

Assistant Under-Secretary of State for Finance and Accountant General
J. A. Hudson

Assistant Secretary (Deputy Accountant General)
J. R. Jameson

Principal
N. Summers (*Part-time*)

Senior Chief Executive Officer (Assistant Accountant General)
J. Comper

Chief Executive Officer
A. W. Thompson

COST INVESTIGATION UNIT

Director (£3,500–4,265)
T. A. J. Warlow

Assistant Director
T. Hollis Hopkins

Cost Accountant
V. J. Delany

ARCHITECTS AND BUILDINGS BRANCH

Curzon Street, W1
Telephone: 01–493 7070

Assistant Under-Secretary of State
J. A. Hudson

Assistant Secretary
P. S. Litton

Chief Architect
W. D. Lacey, CBE**

Assistant Chief Architect
J. L. Kitchin

Principals
R. Dellar   B. C. Peatey
Miss J. A. Gilbey

Principal Architects (Superintending Grade)
B. H. Cox   K. E. Foster
D. L. Medd   J. B. Smith
J. D. Kay   R. L. Thompson

Senior Architects
R. Clynes*   R. L. Fitzwilliam
J. S. B. Coatman   W. A. Fletcher
Miss M. B. Crowley,   D. H. Griffin
  OBE   M. S. Hacker
A. D. G. Devonald   S. C. Halbritter (a)
Miss C. G. Edwards   L. J. P. Halstead

FIG. 34. *British Imperial Calendar and Civil Service List*

Careers Guide: opportunities in the professions, industry and commerce

Prepared by the Central Youth Employment Executive and published annually by H.M.S.O. The work is arranged in sections devoted to particular trades and professions (accountant, barrister, librarian, solicitor) and to openings in particular subjects (chemistry, music, physics). Each section begins with a statement of minimum entry requirements and this is followed by the standard layout of Summary of Work, Qualities and Educational Qualifications Required. Training, Opportunities and Prospects, and finally where to obtain further information.

The guide was first published in 1950, and a new consolidated edition appeared in 1968.

Choice of Careers booklets are also published by H.M.S.O.

Colonial Office List

See Yearbook of the Commonwealth.

Colonial Reports

Issued by the Foreign and Commonwealth Office and published by H.M.S.O. They are illustrated volumes containing a considerable amount of factual information. In 1967, for example (see p. 200), there were Commonwealth Office reports on the Bahama Islands, British Solomon Islands, Cayman Islands, Dominica, Falkland Islands and Dependencies, Gibraltar, Hong Kong, Mauritius, St. Helena, St. Lucia, and Swaziland.

The complete list of reports still available is given in Sectional List No. 69: *Overseas Affairs.*

See also Corona Library.

Commonwealth Office Year Book

See Yearbook of the Commonwealth.

Complete Plain Words

Containing *Plain Words* and *The ABC of Plain Words* by Sir Ernest Gowers. Revised edition by Sir Bruce Fraser (H.M.S.O., 1973). A guide and reference book to the use of English for official and other purposes commissioned by the Treasury.

Corona Library

Prepared for the Foreign and Commonwealth Office by the Central Office of Information, and published by H.M.S.O. It is a series of illustrated volumes dealing with the United Kingdom's dependent territories. Those published so far are:

Hong Kong and *Uganda* by Harold Ingrams.
Sierra Leone by Roy Lewis.
Nyasaland by Frank Debenham.
British Guiana by Michael Swan.
Jamaica by Peter Abrahams.
North Borneo by K. G. Tregonning.
Fiji by Sir Alan Burns.
Swaziland by Dudley Barker.
Basutoland by A. Coates.
Bechuanaland by B. A. Young.
British Honduras by A. R. Gregg.
Western Pacific Islands by A. Coates

The list of Corona Library titles available is given in Sectional List No. 69: *Overseas Affairs.*
See also Colonial Reports.

Diplomatic Service List

Prepared in the Foreign and Commonwealth Office and published annually by H.M.S.O. It describes the organization of Her Majesty's Diplomatic Service and gives biographical notes on its 6000 members (Fig. 35). The work is arranged in five parts as follows:

Part   I   Home Departments
           Lists of Ministers, senior officers and home departments in
           the Foreign and Commonwealth Office.
Part II   British Missions Abroad.
Part III   Consular Districts.
Part IV   Chronological Lists of Secretaries of State, Ministers of
           State, Permanent Under-Secretaries, Ambassadors and High
           Commissioners.
Part V   Biographical Notes and Lists of Staff.

The first edition was published in 1966 following the formation of
H.M. Diplomatic Service on 1 January 1965 by the merger of the Foreign,
Commonwealth and Trade Commissioner Services. The staffs of the
Colonial Office in London were subsequently incorporated. This new work
in fact replaces the *Foreign Office List* which was published from 1806 to
1965.

Documents on British Foreign Policy 1919–1939

A collection of documents from the archives of the Foreign and Commonwealth Office published by H.M.S.O. in three series. The First Series
opens after the signature of the Treaty of Versailles in June 1919, the
Second Series in 1930, and the Third Series covers the period from the
German invasion of Austria in March 1938 to the outbreak of the Second
World War in September 1939. So far, sixteen volumes have been published in Series I, ten in Series II, and Series III is complete in nine volumes
plus an index.

Further particulars are given in Sectional List No. 69: *Overseas Affairs.*

Documents on German Foreign Policy 1918–1945

A collection of documents from captured archives published under the
joint auspices of the British, French and United States Governments.
Originally planned in four series, but Series A and B (Weimar period) along
with the period 1942–45 are only available on microfilm (through the

BIOGRAPHICAL LIST

ABBREVIATIONS

m.	— Married
d.	— Daughter
s.	— Son
CENTO	— Central Treaty Organisation
E.C.S.C.	— European Coal and Steel Community
H.M.O.C.S.	— Her Majesty's Overseas Civil Service
M.E.C.A.S.	— Middle East Centre for Arab Studies
N.A.T.O.	— North Atlantic Treaty Organisation
O.E.C.D.	— Organisation for Economic Co-operation and Development
O.E.E.C.	— Organisation for European Economic Co-operation
P.O.M.E.F.	— Political Office Middle East Forces

STATEMENT concerning the present appointments and some other particulars of the careers of established members of Her Majesty's Diplomatic Service, together with those whose services have terminated within the past year.

A

ABBEY, Donald Alfred; Second Secretary, seconded to the Commonwealth Secretariat since November, 1965; born 7.4.22; H.M. Forces 1941–46; India Office 1947; Commonwealth Relations Office 1947–55; Johannesburg 1956–59; Karachi 1960–62; C.R.O. 1963–65; Second Secretary 1963; m. 1945 Olive Rosalind Pinnell (1 s. 1948; 1 d. 1950).

ABBOTT, Bettie Primrose Tregurtha; Diplomatic Service Administration since 1965; born 31.3.17; Foreign Office 1946; Grade 9.

ABBOTT, David John; Foreign Office since January 1968; born 2.1.39; H.M. Forces 1958–60; Foreign Office 1960; Vice-Consul São Paulo 1964–67; Grade 9; m. 1963 Catherine Teresa Byrne (2 d. 1964, 1967; 1 s. 1965).

ABBOTT, Thomas William; Second Secretary (Information) Melbourne since March 1969; born 15.4.31; Foreign Office 1954; Ankara 1957; Vice-Consul Medan 1958; Foreign Office 1961; Second Secretary 1964; Second Secretary (Information) Abidjan 1965–68; m. 1957 Susan Davis (3 s. 1960, 1962, 1964).

ABRAM, Michael James; Bucharest since July 1968; born 8.11.41; Commonwealth Relations Office 1958; Kampala 1964–67; Grade 9; m. 1964 Christine Dianne Smart.

ACLAND, Antony Arthur; First Secretary Foreign Office since December 1968; born 12.3.30; Foreign Office 1953; M.E.C.A.S. 1954; Dubai, Persian Gulf 1955; Kuwait 1956; Foreign Office 1958–62; Assistant Private Secretary to Secretary of State 1959–62; First Secretary 1961; U.K.

Mission New York 1962–66; Head of Chancery U.K. Mission, Geneva 1966–68; m. 1956 Clare Anne Verdon (2 s. 1958, 1960; 1 d. 1965).

ADAIR, Arthur Robin, cvo (1961); MBE (1947); High Commissioner Brunei since May, 1968; born 10.2.13; Indian Civil Service 1937–47; Commonwealth Relations Office 1947; First Secretary Dacca 1947–50; C.R.O. 1950–52; Colombo 1952–56; C.R.O. 1956–60; Deputy High Commissioner in East Pakistan 1960–64 and Nicosia 1964–67; m. 1952 Diana Synnott (1 s. 1956).

ADAMS, Anthony Peter; Lusaka since September, 1966; born 19.8.26; H.M. Forces 1944–46; Diplomatic Wireless Service 1947–59; Commonwealth Relations Office and Kuala Lumpur 1959–61; Dacca 1961–63; Calcutta 1964–66; Grade 9; m. (1 s. 1954).

ADAMS, Charles Christian Wilfrid; Second Secretary Rio de Janeiro since April, 1966; born 2.6.39; Commonwealth Relations Office 1962; Seconded to Central African Office 1962–64; Assistant Private Secretary to Secretary of State for Commonwealth Relations 1965–66; m. 1965 Elinor Pauline Lepper.

ADAMS, Charles Oliver; Consul Cape Town since May, 1965; born 28.10.13; Home Civil Service 1930–49; H.M. Forces 1941–46; Seconded Control Commission Germany 1946–49; Foreign Office 1949; Bahrain 1951; Vice-Consul Houston 1953; Foreign Office 1957; First Secretary 1963; m. (1) 1942 Gladys Joyce Platt (decd. 1964); (2) 1966 Nanette Ella Maxwell.

ADAMS, Domna; Foreign Office since March 1963 born 19.1.15; Sofia 1938–41; Cairo 1941–42; Shiraz; 1942–43; Tehran 1943–45;

FIG. 35. *Diplomatic Service List*

Public Record Office). Series C (1933–37, in 6 vols.) and Series D (1937–41, in 13 vols.) are published by H.M.S.O.

Further particulars are given in Sectional List No. 69: *Overseas Affairs.*

Flags of All Nations

Originally issued by the Admiralty and latterly by the Ministry of Defence Navy Department, and published by H.M.S.O. The new edition (1955–) will be in three loose-leaf volumes, of which the first two have so far appeared, along with amendments and changes. Parts currently available can be ascertained from Sectional List No. 67: *Ministry of Defence.*

Foreign Office List

See Diplomatic Service List.

Handbook for Industrial Injuries Medical Boards

A loose-leaf work, prepared by the Department of Health and Social Security (1970–), which sets out the statutory provisions governing the proceedings of Medical Boards and guidance in the application of court judgments and decisions of the Commissioner.

Hints to Business Men

Prepared and published by the Department of Trade and Industry. Some sixty pamphlets each dealing with a particular country under such headings as Travel; Hotels, Restaurants and Tipping; Postal, Telegraph, Telephone and Telex Facilities; Economic Factors; Import and Exchange Control Regulations; Methods of doing Business; and Useful Addresses. A guide to further reading is also included.

Histories of the First and Second World Wars

The multi-volume *History of the Great War* is now out of print, but

particulars are still given in Sectional List No. 60: *Histories of the First and Second World Wars.*

The *History of the Second World War* issued by the Cabinet Office and published by H.M.S.O. in many volumes is also detailed in Sectional List No. 60.

India: Transfer of Power 1942–7

A multi-volume collection of official documents concerning the constitutional relations between Britain and India, edited by Nicholas Mansergh and E. W. R. Lumby. The first three substantial volumes (published 1970–1) cover the period up to 12 June 1943.

India Office Library, Guide

The India Office Library is one of the largest orientalist libraries in the world. It is especially important for classical Indological studies and for the study of the British period in India. The *Guide to the India Office Library* by S. C. Sutton published for the Foreign and Commonwealth Office in a second edition by H.M.S.O. in 1967 gives a general conspectus of the Library's European and oriental books, manuscripts, and drawings, and other resources. It also includes an account of the India Office Records which are housed in the same building as the Library.

Industrial Relations Handbook

Prepared by the Department of Employment and now in its third edition (H.M.S.O., 1961, repr. 1964). The subtitle describes its contents as an account of British institutions and practice relating to the organization of employers and workers in Great Britain; collective bargaining and joint negotiating machinery; conciliation and arbitration; and statutory regulation of wages in certain industries.

The first edition was published in 1944.

International Code of Signals

Originally issued by the Board of Trade and published by H.M.S.O. in 1932, this was reprinted in 1962 incorporating the Ministry of Transport's 1952 supplement. A revised code suitable for transmission by all means of communication, including radiotelephony and radiotelegraphy, was published in 1969.

List of Independent Schools in England and Wales
Recognized as Efficient under Rules 16 (List 70)

Issued by the Department of Education and Science and published at regular intervals (latest, 1972) by H.M.S.O. Arranged first by counties, and within counties the names of schools are listed alphabetically with postal addresses indicated. Information given includes the proprietor, date first granted recognition, head master or mistress, fees and number of pupils. Schools in Wales are listed separately.

London Post Offices and Streets

Issued by the Post Office and published annually by H.M.S.O. A supplement to *Post Offices in the United Kingdom (q.v.).*

Mercantile Navy List

Prepared by the Registrar-General of Shipping and Seamen and published by H.M.S.O. with monthly supplements. There are two loose-leaf volumes:

Part I: *Steam and Sailing Vessels.*
Prefatory material includes a list of ports at which mercantile marine business is conducted, local marine boards, chambers of commerce and shipowners' associations, training ships, and Lloyd's agents. Then come two alphabetical lists, one of registered steam vessels and the other of registered sailing and other vessels.

Part II: *Motor Vessels*

In both parts the information given for each vessel is: official number; name and description; port and year of registry; where and when built; material; registered tonnage (net and gross); and owner.

Meteorological Office Publications

The Meteorological Office issues a number of important reference works, of which the following is a selection:

Handbooks, etc.
    Handbook of Aviation Meteorology.
    Handbok of Meteorological Instruments.
    Handbook of Weather Messages.
    Hygrometric Tables.
    Marine Observer's Handbook.
    Meteorological Glossary.
    Ships' Code and Decode Book.
Meteorological Data
    British Rainfall (annual).
    Daily Weather Report.
    Daily Aerological Record.
    Monthly Weather Report.
    Observatories' Year Book.
Climatological Normals or Averages
    Averages of Humidity for the British Isles.
    Averages of Bright Sunshine for Great Britain and Northern Ireland.
Charts of Marine Meteorology and Sea-Surface Currents.
Weather over the Oceans and Coastal Regions.

Some titles are listed in the extract from the 1967 annual catalogue on p. 214; details of all Meteorological Office publications available are given in Sectional List No. 37: *Meteorological Office.*

Nautical Almanac

Produced jointly by H.M. Nautical Almanac Office (Royal Greenwich

Observatory) and the Nautical Almanac Office (United States Naval Observatory) and published annually by H.M.S.O. Its object is to provide, in a convenient form, the data required for the practice of astronomical navigation at sea; and it consists in the main of data from which the *Greenwich Hour Angle* and the *Declination* of all the bodies used for navigation can be obtained for any instant of *Greenwich Mean Time.* The calendar itself is followed by an explanation of its principles and arrangement, a table of standard times, star charts and tables, etc.

This title is now used, in both the United Kingdom and the United States, for the unified edition of the almanacs for surface navigation previously entitled *The Abridged Nautical Almanac* and *The American Nautical Almanac* respectively. The former *Nautical Almanac and Astronomical Ephemeris* (1767–1959) (usually abbreviated to *The Nautical Almanac*) is replaced by the *Astronomical Ephemeris (q.v.).*

Navy List

Compiled by order of the Defence Council and published by H.M.S.O. three times a year – in the spring, summer and autumn. The spring edition is the full edition and is published in March; it contains lists of ships, establishments, and officers of the Fleet. The other editions (June and October) are abridged and contain only the alphabetical list of officers of the R.N., R.M., etc., the list of ships and air squadrons etc., with their key officers; but the autumn edition also contains the seniority lists of R.N., R.M., Q.A.R.N.N.S., and W.R.N.S. officers.

The *Navy List of Retired Officers together with the Emergency List* is published in November every other year.

In August of each year is published the *Appendix to the Navy List: rates of pay, conditions of retirement, entry regulations, etc., etc.*

The *Navy List* was first published in 1814.

Official List

Prepared in the General Register Office pursuant to the Marriage Act, 1949, and published by H.M.S.O. in parts, as follows:

Part I: *List of Registration Officers* (Annual).

Registration Officers are listed under the names of their Registration Districts which are arranged in alphabetical order.

Parts III (*Certified Places of Worship*) and IV (*Naval, Military and Air Force Chapels*). The latest edition is that of 1965, to which there have been Annual Addenda.

Part III contains a list of all places of worship certified to the Registrar General and not subsequently cancelled. Churches and chapels of the Church of England and the Church of Wales are not included. The list distinguishes those which have been registered for marriages, etc.

Part IV contains a list of the service chapels in which marriage may be solemnized according to the rites of the Church of England and those in which marriages may be solemnized according to other rites.

Particulars of Dealers in Securities and of Unit Trusts

Prepared in the Department of Trade and Industry under the Prevention of Fraud (Investments) Act, 1958 and published annually by H.M.S.O. It comprises five lists:

1. Holders of Principals' Licences.
2. Recognized Stock Exchanges.
3. Recognized Associations of Dealers in Securities.
4. Exempted Dealers.
5. Authorized Unit Trust Schemes.

First published in 1960.

Post Office Guide

Issued by the Post Office and sold annually by H.M.S.O. with supplements through the year. Contents include general information on the departments and regions of the Post Office; London postal districts; inland and overseas postal services and charges; telegram, telephone and telex

services; overseas telecommunications; savings services (savings bank, government stock and bonds, savings certificates, premium bonds); and remittance services (postal and money orders, and stamps).

First published in 1856.

Post Offices in the United Kingdom (excluding the London Postal Area) and the Irish Republic

Issued by the Post Office and sold by H.M.S.O. with amendments. Contains the postal and telegraphic addresses of every post office in Great Britain (except London), Northern Ireland, the Channel Islands, the Isle of Man and the Irish Republic, with name of the nearest office paying money orders and telegraph money orders.

See also London Post Offices and Streets.

Postal Addresses

Issued by the Post Office and sold annually by H.M.S.O. with supplements. Includes the correct postal address of more than 20,000 post offices in the United Kingdom (excluding London) and the Irish Republic.

Scientific Research in British Universities and Colleges

Prepared by the Department of Education and Science and the British Council, and published annually by H.M.S.O. in three parts:

    I. Physical Sciences.
   II. Biological Sciences.
  III. Social Sciences (including government departments and other institutions).

In each volume there are a number of subject groups in each of which the universities, etc., are arranged in alphabetical order. The 1967–68 social sciences volume, for example, had the headings Criminology, Economics, History and Philosophy of Science, Human Biology, Human Geography, Industrial Administration, Information Science, Law, Politics, Psychiatry,

Psychology, Social Administration, Social Anthropology, Social Medicine, and Sociology. Names of research directors and descriptive titles of projects are given (Fig. 36) and there are both name and subject indexes.

The first publication in this form was that for 1962—63. It was previously published by the British Council under the title *Scientific Research in Britain* (1951/52—).

Signal Letters of United Kingdom and Commonwealth Ships: for the use of ships at sea and signal stations

Issued by the Department of Trade and Industry and published annually by H.M.S.O. with cumulative supplements through the year. It includes, in the case of ships registered at ports in the United Kingdom, all ships fitted with wireless whose radio call signs have been registered as signal letters, and all ships not fitted with wireless for which signal letters have been registered; and it includes, in the case of ships registered outside the United Kingdom, all ships the signal letters of which have been reported to the Registrar-General of Shipping and Seamen by the Commonwealth authorities concerned. The list also contains the names and distinguishing signal letters of certain unregistered United Kingdom and Commonwealth ships to which signal letters have been allotted.

Star Almanac for Land Surveyors

Prepared by H.M. Nautical Almanac Office in the Royal Greenwich Observatory and published annually by H.M.S.O. It is designed to provide the surveyor with the astronomical data he needs.

First published in 1950.

Surface Water Year Book of Great Britain: hydrometric statistics for British rivers, together with related rainfalls and river water temperature

Issued jointly by the Water Resources Board and the Scottish Development Department and published by H.M.S.O. The 1964—65 edition, pub-

8. Social Anthropology*

5. Belfast: Queen's University

Professor E. Estyn Evans
(Acting Head of Department)

A.C. Tweedie (Miss)	Change and continuity in Bemba Society (1961–66; former Colonial Social Science Research Council)
P.G. Bicknell	Aspects of primitive warfare
R.D. Grillo	Labour force of E. African railways and harbours

12. Cambridge University (*Archaeology and Anthropology*)

Professor M. Fortes	Social anthropology, with special reference to W. Africa
with E. Goody, Ph.D.	Comparative study of fostering and proxy-parental relationships (1966–69; Social Science Research Council)
E.R. Leach, Ph.D.	Anthropology of S. and S.E. Asia
R.F. Fortune	Anthropology of New Guinea
G.I. Jones	Anthropology and administration of W. and S. Africa
J.R. Goody, Ph.D.	Ethnography of W. Africa
	Comparative social institutions (1967–69; Social Science Research Council)
R.G. Abrahams, Ph.D.	Social and political organization in E. Africa
S.J. Tambiah	Sociology of S.E. Asia
D.R. Pilbeam, Ph.D.	Human and primitive evolution

22. Edinburgh University

Professor K. Little (Head of Department)	Modern marriage among "professional" groups in a selected W. African country (1967–69; Social Science Research Council)

49. London University: Birkbeck College

J.S. LaFontaine, Ph.D.	Sociological survey of Leopoldville (now Kinshasa) Congo: sociological characteristics of the city at the period of field work (1962–63) with special emphasis on leadership (1962–67)

53. London University: London School of Economics and Political Science

Professor M. Freedman, Ph.D. (Convener)	Social organization in the Hong Kong New Territories in the 19th century, based mainly on missionary sources (1965–68)
Professor R.W. Firth, Ph.D.	Kinship in N. London: structure and working of extra familial kinship among a set of middle-class families (1961–67; United States National Science Foundation)
	Rank and religion in Tikopia, Polynesia (1966–67; Wenner-Gren Foundation for Anthropological Research)
Professor I. Schapera, D.Sc.	Law-making in Tswana tribès, 1843–1939 (1967)
B. Benedict	Family firms in developing countries
J.A.W. Forge	Social and aesthetic structures of the Abelam, New Guinea (1958–70; Wenner-Gren Foundation for Anthropological Research, Bollingen Foundation)

*see also: 12. Human Geography

FIG. 36. *Scientific Research in British Universities and Colleges*

lished in 1968, contains records relating to over 400 river flow measurement stations and nineteen river temperature stations. A Supplement is published every five years (the first appeared in 1968) and contains descriptions, information and explanations which are not likely to change materially from year to year and therefore do not merit annual publication. Thus, one supplement and five annual numbers of the Year Book constitute one complete volume.

The first edition, for 1935–36, was published in 1938.

Yearbook of the Commonwealth

Prepared in the Foreign and Commonweath Office and published by H.M.S.O. It contains essential information about all the countries constituting the Commonwealth today, including the member nations, associated states and dependencies. Background information not readily available elsewhere is provided on the constitutional development of the Commonwealth and the countries comprising it, and on Commonwealth trade and the organisation of British government relations with other Commonwealth countries. Information is also included on the Commonwealth Secretariat, Commonwealth regional organizations, diplomatic representation and currencies; and particulars are given of more than 180 committees, societies and organizations in Britain with Commonwealth interests or links.

Formerly published under the title of *Commonwealth Office Year Book* (1967–68), it continues the *Colonial Office List* which lasted from 1862 to 1966.

CHAPTER 14

Statistics

IN 1949 a series of *Studies in Official Statistics* began and the collection which has since built up constitutes a valuable reference guide to statistical sources and methods. The following have so far been published.

1. *The Interim Index of Industrial Production* (1949).
2. *The Index of Industrial Production* (1952).
3. *National Income Statistics: sources and methods* (1956).
4. *The Length of Working Life of Males in Great Britain* (1959).
5. *New Contributions to Economic Statistics* (1959).
6. *Methods of Construction and Calculations of the Index of Retail Prices* (1967).
7. *The Index of Industrial Production: method of compilation* (1960).
8. *Input–Output Tables for the United Kingdom, 1954* (1961).
9. *New Contributions to Economic Statistics (Second Series)* (1962).
10. *New Contributions to Economic Statistics (Third Series)* (1964).
11. *List of Principal Statistical Series Available* (1965). Replaced by no. 20.
12. *New Contributions to Economic Statistics (Fourth Series)* (1967).
13. *National Accounts Statistics: sources and methods* (1968).
14. *Agricultural and Food Statistics: a guide to official sources* (1969).
15. *New Contributions to Economic Statistics* (1970).
16. *Input–Output Tables for the United Kingdom 1963* (1970).
17. *The Index of Industrial Production and Other Output Measures* (1970)
18. *Qualified Manpower in Great Britain: the 1966 Census of Production* (1971).
19. *New Contributions to Economic Statistics* (1972).
20. *List of Principal Statistical Series and Publications* (1972).

No. 20, the *List of Principal Statistical Series and Publications,* replaces No. 11. The information it contains relates to the situation as at the beginning of February 1972. The main arrangement is by subject, and there is a separate alphabetical list of publications and a detailed subject index. Additions and amendments are reported in *Statistical News: developments in British official statistics,* which commenced publication in 1968 and is issued quarterly by the Central Statistical Office. A particularly useful feature is an index which cumulates in each new issue.

A revised and enlarged edition of Joan Harvey's *Sources of Statistics* was published in 1971. Its emphasis is on British statistics and it has the advantage of being relatively up to date and having a good index.

The guide which follows begins with general compilations and goes on to deal with specialized sources under subject headings arranged alphabetically.

General Compilations

The single most useful compilation is the *Annual Abstract of Statistics* produced since 1946 by the Central Statistical Office (Fig. 37). It contains figures on the physical aspects of the country including the climate; data on population and social conditions; production and trade figures; statistics on the nation's income and expenditure; tables on transport and communications; as well as information on such things as personal incomes, banking, the cost of living and so forth. Many of the tables are summarized from more detailed compilations, and a particularly useful feature of the *Annual Abstract* is the direction it provides to these other sources. From 1840 to 1938 this document was issued by the Board of Trade under the title *Statistical Abstract for the United Kingdom.* Monthly updatings, where available, have appeared since 1946 in the *Monthly Digest of Statistics* also produced by the Central Statistical Office. Figures for the period 1939–45 are available in the *Statistical Digest of the War* which was published by H.M.S.O. in 1951 as a companion to the official *History of the Second World War.*

Another general publication is *Economic Trends* which again is compiled by the Central Statistical Office (1953–). In addition to authoritative articles on economic subjects it contains data on employment,

University students
Great Britain
Academic years

TABLE 122

Number

		1957/58	1958/59	1959/60	1960/61	1961/62	1962/63	1963/64	1964/65	1965/66	1966/67	1967/68
New students admitted (full time only)[1]:												
Men		20,646	21,236	20,823	21,464	22,964	23,956	24,666	27,609	37,166	37,890	40,539
Women		7,030	7,041	7,194	8,046	9,196	9,721	10,107	11,959	15,059	15,685	16,588
Students taking courses (full and part time)[2]:												
Men		85,576	89,080	92,339	96,423	100,330	101,410	106,402	115,460	133,963	147,797	159,354
Women		26,402	27,003	27,602	29,107	31,592	34,018	36,571	41,328	47,089	52,927	58,275
Full time students[3]:												
Total:	Men	71,855	75,879	79,037	81,330	84,425	87,654	92,636	100,381	124,087	134,443	144,956
	Women	23,587	24,325	24,972	26,369	28,718	31,350	33,809	38,330	44,520	49,760	54,716
Advanced:	Men	11,278	11,872	13,364	14,305	15,612	16,754	18,255	20,209	22,568	25,397	27,484
	Women	2,791	2,967	3,285	3,531	3,750	4,039	4,300	5,358	5,860	6,576	7,535
First degree:	Men	57,129	60,670	62,561	63,409	65,420	67,578	71,026	77,692	98,349	106,989	115,542
	Women	19,558	20,135	20,522	21,590	23,799	26,192	28,443	31,366	37,080	41,819	45,919
First diploma:	Men	2,856	2,864	2,628	2,950	2,737	2,562	2,602	1,705	2,159	1,090	1,049
	Women	1,081	1,064	977	1,008	951	850	788	1,253	1,170	999	858
Others:	Men	592	473	484	666	656	760	753	775	1,011	967	881
	Women	157	159	188	240	218	269	278	353	410	366	404
Part-time students[4]:												
Total:	Men	13,671	13,201	13,302	15,093	15,905	13,756	13,766	15,079	9,876	13,354	14,398
	Women	2,815	2,678	2,630	2,738	2,874	2,668	2,762	2,998	2,569	3,167	3,559
Advanced:	Men	4,577	4,523	4,688	5,183	5,224	5,418	5,629	6,533	6,626	10,766	11,733
	Women	889	945	949	1,051	1,105	1,097	1,185	1,344	1,313	1,771	2,061
First degree:	Men	1,140	1,192	1,106	1,105	1,057	964	1,001	1,030	1,753	1,434	1,195
	Women	371	349	359	348	340	348	350	336	404	552	599
First diploma:	Men	1,066	936	993	818	912	676	650	477	565	334	472
	Women	111	100	87	136	131	105	116	175	117	95	85
Occasional:	Men	6,888	6,550	6,515	7,987	8,712	6,698	6,486	7,039	932	820	998
	Women	1,444	1,284	1,235	1,203	1,298	1,118	1,111	1,143	735	749	814
Country of home residence of full-time students:												
United Kingdom		85,280	90,004	93,358	96,091	100,122	105,629	112,659	124,228	153,629	167,884	184,887
Other Commonwealth countries		6,180	6,084	6,443	6,932	7,533	7,602	7,562	7,831	8,481	8,836	7,836
Foreign countries		3,982	4,116	4,208	4,676	5,488	5,773	6,224	6,652	7,376	8,079	7,398
University residence of full-time students[5]:												
Colleges and hostels:	Men	16,073	17,103	18,087	19,108	20,920	22,932	26,821	31,257	39,236	44,371	48,363
	Women	9,101	9,507	10,007	10,366	10,850	11,663	12,500	13,722	16,422	19,592	22,120
Lodgings:	Men	37,402	40,412	42,730	44,151	46,153	47,460	48,316	50,802	59,926	64,351	69,519
	Women	8,835	9,288	9,558	10,463	12,229	13,932	15,462	17,860	20,758	21,997	24,043
At home:	Men	18,380	18,364	18,220	18,071	17,302	17,262	17,499	18,322	22,862	23,963	24,394
	Women	5,651	5,530	5,407	5,540	5,639	5,755	5,847	6,748	7,524	8,132	8,345

[1] Excluding students undertaking courses 'not of a university standard': in 1965/66, 227 men and 187 women; in 1966/67, 226 men and 126 women; in 1967/68, 219 men and 118 women. [2] Excluding students undertaking courses 'not of a university standard': in 1965/66, 4,775 men and 663 women; in 1966/67, 2,100 men and 530 women; in 1967/68, 1,416 men and 454 women. [3] Excluding students undertaking courses 'not of a university standard': in 1965/66, 619 men and 260 women; in 1966/67, 428 men and 168 women; in 1967/68, 321 men and 128 women. [4] Excluding students undertaking courses 'not of a university standard': in 1965/66, 4,156 men and 403 women; in 1966/67, 1,672 men and 362 women; in 1967/68, 1,095 men and 326 women. [5] From 1965/66, figures include those students on courses 'not of a university standard', but not those sandwich students undertaking the industrial part of their training away from the university or college at the time of the student count, which is the end of the autumn term (31 December). Prior to 1965/66 the student count took place at the end of the academic year.

Source: University Grants Committee.

FIG. 37. *Annual Abstract of Statistics.*

production, prices and so forth both in tabular form and by way of graphs. Despite the many other statistical publications, both general and special, the weekly *Trade and Industry* which has been published since 1886, continues to be an invaluable source; it frequently contains figures which would be extremely difficult to obtain elsewhere.

Historical data on a large number of subjects — population, production,

finance, etc. − are contained in the *Abstract of British Historical Statistics* by B. R. Mitchell and Phyllis Deane (1962) and the *Second Abstract of British Historical Statistics* by B. R. Mitchell and H. G. Jones (1971).

Agriculture

Agricultural Statistics: United Kingdom began with an issue for 1939−44, and its coverage is indicated in its subtitle: *Agricultural Censuses and Production with Separate Figures for England and Wales, Scotland, Great Britain and Northern Ireland; Price Indices for Main Agricultural Products and Materials.* In addition, there are the separate publications *Agricultural Statistics, England and Wales* and *Agricultural Statistics, Scotland.* More specialized publications include the *Register of Potato Crops Certified*, the *Annual Review and Determination of Guarantees* and *Farm Incomes in England and Wales.* Much useful information is contained in *A Century of Agricultural Statistics: Great Britain 1866−1966* (1968), the centennial report of the Ministry of Agriculture, Fisheries and Food.

Aid

Britain's overseas aid expenditure is detailed in the Ministry of Overseas Development's *British Aid: statistics of official economic aid to developing countries* (1961−).

Balance of Payments

United Kingdom Balance of Payments popularly called the "Pink Book" or the "Orange Book", is compiled at the Central Statistical Office. Now a Non-Parliamentary Publication, this was issued between 1946 and 1962 as a Command Paper. Quarterly estimates are published in the Office's monthly *Financial Statistics* as well as in *Trade and Industry* and *Economic Trends.*

Civil List

This is the term used for the financial provisions which include the Sovereign's personal income and that of other members of the Royal Family. The provisions are set out in a special Act promulgated at the time of the Sovereign's accession (Civil List Act, 1952).

Communications

Since 1967 the Post Office has published annually its *Post Office Telecommunications Statistics*. Other convenient sources are the annual reports of the B.B.C. and the I.T.A., Cable and Wireless Ltd., and the Post Office.

Companies

Each year the Department of Trade and Industry issues six publications concerning companies. First there are the *Companies General Annual Report* (1891–) and *Companies Assets, Income and Finance* (1957–). Then there are two titles in the Business Monitor Miscellaneous Series: M3 *Company Finance* (annual), and M7 *Acquisitions and Mergers of Companies* (quarterly). As regards bankruptcy, the *Bankruptcy General Annual Report* has been issued since 1883 and *Bankruptcy and Companies* (*Winding-up*) *Proceedings* since 1926–27. In addition, *Trade and Industry* has quarterly figures of bankruptcy orders. A Central Register of Businesses is maintained by the Government Statistical Service; it is a list of names and addresses, held on a computer, classified by industrial activity, location, size and so forth.

Crime

There is a guide to criminal statistics by T. S. Lodge in M. G. Kendall's *The Sources and Nature of the Statistics of the United Kingdom* (1952–57). The principal official sources are *Criminal Statistics, England and Wales* started last century and currently presented annually by the Home Office, and the Scottish Home and Health Department's *Criminal*

Statistics, Scotland (1925–) also issued annually. In addition to the annual *Report on the Work of the Prison Department* (formerly *Prisons and Borstals*) and *Prisons in Scotland* (1927–) there are other statistics relating to particular crimes, for example *Offences of Drunkenness* (1964–) and *Offences Relating to Motor Vehicles* (1950–). Another recently inaugurated compilation is the *Report of the Criminal Injuries Compensation Board,* again issued by the Home Office.

Customs and Excise

Statistics relating to purchase tax (as from 1973–74, value added tax) and other duties are covered by the *Report of the Commissioners of Her Majesty's Customs and Excise* (1909/10–).

Education

Educational statistics used to be included in the Ministry's (now Department's) annual reports (1928–), but in 1961 they began to be published separately as *Statistics of Education* which itself is in several parts, e.g. vol. 1: *Schools;* vol. 5: *Finance and Awards.* The Ministry's report for 1950 was entitled *Education 1900–1950* and contained a wealth of retrospective data. Scottish statistics are available in the annual *Scottish Educational Statistics* (1966–). The new publication *Education Statistics of the United Kingdom* (1967–) includes in its introduction a section on sources of United Kingdom education statistics.

(*See also* Universities.)

Estimates

Supply Estimates for the coming year are published both as a single volume and in separate volumes for each of the eleven classes, as follows:

  I Government and Exchequer.
  II Commonwealth and Foreign.
  III Home and Justice.

IV Transport, Trade and Industry.
 V Agriculture.
VI Local Government, Housing and Social Services.
VII Education and Science.
VIII Museums, Galleries and the Arts.
 IX Public Buildings and Common Governmental Services.
  X Smaller Public Departments
 XI Miscellaneous.

An index to the whole is also available separately as well as in the consolidated volume.

Defence Estimates are issued by the Ministry of Defence.

All the estimates are issued before the Budget as a Command Paper entitled *Estimates [year]* : *Memorandum by the Financial Secretary to the Treasury.* Discussion of the estimates naturally takes up a good deal of time in the House where they are debated with the Deputy Speaker in the Chair. *Hansard* reports these debates in full.

Funds needed to carry on the business of civil and military affairs before the full estimates can be approved are provided by means of Votes on Account. These are presented to the House in the form of a House of Commons Paper entitled *Vote on Account: Civil Estimates and Defence (Central) Estimate* which is prepared by the Treasury.

Supplementary Estimates, both Supply and Defence are published and are considered by a special Subcommittee on Supplementary Estimates, whose reports are included in the series of *Reports of Estimates Committees.* Legal provision for meeting excess expenditure is made, when necessary, by passing an *Excess Vote.*

The main estimates as approved by the House are detailed in the Appropriation Act. The Consolidated Fund Act, on the other hand, covers the *Votes on Account, Supplementary Estimates* and *Excess Votes.*

(*See also* National Income and Expenditure.)

Family Expenditure

See Personal Expenditure.

Finance

Financial Statistics, is produced monthly by the Central Statistical Office and provides data on central and local government, banks, companies, stock exchange business and so forth.

Fire Services

The principal source of data on fires attended by brigades is *United Kingdom Fire and Loss Statistics* (1960–); and various other statistics are given in the *Report of Her Majesty's Chief Inspector of Fire Services* (1948–) and the *Report of Her Majesty's Inspector of Fire Services for Scotland.*

Fisheries

Sea Fisheries Statistical Tables dating back to 1888 are an important source. *Scottish Sea Fisheries Statistical Tables* (1922–) are of more recent origin and are supplemented by data contained in *Fisheries of Scotland,* the annual report of the Department of Agriculture and Fisheries for Scotland. Other relevant titles are the *Annual Report of the Herring Industry Board* (1935–) and the *Annual Report and Accounts of the White Fish Authority* (1951/51–).

Food

Food Statistics: a guide to the major official and unofficial United Kingdom Sources, a 53-page booklet, was published by the National Economic Development Office in 1969.

(*See also* Personal Expenditure.)

Forestry

Aside from data in the *Annual Abstract of Statistics* there are tables in the *Annual Report of the Forestry Commissioners* (1919/20–).

Gambling

Betting, Gambling and Lotteries Act 1963: Permits and Licences includes data on bookmakers' and betting office permits.

Health and Social Security

Current data is published in the *Annual Report of the Department of Health and Social Security* (1968–) which superseded the *Annual Report of the Ministry of Social Security,* the *Report of the Ministry of Pensions and National Insurance* and the *Report of the National Assistance Board.* Coverage extends from family allowances and maternity benefits to legal aid and war pensions. A new publication is the Department of Health and Social Security's annual *Health and Personal Social Services Statistics* (1969–). Earlier material is the subject of *Social Security Statistics* published by H.M.S.O. in 1961 as No. 5 in the series of *Guides to Official Sources.* Scotland is covered by the annual *Health and Welfare Services in Scotland* (1962–) issued by the Scottish Home and Health Department, and by *Scottish Health Statistics* (1961–).

As regards the cost of operating the National Health Service, returns are made under the provisions of the National Health Service Acts 1946 to 1961 and the National Health Service (Scotland) Acts 1947 to 1961, and are published as House of Commons Papers. They provide summarized accounts of the regional hospital boards, other management boards and committees, and the respective dental estimates boards.

Details on the use of hospitals are given in the *Report on Hospital In-patient Enquiry* produced by the General Register Office and the Department of Health and Social Security and published by H.M.S.O. since 1960. This information was previously published as a supplement to the *Registrar General's Statistical Review of England and Wales.* Scotland has its own *Scottish Hospital In-Patient Statistics* (1963–) produced by the Scottish Home and Health Department.

Financial matters are dealt with in the Department of Health and Social Security's *National Health Service: Hospital Costing Returns,* issued annually, and the Scottish Home and Health Department's *National Health Service, Scotland: Analysis of Running Costs of Scottish Hospitals.*

A specialized compilation, the *Digest of Pneumoconiosis Statistics* is produced annually by the Ministry of Power.

Housing

As from 1972 *Housing Statistics: Great Britain* and the *Monthly Bulletin of Construction Statistics* have been amalgamated to form a new quarterly publication, *Housing and Construction Statistics*. Other figures are given in the quarterly *Local Housing Statistics: England and Wales* and the annual *Statistics of Decisions on Planning Applications* which began in 1962. Figures for Scotland are given in the annual *Scottish Development Department Report* (Command Paper), and *Housing Returns for Scotland* which is issued quarterly by the Scottish Development Department.

Accounts prepared under the terms of the Housing Act 1964 and, for Scotland, the Housing Act, 1961, and Housing (Scotland) Act, 1962, are published as House of Commons Papers; they provide figures of sums received by the ministries responsible for housing from the Consolidated Fund, the Housing Corporation and housing associations in respect of interest and repayment of advances. Reports from new towns and accounts prepared pursuant to the New Towns Acts of 1946 and 1965 are also published as House of Commons Papers.

Imports and Exports

Statistics on foreign trade are provided by the *Annual Statement of the Overseas Trade of the United Kingdom*. Dating back to the middle of the nineteenth century, the *Annual Statement* now comprises five volumes. It is compiled by H.M. Customs and Excise which also issues annually *Protective Duties: values or quantities of imported goods entered for home use in the United Kingdom and receipts of duty*. Up-to-date figures are reported in the monthly *Overseas Trade Accounts of the United Kingdom* prepared at the Department of Trade and Industry. Formerly called *Accounts Relating to the Trade and Navigation of the United Kingdom,* this too dates back to the middle of the nineteenth century. Another of the Department's annual compilations *The Commonwealth and the Sterling Area: statistical abstract,* which supeiseded the *Statistical Abstract for the*

Commonwealth, was discontinued after the 1967 edition. Recent figures are included in *Trade and Industry.*

Inland Revenue

Statistics on direct taxation are included in the *Annual Reports of the Commissioners of Inland Revenue* (1857/58–). Since 1970 the statistical material of general economic interest has been published separately in the new *Inland Revenue Statistics.* The Board also publish the results of quinquennial surveys of personal incomes analysed by source, range, family circumstances and region. The latest edition is *Inland Revenue Survey of Personal Incomes 1969–70.*

Insurance

Dating back to 1871 the Department of Trade and Industry's *Life and other Long Term Insurance Business; full accounts and statements deposited with the Board of Trade* formerly also included data on some of the forms of insurance covered since 1949 by its *Insurance Business: summary accounts and statements deposited with the Board of Trade.* These two publications have now been superseded by *Insurance Business, annual report* (1967–) and *Insurance Business Statistics* (1964/66–). *Trade and Industry* has quarterly figures of the transactions of insurance companies and pension funds.

The *Report of the Chief Registrar of Friendly Societies* (1875–) is in five parts – 1: General; 2: Friendly Societies; 3: Industrial and Provident Societies; 4: Trade Unions; and 5: Building Societies. They record registrations, legal cases and so forth. Industrial life insurance is the subject of the annual *Report of the Industrial Assurance Commissioner* (1875–).

Iron and Steel

Financial statistics on iron and steel are published in the *Annual Report and Accounts of the British Steel Corporation.* The BSC's *Annual Statistics for the Corporation* includes statistics on the manufacture of iron and steel products.

Judiciary

There are two publications to note here. First is *Judicial Statistics, England and Wales: Civil Judicial Statistics; Statistics relating to the Judicial Committee of the Privy Council, the House of Lords, the Supreme Court of Judicature, County Courts and other Civil Courts.* Second is the Scottish equivalent, *Civil Judicial Statistics (Scotland) (including Licensing and Bankruptcy): Statistics relating to the House of Lords (Scottish Appeals): the Court of Session; Sheriff Courts and other Civil Courts; Licensing Courts; Certain Legal and Public Departments, Bankruptcy; Court Fees and Fees taken by the Departments for the Year.*

Labour

The main sources of labour statistics are the monthly *Department of Employment Gazette* (1893–) and the *British Labour Statistics Yearbook* (1969–) which contain statistics on wages and earnings, prices, employment and unemployment, industrial disputes, accidents, etc. Historical runs of data are contained in the volume *British Labour Statistics, historical abstract 1886–1968.* Detailed earnings statistics are now published in the *New Earnings Survey* (1968–) and in the Inland Revenue's *Survey of Personal Incomes.* Another useful compilation is the Department of Employment's annual *Time Rates of Wages and Hours of Work.*

Local Authorities

Figures on the annual income and expenditure of local authorities may be had from the Ministry of Housing and Local Government's annual *Local Government Financial Statistics* (1934/35–). For Scotland there are the Scottish Development Department's *Local Financial Returns (Scotland)* (1961–).

(*See also* Rates.)

Minerals

Responsibility for producing statistical data on the mineral industry

rests with the Natural Environment Research Council and these it publishes in its *Statistical Summary of the Mineral Industry.*

National Income and Expenditure

National Income and Expenditure, the "Blue Book", is compiled annually in the Central Statistical Office and its scope ranges from taxation to the gross national product. Immediately following the Budget Speech (see p. 106) the Treasury issues the *Financial Statement and Budget Report* as an H.C. Paper; it is in the form of a Return to an Order of the Honourable the House of Commons for a Statement of Revenue and Expenditure as laid before the House by the Chancellor of the Exchequer when opening the Budget. Recently the *Consolidated Fund and National Loans Fund Accounts* (1968/69–) have taken the place of the *Public Income and Expenditure* account, and the *Consolidated Fund and National Loans Fund Accounts Supplementary Accounts* have replaced the *National Debt Return* and the *Financial Accounts of the United Kingdom.* A useful guide is provided by Studies in Official Statistics No. 13: *National Accounts Statistics: sources and methods* (1968).

(*See also* Estimates.)

Personal Expenditure

The Department of Employment and Productivity's *Family Expenditure Survey* (1957/65–) provides data on the earnings of individuals and expenditures of households, while expenditure on food is covered by *Domestic Food Consumption and Expenditure* (1950–64) which was retitled *Household Food Consumption and Expenditure* (1965–).

Personal Incomes

See Labour.

Police

There are no separately published statistics relating to the police but the *Annual Report of Her Majesty's Chief Inspector of Constabulary,* the *Report of the Commissioner of Police of the Metropolis* and the *Report of Her Majesty's Chief Inspector of Constabulary for Scotland* all contain statistical data; and all began last century.

Population

Under this heading the various editions of the Census are the most important sources. They have been published every ten years (except for 1941) since 1801. Until 1861 they covered Great Britain, but since then there has been a separate census for Scotland. Responsibility for England and Wales rests with the General Register Office, and for Scotland with the General Register Office, Scotland. The most recent full censuses were made in 1971 and these were preceded in 1966 by two sample censuses. one for England and Wales and one for Scotland. Their range is quite remarkable, extending to such things as scientific and technical qualifications, Commonwealth immigrants in the conurbations and fertility tables. A useful guide to the early censuses is *Census Reports of Great Britain 1801–1931* (*Guides to Official Sources,* No. 2.) published by H.M.S.O. in 1951. Available census reports are listed in Sectional List No. 56 (see pp. 23-5). Estimates of population are published in the *Registrar General's Annual Estimates of Population of England and Wales and of Local Authority Areas,* and in the *Annual Estimates of the Population of Scotland.*

Each year the General Register Office issues the *Registrar General's Statistical Review of England and Wales* in three parts: I *Tables, medical,* II *Tables, population* and III *Commentary.* New editions of the *Supplement on Cancer* are also published. The information these provide relates to such things as the number of births, marriages and deaths, and includes ages and causes of the latter. Scotland's figures appear in the *Annual Report of the Registrar General for Scotland.* Both offices issue weekly and quarterly figures.

Demographic statistics for various periods are provided in vol. II of the *Report of the Royal Commission on Population 1950* (Cmd. 7695).

Migration statistics are the subject of *External Migration: a study of the available statistics* by N. H. Carrier and J. R. Jeffrey, which was published by H.M.S.O. in 1953 as No. 6 in the series of *Studies on Medical and Population Subjects* produced by the General Register Office. Current figures appear in the following Home Office compilations published annually as Command Papers by the Stationery Office:

Control of Immigration. Statistics (1962–).
Statistics of Foreigners Entering and Leaving the United Kingdom (1939/51–).
Statistics of Persons Acquiring Citizenship of the United Kingdom and Colonies (1964–).

Power

The Ministry of Fuel and Power's *Statistical Digest* began with an issue covering the years 1938–43; thereafter it and its successors the Ministry of Power's *Statistical Digest* and the present Department of Trade and Industry *Digest of Energy Statistics* (1968/69–) have been published annually. In addition to giving production figures for such as coal, gas and electricity the Digest provides data on capital expenditure and employment in the fuel industries. Statistical tables are also published in vol. 2 of the National Coal Board's *Report and Accounts*.

Prices

Index numbers of wholesale prices are given each month in *Trade and Industry* and the *Monthly Digest of Statistics*. As regards retail prices, H.M.S.O. has published a guide entitled *Method of Construction and Calculation of the Index of Retail Prices* (*Studies in Official Statistics* No. 6, 4th edn. 1966). The index itself appears monthly in the *Department of Employment Gazette* and in more summary fashion in *Trade and Industry*. *National Income and Expenditure* includes a consumers' price index. The first of a new series of special indices of retail prices for one-person and two-person pensioner households were published in the *Employment and Productivity Gazette* for June 1969.

Production

Here the principal sources are the *Reports of the Census of Production* (1907–) which is described in *Guides to Official Sources*, No. 6 *Census of Production Reports* (H.M.S.O., 1961). Since their inception there have been censuses in 1907, 1912 (not published), 1924, 1930, 1935, 1948, 1954, 1958, 1963 and 1968. The 1968 census has 171 reports. Commencing with the 1970 census, the *Census of Production Reports* are being published annually as part of the *Business Monitor* series. An index of industrial production is included in *Trade and Industry*, the *Monthly Digest of Statistics* and the *Annual Abstract of Statistics*.

Rates

Rates and Rateable Values in England and Wales (1921–) is a joint annual publication of the Department of the Environment and the Welsh Office. A corresponding publication for Scotland, *Rates and Rateable Values in Scotland* (1938–), is prepared by the Scottish Development Department.

Regional Statistics

Subjects such as population and employment, production, and family expenditure for which regional figures are available are included in the *Abstract of Regional Statistics*, which has been issued annually since 1965 by the Central Statistical Office. But a particular difficulty with statistics of this kind is that of ensuring compatibility between the figures for different regions. The Welsh Office compiles its own *Digest of Welsh Statistics* (1954–), and Scotland is served by the *Scottish Abstract of Statistics* (annual, 1971–) and the *Scottish Economic Bulletin* (half-yearly, 1971–).

Science and Technology

Statistics of Science and Technology is a joint publication of the De-

partment of Education and Science and the Department of Trade and Industry.

Social

Social Trends (1970–) contains statistics on population, employment, leisure, personal income and expenditure, education, the environment, and housing.

Standard Industrial Classification

The S.I.C. was first published in 1948; there was a second edition in 1958, a reprint with a few amendments a few years later, and a new revised edition in 1968.

Taxation

See Inland Revenue.

Trade

The first *Census of Distribution and Other Services* was a short report for 1950, and this was followed by three further volumes for that year covering 1: *Retail and Service Trades, Area Tables;* 2: *Retail and Service Trades, General Tables:* and 3: *Wholesale Trades.* Since then there have been censuses of different depth in 1957, 1961, 1966 and 1971. More up-to-date figures appear in *Trade and Industry* and later selectively in the *Digest of Statistics* and the *Annual Abstract of Statistics.*

Transport

All forms of transport are included in the Department of Environment's annual compilation called *Passenger Transport in Great Britain* (1962–) which replaces *Public Road Passenger Statistics* (1949–62).

Railway statistics are given in the *Annual Report and Accounts of the British Railways Board* and in *Railway Accidents*.

Data on roads are provided by the Department of the Environment's *Highway Statistics* (1963–) (previously *Road Motor Vehicles*, 1951–62); by the annual *Roads in England*; and by *Road Accidents* also published annually.

For air transport the new *Business Monitor: Civil Aviation series* (1968–) is available; their titles are: *Airport Activity, Air Passengers, Air Freight and Mail, Airlines, Airline Operations* and *Domestic Passenger Traffic. Accidents to Aircraft on the British Register* is issued annually by the Department of Trade and Industry.

For shipping there is the *Digest of Port Statistics* (1964–) sold by H.M.S.O. but published by the National Ports Council, and the Department of Trade and Industry's *Shipping Casualties and Deaths: vessels registered in the United Kingdom*. The various statistics relating to the fishing industry (see p. 256) and to external trade (see pp. 258-9) are also relevant.

Universities

Statistics of Education 1966, vol. 6: Universities is the first occasion on which the University Grants Committee has used the larger format of the *Statistics of Education* series. It takes the place of the U.G.C.'s *Returns from Universities and University Colleges* which were published in Command Paper form up to the issue for 1965–66. The U.G.C. also issue an *Annual Survey and Review of University Development*.

CHAPTER 15

National Archives

The Public Record Office

The Public Record Office is a government department having statutory custody of public records. It was originally established to carry out the provisions of the Public Record Office Act, 1838, under which the Master of the Rolls was given responsibility for keeping the public records. There were further Public Record Office Acts in 1877 and 1898 and then in 1954 came the Report of the Committee of Departmental Records (Cmd. 9163). This Committee, under the chairmanship of Sir James Grigg, led to the Public Records Act, 1958, which repealed the earlier Acts and transferred the direction of the P.R.O. from the Master of the Rolls to the Lord Chancellor. It empowered him to appoint a Keeper of Public Records to take charge under his direction of the Public Record Office and suggested that this officer might compile and make available indexes and guides to, and calendars and texts of, the public records. It also laid down guidelines for the selection of documents and in particular stipulated that all public records created before the year 1660 should be included among those selected for permanent preservation. As far as more recent records were concerned these should not normally be available for public inspection until they had been in existence for fifty years. But this was later reduced to thirty years by the Public Records Act 1967.

Originally confined to court records, the term "public records" has been extended to include administrative records of government departments. Indeed the term is now more generally understood to refer only to the latter.

LISTS AND INDEXES

From the time of the 1838 Act until 1856 brief calendars were usually

published as appendices to the Deputy Keeper's Reports, but thereafter they began to appear separately. The parallel series of *Chronicles and Memorials of Great Britain and Ireland during the Middle Ages* (the "Rolls Series") continued until 1890 when both it and the appendices to the Deputy Keeper's Reports were abandoned in favour of the P.R.O.'s series of lists and indexes.

In continuation of this programme of listing and describing, and in compliance with the 1958 Act, various forms of publication are currently undertaken by the Public Record Office, and these are summarized in Sectional List No. 24: *British National Archives* as follows:

(a) Transcript. This is a full text, in which the abbreviations of the original manuscript have been extended wherever this could be done with certainty.
(b) Calendar. This is a précis, usually in English, and full enough to replace the original for most purposes.
(c) Descriptive list. This provides short abstracts of documents too voluminous for fuller treatment.
(d) Index. This comprises alphabetically arranged references to people, places or subjects mentioned in the records.
(e) List. This varies from an attenuated descriptive list to a simple enumeration of the units composing a class of records.
(f) Catalogue. This is a descriptive list containing records of similar content drawn from different groups for a special purpose, such as a public exhibition

All of these are represented in Sectional List No. 24 which is arranged under twelve headings:

    I Public Record Office Calendars, guides, etc.

    II Public Record Office Lists and Indexes.

    IIa Public Record Office Lists and Indexes, Supplementary Series.

    III Public Record Office Privy Council Registers.

    IV Rerum Britannicarum Medii Aevi Scriptores (Chronicles and Memorials of Great Britain and Ireland during the Middle Ages).

    V Publications of the Record Commissioners, etc.

    VI Works in Facsimile.

    VII Micro-Opaque Cards.

    VIII House of Lords Record Office Publications.

    IX Miscellaneous Publications.

    X Ireland.

    XI Northern Ireland.

XII Scotland.

The list concludes with an analytical index.

A good starting point is the general *Guide to Public Records, Part I: Introductory* (1949). Then there are three volumes of the *Guide to the Contents of the Public Record Office:* Vol. I *Legal Records,* etc. (1963); Vol. II *State Papers and Departmental Records* (1963); and Vol. III *Documents Transferred to the Public Record Office 1960–1966* (1969).

A number of further guides to official papers have been issued in the series of Public Record Office Handbooks. They are:

1. *Guide to Seals in the Public Record Office* (2nd edn. 1968).
2. *Domesday Re-bound* (1954).
3. *The Records of the Colonial and Dominions Offices* (1964).
4. *Lists of Cabinet Papers, 1880–1914* (1964).
5. *Shakespeare in the Public Records* (1964).
6. *List of Papers of the Committee of Imperial Defence, to 1914* (1964).
7. *List of Documents relating to the Household and Wardrobe, John to Edward I* (1964).
8. *List of Colonial Office Confidential Print, to 1916* (1965).
9. *List of Cabinet Papers, 1915 and 1916* (1966).
10. *Classes of Departmental Papers for 1906–1939* (1966).
11. *The Records of the Cabinet Office to 1922* (1966).
12. *The Records of the Forfeited Estates Commission* (1968).
13. *The Records of the Foreign Office 1782–1939* (1969).
14. *Records of Interest to Social Scientists 1919 to 1939: introduction* (1971).
15. *The Second World War: a guide to documents in the Public Record Office* (1972).

The scope of this series, originally called "Sectional Guides", has been expanded to embrace not only guides to specific categories of records but also works of other kinds serving to elucidate the public records or to facilitate research in them.

Most of the calendars listed in the sectional list have been reprinted by Kraus Reprint. They include those of the Chancery Records, the Exchequer Records, the Judicial Records, and the Domestic and Foreign State

Papers. Kraus have also reprinted most of the Public Record Office Lists and Indexes, the Privy Council Registers, and the Chronicles and Memorials.

In 1965 the List and Index Society was formed to distribute volumes of photographic copies of unpublished lists which have been compiled in the Search Room of the Public Record Office. The copies are sent only to subscribing members of the Society, of which the Secretary's address is c/o Swift Ltd., 5–9 Dyers Buildings, Holborn, London E.C.1. A list of particular interest is vol. 1 of the Special Series entitled *List of House of Commons Sessional Papers 1701–1750*, edited by Sheila Lambert (1968). It describes the two official collections of eighteenth-century Commons Papers, the Abbot Collection and the so-called "First Series", and two unofficial collections in the British Museum. Particulars are then given of lists and finding aids both generally and under the headings Bills, Reports of Commissioners, Reports of Committees, and Accounts and Papers.

The Public Record Office reproduces documents, lists and so forth by a number of photographic processes, and has also microfilmed the Memoranda Rolls of the Exchequer for the period 1217–1307. A typescript index to these rolls is now being compiled, and a copy of each successive instalment can be purchased as and when available. In addition, there is a growing stock of microfilm copies of various groups of records from which duplicate copies can be supplied. For a list of the films available in this way and for further information inquiries should be addressed to the Secretary, Public Record Office, Chancery Lane, London W.C.2.

Inquiries concerning Scottish records should be addressed to the Curator of Historical Records, Scottish Record Office, H.M. General Register Office, Edinburgh 2.

It is not perhaps generally known that the Record Office holds a good many maps and plans and that it is possible to have photographic copies made of them. In 1967 the P.R.O. issued the first part of its catalogue of *Maps and Plans in the Public Record Office* covering the *British Isles, c. 1410–1860*.

The P.R.O.'s publishing policy is reviewed periodically in collaboration with a committee of specialist historians from the universities set up by the Advisory Council on Public Records. New ways of making public records available to researchers are constantly being sought. Recently, for example, as an experiment to test demand, the P.R.O. prepared a set of

microcards of certain unpublished material including the Privy Council Registers, Charles I, 1631—1637, and various Search Room Lists.

RECORDS NOT IN THE P.R.O.

A guide to users of the Public Record Office draws attention to the fact that certain classes of public records are held elsewhere than in the P.R.O. For some records, including those of quarter sessions, the Lord Chancellor has appointed local repositories as the place of deposit. A few government departments maintain their own records and provide facilities for their inspection; in particular the Principal Probate Registry (Somerset House, W.C.2) which contains registrations of wills, and the Foreign and Commonwealth Office so far as concerns the records of the former India Office (see p. 240).

The following are indicated as the chief places where official documents not covered by the Public Records Act, 1958, are preserved:

The Record Office, House of Lords, London S.W.1 (records of Parliament);

The General Register Office, Somerset House, London W.C.2 (registration of births, marriages and deaths in England and Wales);

The Scottish Record Office, General Register House, Edinburgh 2 (records of the Kingdom of Scotland to 1707; legal registers, including testaments; records of the Scottish courts and departments; records of the Church of Scotland; certain local records and collections of family muniments);

The General Register Office of Births, Deaths and Marriages (Scotland), New Register House, Edinburgh 2;

The Public Record Office of Northern Ireland, Law Courts Building, May Street, Belfast (the records of the Northern Ireland courts and departments, and collections of privately deposited papers);

The Registrar-General's Office for Northern Ireland, Fermanagh House, Ormeau Avenue, Belfast.

ROYAL COMMISSION ON HISTORICAL MANUSCRIPTS

Various collections of papers which a researcher might expect to find in

the Public Record Office remain in private hands or have been given, sold or lent to institutions, notably to the British Museum's Department of Manuscripts, Bloomsbury, London W.C.1. Information on the present whereabouts of such collections should be sought from the Royal Commission on Historical Manuscripts, Quality Court, Chancery Lane, London WC2A 1HP.

This standing Royal Commission was set up in 1869, and in 1959 was reconstituted with extended powers. In the terms of its Royal Warrant the task of the Commissioners is to

> make enquiry as to the existence and location of manuscripts, including records or archives of all kinds, of value for the study of history, other than records which are for the time being public records by virtue of the Public Records Act; with the consent of the owners or custodians reproduce and publish or assist the publication of such reports; record particulars of such manuscripts and records in a National Register thereof; promote and assist the proper preservation and storage of such manuscripts and records; assist those wishing to use such manuscripts or records for study or research; consider and advise upon general questions relating to the location, preservation and use of such manuscripts and records; promote the co-ordinated action of all professional and other bodies concerned with the preservation and use of such manuscripts and records; carry out in place of the Public Record Office the statutory duties of the Master of the Rolls in respect of manorial and tithe documents.

Publications of the Commission are recorded in Sectional List No. 17: *Publications of the Royal Commission on Historical Manuscripts.*

The Commission's National Register of Archives records documents held by individuals and institutions, and issues an annual *List of Accessions to Repositories.*

RECORDS OF PARLIAMENT

A major new work is M. F. Bond's *Guide to the Records of Parliament* (H.M.S.O., 1971). This is the first comprehensive guide to the records of Parliament to be published. It describes the records of both Lords and Commons, and also other important classes of documents preserved within the Palace of Westminster. Special attention is given to manuscript material; but descriptions are also included of publications such as the Journals of the two Houses and the later Sessional Papers. The guide concerns proceedings in Parliament from the fifteenth century to the pre-

sent day and the records it describes total several million items. Nearly all of the documents are available for consultation in the Record Office of the House of Lords: the publication therefore serves as a guide to the House of Lords Record Office.

References to calendars of House of Lords manuscripts are given in Sectional List No. 17 (*supra*). They first appeared in the *Inspectors' Reports to the Commissioners* which, as appendices to the *Commissioners' Reports to the Crown,* were bound up therewith and issued as Command Papers, i.e.

First Report	C.55	(1870)
Second Report	C.441	(1871)
Third Report	C.673	(1872)
Fourth Report	C.857	(1874)
Fifth Report	C.1432	(1876)
Sixth Report	C.1745	(1877)
Seventh Report	C.2340	(1879)
Eighth Report	C.3040	(1881)
Ninth Report	C.3773–I	(1883)

Next they were printed as separate appendices to the Reports to the Crown, i.e.

Eleventh Report	App. II 1678–88 C.5060–1 (1887)
Twelfth Report	App. VI 1689–90 C.5889–III (1889)
Thirteenth Report	App. V 1680–91 C.6822 (1892)
Fourteenth Report	App. VI 1692–93 C.7573 (1894)

Since 1900 they have been issued independently of the Commissioners, as House of Lords Papers in a New Series, i.e.

N.S.I	1693–95	H.L.5 of 1900
N.S.II	1695–97	H.L.18 of 1903
N.S.III	1697–99	H.L.175 of 1905
N.S.IV	1699–1702	H.L.7 of 1908
N.S.V	1702–04	H.L.62 of 1910
N.S.VI	1704–06	H.L.142 of 1912
N.S.VII	1706–08	H.L.1 of 1921
N.S.VIII	1708–10	H.L.40 of 1922

N.S.IX	1710–12	H.L.92 of 1948
N.S.X	1712–14	H.L.35 of 1953
N.S.XI	Addenda	
	1514–1714	H.L.123 of 1962
N.S.XII	1714–18	(In preparation)

Information concerning photographic copies of documents in the House of Lords Record Office can be obtained from the Clerk of the Records, House of Lords, London S.W.1.

CHAPTER 16

Obtaining H.M.S.O. Publications

HER MAJESTY'S STATIONERY OFFICE

Early in each parliamentary session the Controller of the Stationery Office is appointed Printer and Publisher to Parliament, and he receives similar appointments from the Parliament of Northern Ireland. He is also Queen's Printer of Acts of Parliament. In him too is vested the Crown copyright in all official documents, published and unpublished. The office dates back to 1786 when John Mayor was installed as Superintendent of the newly created Stationery Office. Though H.M.S.O. is now most widely known through its role as publisher for Parliament and the Government it is in fact responsible for the supply of stationery, books, periodicals and office machinery not only to government departments but also to the armed services and a number of other national institutions including the health and hospital services.

An account of the history and activities of the Stationery Office was the subject of an address given by Sir John R. Simpson (Controller from 1954 to 1961) to the Stationers' and Newspaper Makers' Company in 1961; and an updated version was published by H.M.S.O. in 1967 in the form of a booklet entitled *Her Majesty's Stationery Office*.

Today H.M.S.O. publishes for sale some 6500 items a year for Parliament, government departments, museums and other public bodies in the United Kingdom. It prints about 30,000,000 copies a year of its priced books and pamphlets of which a substantial proportion are produced on its own presses. It always has about 90,000 titles in print and every year sells about £2,500,000 worth of publications at home and overseas. In 1911 it opened its first bookshop, selling direct to the public, in Edinburgh; and the shop's success led to the opening of others a few years later.

GOVERNMENT BOOKSHOPS

Each government bookshop carries a comprehensive stock of current titles, of which it displays a varied selection of those considered to be more important and to have a wide general appeal. They are bookshops in the normal sense, where the customer may inspect the publications displayed, make inquiries about stock and other items and place orders for any of the 90,000 titles in print at any given time.

ENGLAND

Birmingham B1 2HE: 258 Broad Street (phone 021–643 3740 and 3757).

Bristol BS1 3DE: 50 Fairfax Street (phone 0272–24306).

London WC1V 6HB: 49 High Holborn (Callers only) (phone 01–928 6977 ext. 423).

London SE1 9NH: PO Box 569 (Trade and London area mail orders) (phone 01–928 6977: telephone order section).

Manchester M60 8AS: Brazennose Street (phone 061–834 7201).

SCOTLAND

Edinburgh EH2 3AR: 13a Castle Street (phone 031–225 6333).

WALES

Cardiff CF1 1JW: 41 The Hayes (phone 0222–23654).

NORTHERN IRELAND

Belfast BT1 4JY: 80 Chichester Street (phone 0232–34488)

Publications may also be obtained through booksellers. The following is a list of those in the United Kingdom and the Republic of Ireland who act as official agents. Copies of recent titles are normally in stock, and special arrangements have been made for those not held to be obtained promptly.

Official Agents in the United Kingdom

	Agent	*Telephone number*
Aberdeen	A. & R. Milne & Wyllies (Booksellers) 247 Union Street	0224 24344

Bournemouth	W. H. Smith & Son Ltd.	
	The Square	0202 25342
Brighton	Combridge's (Hove) Ltd.	0273 735121 and
	56 Church Road	738060
Cambridge	W. Heffer & Sons Ltd.	
	20 Trinity Street	0223 58351
Canterbury	The Pilgrim's Bookshop	
	29 St. Margaret Street	0227 66617
Colchester	A. T. Shippey Ltd.	
	47 Head Street	0206 72284/5
Cork	Eason and Son Ltd.	
	111 Patrick Street	20477
Coventry	Church Book Shop	
	27 Trinity Street	0203 22844
Derby	The Central Education Co. Ltd.	
	36–38 St. Peter's Churchyard	0332 46024
Dublin	Eason and Son Ltd.	
	40–41 Lower O'Connell Street	41161
Dumfries	Blacklock, Farries and Sons	
	18–26 Church Crescent	0387 4288/9
Dundee	J. Menzies & Co. Ltd.	
	8 Whitehall Street	0382 25439
Durham	House of Andrews	
	73–75 Saddler Street	0385 2359
Exeter	Wheatons	
	143 Fore Street	0392 52456
Farnham	Hammicks Bookshop	
	Downing Street	0251 24666
Glasgow	John Smith & Sons	
	57–61 St. Vincent Street	041 221 7472
Hull	A. Brown & Sons Ltd.	
	24–28 George Street	0482 25413
Inverness	Melven's Bookshop	
	29 Union Street	0463 33500
Leeds	Austick's Bookshop	
	25 Cookridge Street	0532 22623
Leicester	The University Bookshop	
	Mayor's Walk	0533 26514

Liverpool 2	Parry Books Ltd.	
	The University Bookshop	
	Alsop Building	051 709 8146 or
	Brownlow Hill	6512 (H.M.S.O. line)
Maidstone	W. H. Smith & Son Ltd.	
	11 High Street	0622 54264/5
Middlesbrough	Boddy's Bookshop	
	165 Linthorpe Road	0642 47568
Newcastle-upon-Tyne	The Bible House	
	14 Pilgrim Street	0632 20335
	Thorne's Students'	
	Bookshop Ltd.	
	63–67 Percy Street	0632 24345
Northampton	C. B. Savage Ltd.	
	99–105 Kettering Road	0604 37883
Norwich	Jarrold & Sons Ltd.	
	London Street	0603 60661
Nottingham	Sisson and Parker Ltd.	
	Wheeler Gate	0602 43531
Oxford	B. H. Blackwell Ltd.	
	50 and 51 Broad Street	0865 49111–4
Reading	William Smith	
	(Booksellers) Ltd.	
	35–41 London Street	0734 54227
Sheffield	W. Hartley Seed	0742 78315 or
	154–160 West Street	22035 (H.M.S.O. line)
Southampton	John Adams Bookservice Ltd.	
	103 St. Mary Street	0703 23722
Stoke-on-Trent	Webberley Ltd.	
	Percy Street, Hanley	0782 25256/7/8
Swansea	Uplands Bookshop Ltd.	
	4 Gwydr Square	
	Uplands	0792 57050
	Singleton Bookshop	
	College House	
	Singleton Park	0792 25149

Wakefield	The Eagle Press	
	18 Wood Street	0924 72603
Wolverhampton	Bookland & Co. Ltd.	
	13 and 15 Lichfield Street	0902 23141

Official Agents Outside the United Kingdom

Argentina: Carlos Hirsch, Florida 165, Buenos Aires.

Australia: Australian Government Publishing Service, Treasury Building, Canberra, ACT 2600 (P.O. Box 84).

Barker's Bookstore, 196 Edward Street, Brisbane, Qd 4001 (P.O. Box 1676).

Carroll's Pty. Ltd., 566 Hay Street, Perth, WA 6001 (P.O. Box M 594).

Grahame Book Co. Pty. Ltd., 2 Denison Street, Sydney, NSW 2060 (P.O. Box 495).

Thomas C. Lothian Pty. Ltd., 4 Tattersalls La., Melbourne, Victoria 3000 (and at Sydney, Brisbane and Adelaide).

O.B.M. Pty. Ltd., 36 Elizabeth Street, Hobart, Tasmania.

Technical Book & Magazine Co. Pty. Ltd., 289 Swanston Street, Melbourne, Victoria 3000.

Austria: English Reading Room, Stephansplatz 8, 1010 Vienna 1.

Canada: Information Canada, Ottawa, K1A OS9 (and at Halifax, Montreal, Toronto, Vancouver & Winnipeg).

Denmark: Arnold Busck, Købmagergade 49, Copenhagen.

Finland: Akateeminen Kirjakauppa, Keskuskatu 2, Helsinki 10.

France: W. H. Smith & Son, 248 rue de Rivoli, Paris.

Idea Books, 24 rue du 4 Septembre, Paris 2e.

Germany: Elwert & Meurer, 1 Berlin 62, Hauptstrasse 101.

Alexander Horn, Spiegelgasse 9 (Pariser Hof), Wiesbaden.

Hans Heinrich Petersen (trade only), P.O. Box 265, Borsteler Chaussee, 85 Hamburg 61.

W. E. Saarbach GmbH, Follerstrasse 2, Cologne 1.

Greece: G. C. Eleftheroudakis S.A., International Bookstore, 4 Nikis Street, Athens (T—126).

Gulf Area: All Prints Distributors & Publishers, Fahd El Salem Street, Kuwait (P.O. Box 1719) (and at Abu Dhabi, P.O. Box 857).

Guyana: Booker's Stores Ltd., 19 Water Street, Georgetown.

Hong Kong: Swindon Book Company, 13 Lock Road, Kowloon.

Iceland: Snaebjorn Jonsson, P.O. Box 1131, Hafnarstraeti 9, Reykjavik.

India: British Information Services, Chanakyapuri, New Delhi 110021.

    Higginbothams Ltd., 2 Mount Road, Madras (and at Bangalore).

    The Oxford Book & Stationery Co., Scindia House, New Delhi; and 17 Park Street, Calcutta 16.

Israel: Steimatzky's Agency Ltd., P.O. Box 628, Citrus House, Tel Aviv.

Italy: The Lion Bookshop, 181 Via del Babuino, Rome.

Jamaica: Sangster's Bookstore, 91 Harbour Street, Kingston

Japan: Maruzen Co. Ltd., 3–10 Nihinbashi 2–Chome Chuo-ku, Tokyo 103.

Kenya: E. S. A. Bookshop Ltd., P.O. Box 30167, Church House, Government Road, Nairobi.

Lebanon: Uncle Sam's Bookshop, Bakhaazi Building, Jeanne d'Arc Street, Beirut.

Malaysia: Jack Chia – MPH Ltd., 278 Jalan Brickfields, Kuala Lumpur.

    Jubilee (Book) Store Sdn Bhd, 97 Jalan Tuanku

    Abdul Rahman, Kuala Lumpur (P.O. Box 629).

Mexico: Cía Internacional de Publicaciones S.A. de C. V.

Netherlands: Dekker & Nordemanns Wetenschappelijke Boekhandel NV, OZ voorburgwal 243, Amsterdam-C.

    Martinus Nijhoff NV, Lange Voorhout 9, The Hague (P.O. Box 269).

    NV Swets & Zeitlinger, Keizersgracht 471, Amsterdam.

New Zealand: Thomas C. Lothian Pty. Ltd., 88 Nelson Street, Auckland 1 (P.O. Box 8220).

    Whitcombe & Tombs Ltd., P.O. Box 1894, Wellington C 1 (and at Auckland, Christchurch, Dunedin, Hamilton, Invercargill, Lower Hutt, and Timaru).

Nigeria: C. S. S. Bookshops, 50 Yakubu Gowon Street, Lagos (P.O. Box 174); P.O. Box 34 Port Harcourt;

    Sudan United Mission Bookshop, Maiduguri.

Norway: Ed. B. Giertsen A/S, P.O. Box 217, Bergen.

    J. G. Tanum & Cammermeyer, Karl Johansgt 43, Oslo.

Pakistan: Mirza Book Agency, 65 Shahrah Quaid-E-Azam, Lahore 3 (P.O. Box 729).

Portugal: Empresa Nacional de Publicidade, Largo do Chiado 9, Lisbon.

Sierra Leone: Sierra Leone Diocesan Bookshop, P.O. Box 104, Freetown (UK Office: 85 Rowlands Road, Worthing, Sussex).

Singapore: Jack Chia — MPH Ltd., 71 Stamford Road, Singapore 6 (P.O. Box 347).

Spain: Pamel S.A., Taquigrafo Garriga 156, Barcelona 15.

Sri Lanka: H. W. Cave & Co. Ltd., P.O. Box No. 25, Colombo.

Sweden: C. E. Fritzes Hovbokhandel, Fredsgatan 2, Stockholm 16.

Switzerland: Buchhandlung Hans Huber, Markygasse 9, Bern Librairie Payot, 6 rue Grenus, 1211 Geneva 11.

　　Kurt Stäheli & Co., Bahnhofstrasse 70, 8021 Zurich.

　　Wepf & Co., Eisengasse 5, Basel.

Tanzania: Duka la Vitabu (Tanzania), Dar es Salaam Bookshop, (P.O. Box 9030) (and at Lindi, Tanga, and Zanzibar).

Trinidad: Stephens, Frederick Street, Port of Spain (P.O. Box 497).

Uganda: Uganda Bookshop, P.O. Box 7145, Kampala (and at Jinja, Mbale, Gulu, Fort Portal, Kabale, Masaka, Mbarara, Soroti, and Tororo).

USA: Pendragon House Inc., 220 University Avenue, Palo Alto, California 94301.

Yugoslavia: Jugoslovenska Knjiga, Terazije 27, Belgrade.

Catalogues of official publications may be inspected at major British Consulates throughout the world, and in case of difficulty in obtaining documents overseas, they may be ordered direct from H.M.S.O., P.O. Box 569, London SE1 9NH. Consignments are usually sent by book post, unless special instructions are given. Carriage, which is extra, may be calculated at approximately 7 per cent of the value of the consignment.

STANDING ORDERS

Certain publications which are of a recurring nature, or form part of a recognizable series or group, can be supplied automatically as published. This Standing Order Service is available to customers who open or already have accounts with the Stationery Office. Standing orders can be accepted under general headings such as Civil Aviation or Agriculture, or they can be more specific, for example each issue of a department's annual report, each print of a Bill progressing through Parliament until it becomes an Act, then all regulations subsequently made under the Act. While standing

orders can be entered by subject, they cannot be entered for all the publications of a particular department. Details of classes of publications accepted under these arrangements and advice on methods of payment can be obtained from Her Majesty's Stationery Office, P.O. Box 569, London SE1 9NH, to which address orders should also be sent. It is normally possible for a subscription to a periodical or a standing order for selected publications as they appear to commence about two weeks after instructions and payment have been received. In the catalogues the inclusive price of cost and postage is always shown in brackets (see Figs. 3—6); remittances should be made payable to H.M.S.O. when orders are made direct by post.

SELECTED SUBSCRIPTION SERVICE

In 1969 a new Selected Subscription Service was put into operation by H.M.S.O. with a view to reducing the detailed selection, invoicing and accounting work involved both for itself and for its customers in meeting large numbers of individual orders for Stationery Office publications. In return for one inclusive payment of £2352 (April 1973) H.M.S.O. will supply to subscribers to this service one copy of all government publications less the following:

- (i) forms and posters;
- (ii) *House of Commons Votes and Proceedings;*
- (iii) *House of Lords Minutes of Proceedings;*
- (iv) periodicals available on normal subscription terms;
- (v) services' regulations, manuals, licences and amendments (including those issued by the Department of Trade and Industry in respect of civil aviation);
- (vi) separately published maps and charts;
- (vii) art reproductions;
- (viii) Aeronautical Research Council *Current Papers* and *Reports and Memoranda;*
- (ix) *Defence Specifications and Aerospace Material Specifications;*
- (x) *Statutes in Force*
- (xi) all reprints.
- (xii) 'Agency' publications which H.M.S.O. sells but does not publish.

Included in the annual cost of the service are the bound volumes of *Hansard*, all Acts of Parliament (both individually and in volumes) and all statutory instruments (both individually and in volumes). Subscribers also receive a free service of index cards, each daily batch following some three to four working days after the associated publications. Those who do not require copies of individual statutory instruments as published may enter a subscription at the reduced annual rate of £2256 and still receive the bound volumes. Hitherto, subscribers who placed bulk standing orders received a delivery note listing the items in each daily consignment. This is not included in the new service, but subscribers are assured by H.M.S.O. that their handling system will ensure that all published items except the excluded categories will be dispatched.

The subscription year runs from 1 April to 31 March; a new customer may join on the first day of any month but his first year's subscription will run only to 31 March and the amount payable will be assessed *pro rata* to the annual subscription. There will not normally be any refund of subscriptions to customers wishing to contract out of the scheme during the course of a year, and returns for credit cannot be allowed. The subscription rate for the service will be reviewed annually by H.M.S.O. and renewal order forms showing the subscription for the year commencing 1 April sent to subscribers in February each year. It is, however, intended to hold the price for as many years as possible. "We would not", say the publishers "alter it on account of a comparatively minor 'loss' or 'profit' to H.M.S.O. in any one year."

LIBRARY DISCOUNTS

A discount of fity per cent is given by H.M.S.O. on orders from rate-supported public libraries for all Parliamentary Papers and Non-Parliamentary Publications published by the Stationery Office.

OUT-OF-PRINT PUBLICATIONS

H.M.S.O. will supply photocopies of out-of-print items at 5p per page of text and 7½p per page carrying an illustration.

PERIODICALS

A number of serial publications may be obtained on a subscription basis; indeed this is the only way in which some titles can be ordered, as they are not included in bulk purchase schemes such as the Selected Subscription Service described above. Those which H.M.S.O. treat in this way are listed at the end of every issue of the annual *Catalogue of Government Publications* and in Sectional List No. 28: *Periodicals and Subscription Rates*. The current titles are as follows:

Abstracts of Efficiency Studies in the Hospital Services (Q).
Accidents, How They Happen and How to Prevent Them (Q).
ADAS Quarterly Review. Journal of the Agricultural Development Advisory Service (Q).
Air Force Law, Manual of, Amendements (Irr.).
Air Pilot, Amendment Service Supplements and NOTAMS.
Allowance Regulations for the Army, Amendments. (Irr.).
Army Pay Warrant, Amendments. (Irr.).
British Library Review.
Building Research Station Digests (2nd Series) (M.).
Building Science Abstracts (M.).
Business Monitor, Civil Aviation Series.
Business Monitor, Production Series
Business Monitor, Miscellaneous Series. } (A. M. and Q.).
Business Monitor, Service and Distributive Series.
Construction Indices, Monthly Bulletin of.
Contents of Recent Economic Journals (W.).
Court of Session, Edinburgh:
    Abstracts of Petitions for the Appointment of Executors.
    Abstracts of Petitions for the Service of Heirs and Edictal Citations for Summonses in the Supreme Court and Inferior Courts.
    General Minute Book of the Court of Session.
Customs and Excise Tariff and Supplement. Amending Supplement. (Irr.).
Directory of Employers' Associations, Trade Unions Joint Organization, etc., Amendments (Irr.).
Economic Trends (M.).

Edinburgh Gazette. (twice W). (Obtainable only from H.M. Exchequer, 102 George Street, Edinburgh 2).

Employment and Productivity Gazette. (M.).

Financial Statistics (M.).

General Aviation Flight Guide Amendment Service (Irr.).

H.M. Ministers and Heads of Public Departments, List of (5 issues p.a.).

Hospital Abstracts (M.).

Housing and Construction Statistics (Q.).

Journal of Administration Overseas. (Q.).

London Diplomatic List. (Bi-M).

London Gazette Supplements and Indices (4 times Weekly).

Marine Observer. (Q.).

Meteorological Magazine. (M.).

Military Law, Manual of, Amendments. (Irr.).

Overseas Trade Statistics of the United Kingdom. (M.).

Plant Pathology. (Q.).

Plant Varieties and Seeds Gazette. (M.).

Probation and After Care Directory. Amendment Lists (M.).

Project Magazine.

Queen's Regulations and Air Council Instructions for the RAF, Amendments. (Irr.).

Queen's Regulations for the Army and the Royal Army Reserve. (Irr.).

Registrar-General's Returns of Births, Deaths and Marriages: . . . . . .
    England and Wales:
        Weekly (Births, Deaths, Infectious Diseases and Weather Report).
        Quarterly. (Births, Deaths and Marriages, etc.).
    Scotland:
        Weekly.
        Quarterly.

Registry of Ships, Supplements. (M.).

Statistical News. (Q.).

Statistics, Monthly Digest of

Statutory Instruments, Lists.

Survey of Current Affairs. (M.).

Tax Case Leaflets and Profits Tax Leaflets. (Irr.).

Tax Cases Reports. Volume of 12 parts. (Irr.).

Trade and Industry (incorporating the Board of Trade Journal. (W.).

Traffic Cases. (Irr.).

Trends in Education. (Q.).

Tropical Science. (Q.).

Wages and Hours of Work, Changes in Rates of (M.).

Water Pollution Abstracts (Formerly Summary of Current Literature. (M.).

Weather Report (including Annual Summary). (M.).

Irr. = irregular, M = monthly, Q = quarterly, W = weekly.

Some of the titles, particularly those relating to statistics, have been described in the appropriate chapters, and others such as *Kew Bulletin* and *Trends in Education* need no explanation. Two titles which stand out are the *London Gazette* and the *Edinburgh Gazette.* The former is perhaps most widely known for its (separately priced) supplements listing honours and awards. Both contain public and legal notices, company liquidations and bankruptcies. The remainder range from *Soldier,* a popular magazine, to technical abstracting journals like *Building Science Abstracts* and *Water Pollution Abstracts.*

H.M.S.O. AS SALES AGENT

The Stationery Office acts as sales agent for certain public bodies whose publications are listed in the official catalogues (though omitted from the select list on pp. 197-228). The bodies concerned include the following:

Agricultural Research Council
British Antarctic Survey
British Council
British Film Institute
British Museum
British Travel Association
British Waterways Board
Countryside Commission for Scotland
Crown Agents for Overseas Governments and Administrations

Highlands and Islands Development Board
National Building Agency
National Gallery, London
National Ports Council
Science Research Council
United Kingdom Atomic Energy Authority

H.M.S.O. also acts as United Kingdom distributor for sale publications of the United Nations, UNESCO, the World Health Organisation, the Food and Agriculture Organisation and other specialized agencies of the U.N.; and for the Organisation for Economic Co-operation and Development (O.E.C.D.), the European Communities and several other international organizations, e.g.

Council of Europe
Customs Co-operation Council
General Agreement on Tariffs and Trade (G.A.T.T.)
International Atomic Energy Agency (I.A.E.A.)
International Customs Tariff Bureau
International Civil Aviation Organisation (I.C.A.O.)
International Institute of Administrative Science
International Monetary Fund (I.M.F.)
Western European Union (W.E.U.)
World Meteorological Organisation (W.M.O.)

Publications of these and other institutions handled by the Stationery Office are listed in *International Organisations and Overseas Agencies Publications,* a catalogue sold annually by H.M.S.O. Subject lists and information are supplied free on application to P.O. Box 569, London SE1 9NH.

REPRINTS AND MICROTEXTS

Very many older British official publications are being made available either as reprints on paper or in microtext editions. Details will be found under the heading "Great Britain" in *Guide to Reprints* and *Guide to Microforms in Print,* both published annually by the National Cash Register Company.

CROWN COPYRIGHT

For a brief account of Crown Copyright see John E. Pemberton's "Crown Copyright," *Library World,* vol. lxxi, no. 838, pp. 307-8, 1970.

H.M.S.O. SERVICES WORKING PARTY

In November 1970 Mr. J. P. Morgan, H.M.S.O.'s Director of Publications addressed a meeting of librarians at the Library Association headquarters in London, and his offer to discuss problems of mutual interest matched a need previously expressed by librarians for some kind of Stationery Office users' council. As a result, an H.M.S.O. Services Working Party, with representation from the Library Association, Aslib and the British and Irish Association of Law Librarians, was set up and held its first meeting in September 1971. Improvements have since been made in publicizing the many valuable services operated by H.M.S.O. The secretary of the Working Party is R. Howes, FLA, 36 Limes Avenue, Aylesbury, Buckinghamshire.

CHAPTER 17

Non-H.M.S.O. Official Publications

SPECIAL difficulties are presented by the literature which is issued direct-ly by the government department in which it originates. They arise be-cause no machinery exists for the centralized recording of the documents concerned. Unlike those publications which are handled by H.M.S.O., they are not covered by any comprehensive catalogue service: there is no single source for the enquirier to consult.

A common misconception that *all* official papers are published by H.M.S.O. could imply that a good deal of departmental literature is failing to reach its full potential readership. Departments in fact publish at least as much by themselves as they channel through H.M.S.O. Distribution tends to be made on the basis of mailings to "target" bodies, and whilst this may satisfy a department's immediate objectives and enable it to discharge specific obligations, it is quite ineffective in the wider context of public interest.

In order to publicize and increase access to the considerable body of non-listed material in the libraries of government departments the Social Science Research Council sponsored a survey of their holdings, and the catalogue which resulted is published by Political Reference Publications under the title *Guide to Government Data*. As regards serials, the State Paper Room of the British Museum has compiled a *Check List of British Official Serial Publications* which it issues periodically in revised and updated editions.

A very few non-H.M.S.O. departmental publications appear in the *British National Bibliography* and anyone wishing to keep informed of what is being issued currently is therefore obliged to make direct contact with the relevant departments. The following brief survey of departmental publishing activity does not claim to be exhaustive. Its two-fold purpose is

to reveal something of the large reservoir of official publications which lies outside the domain of H.M. Stationery Office, and to specify some of the means whereby it may be tapped.

Admiralty (Ministry of Defence)

Superintendent of Sales, Hydrographic Supplies Establishment, Taunton, Somerset.

Admiralty charts and hydrographic publications are obtainable from the Hydrographic Supplies Establishment (as above), or from their principal agents. The principal London agent is J. D. Potter Ltd., 145 The Minories, London EC3. An annual catalogue is published.

Agriculture, Fisheries and Food (Ministry)

Publications), Tolcarne Drive, Pinner, Middlesex, HA5 2DT.
  (Fisheries publications are also available from the Fisheries Laboratory, Lowestoft, Suffolk.)

Issues a printed catalogue every six months called *Agriculture, Fisheries and Food: catalogue of departmental publications* in the same format as the H.M.S.O. Sectional Lists. Most of the items listed belong to series — Advisory Leaflets, Profitable Farm Enterprises, Performance Trial Reports, etc. — and are arranged in subject groups. A detailed index is included.

British Council

Publications and Recorded Sound Department, Albion House, 59 New Oxford Street, London, WC1A 1BP.

The Council's publications are listed in an appendix to its annual report, some being indicated as published by commercial publishers, e.g. *English Language Teaching* published three times a year by the Oxford University Press; *Language-Teaching Abstracts* quarterly by the Cambridge University Press; *Scientific and Learned Societies of Great Britain: a hand-*

book by Messrs Allen & Unwin; and booklets on various aspects of Britain by the Longman Group Ltd.

Central Office of Information

Hercules Road, London, SE1 7DU.

The Central Office of Information produces material in the main communications media for other government departments. Three divisions are concerned with printed word: Overseas Press and Radio, Publications and Design Services, and Reference. Press material, consisting of news and features, is not available in Britain. The non-H.M.S.O. items issued by the Publications and Design Services Division are in the main concerned with Government publicity campaigns — decimalization, road safety, VAT, legal aid, recruitment, and so forth — and usually have a relatively short life, during which they are circulated through various outlets such as government departments, the Post Office, local authorities or by direct mail. There are also trade promotion publications prepared exclusively for use overseas. Since all these free publications serve specific purposes, distribution is arranged direct to the target readership. No catalogues are issued and no stocks maintained after a particular campaign has come to an end. Reference material, prepared primarily for use in the overseas information services, is on sale in Britain, some titles through H.M.S.O. and some direct from the Distribution Unit (Room 420) Reference Division, at the above address. An annual Sales List (with quarterly supplements), listing reference material in print, is available free from that address.

Central Statistical Office

Press and Information Service, Great George Street, London, SW1P 3AQ.

Virtually all the C.S.O.'s publications are published by H.M.S.O. *Facts in Focus,* a popular paperback compendium of statistics, is produced jointly by Penguin and H.M.S.O. *United Kingdom in Figures* and *Government Statistics* are small pamphlets produced annually, and *Profit from Facts* a rather more substantial booklet — all available directly from the above address.

Civil Service Department

Central Management Library, Whitehall, London SW1A 2AZ.

The Central Management Library has compiled a complete catalogue of C.S.D. publications not published by H.M.S.O. It is arranged by subject, and the intention is to revise and update it annually. Also available from the Library is a monthly list entitled *Published by CSD* which indicates the addresses from which listed non-H.M.S.O. items may be obtained.

Countryside Commission

1 Cambridge Gate, Regent's Park, London, NW1 4JY.

Issues a *Catalogue of Publications* which includes a list of *Countryside Commission Papers* obtainable on request from the Commission, mostly free of charge. Also listed is a range of free publicity material including, for example, the Country Code, posters and long-distance footpath maps and folders. See also under Department of the Environment.

Countryside Commission for Scotland

Battleby, Redgorton, Perth, PH1 3EW.

A duplicated list of non-H.M.S.O. publications obtainable from the Commission includes information sheets on such topics as access agreements and country parks; reports on studies or conferences undertaken or sponsored by the Commission; and publications intended for those using the Scottish countryside for leisure.

Customs and Excise (H.M.)

General Information Section, Room 024, King's Beam House, Mark Lane, London, EC3R 7HE.

H.M. Customs and Excise publish several hundred free Public Notices on all aspects of Customs & Excise work where it is necessary to make information generally available. No catalogue of these Public Notices is

issued, but information about them, and the Notices themselves, are obtainable from the General Information Section. Appropriate selections of these Notices are also available at local Customs & Excise Offices.

Defence (Ministry)

Old War Office Building, Whitehall, London, SW1.

All M.O.D. publications not handled by H.M.S.O. have some degree of security restriction which precludes listing in catalogues, book lists, etc. The only exceptions to this are the items produced by the three Service public relations branches as recruiting literature.

Education and Science (Department)

Elizabeth House, York Road, London, SE1 7PH.

H.M.S.O. publishes an *Index to Department of Education and Science Circulars and Administrative Memoranda,* in which the majority of the items listed are available directly from the DES at the above address. In addition, the Department itself issues other lists, for example a *List of Reports on Education Currently Available from the Information Division* (Elizabeth House); a list issued by the Architects and Building Branch which includes many items on educational building obtainable from the D.E.S. Publications Despatch Centre, Honeypot Lane, Stanmore, Middlesex; and a list of *Current Educational Research Projects Supported by the D.E.S.* Other non-H.M.S.O. publications are listed in the Department's annual report.

Employment (Department)

Information Section, 8 St. James's Square, London, SW1 4JB.

The Department issues a large number of booklets, especially items which explain the provisions of industrial legislation. They are listed in the periodically revised *List of Current Publications of the Department of Employment.* Most are available free from any Employment Exchange,

but certain titles are indicated as obtainable only from St. James's Square.

Environment (Department)

2 Marsham Street, London, SW1P 3EB
(and other addresses below).

The non-H.M.S.O. publications of the Department of the Environment including those of the Property Services Agency cover a wide variety of topics. In 1971 for example, 350 items were published by the Department itself (not including those issued by the Department's research establishments, and by the Countryside Commission and Water Resources Board). They ranged from massive works like the "Enviro System" — a four volume description of a computerised system for dealing with bills of quantities, and costing £35 — to unpaged, unpriced pamphlets such as the "Green Cross Code" and "Finding a Home to Rent". The subjects embraced included Bridge Design, Building and Construction, Camping, Computer programs, European transport policy, Furniture, Goods Vehicles, Housing, International Road Haulage, Local government, Mathematical and Time research, Planning (Town, Country and Regional), Pollution, Railway accidents, Roads, Road safety, Traffic and Transport.

Non-H.M.S.O. publications of the Department's research establishments cover research in Building and Construction, Fire and its Causes, Forest Products, Hydraulics, Road Construction and Transport. In 1961 these establishments published 380 items between them, and in the same year the Countryside Commission and Water Resources Board published over twenty.

The Map Library of the Department is responsible for the publication of a number of maps which do not bear the H.M.S.O. imprint. In 1971, 97 such maps were produced on such subjects as Agricultural Land Classification, Airports and Airport Traffic, Cars per Household, Crops per Acre, Employment in Different Occupations, Highway Networks, Housing, Local Government Boundaries, Regional Employment and Unemployment, Regional Planning, and Transport.

There is no central issue point for these publications and enquiries concerning them must be made to the Library (Room P3/178), Department of the Environment, 2 Marsham Street, London SW1P 3EB. The

Library has recently issued an *Annual List of Publications* for 1971 and this is intended as the first of a series of such lists. Section 2 of the *Annual List* enumerates all non-H.M.S.O. publications of the Department itself and in each case gives the address where the item can be obtained. Sections 6, 7, and 8 are devoted to publications of the research establishments, the Countryside Commission and Water Resources Board, and the Map Library. These bodies issue their own publications and the *Annual List* gives the address for each of them. It is obtainable from: Department of the Environment Sub-Library, Room 414, Government Building, Bromyard Avenue, Acton, London, W3.

Current information on Department of the Environment publications is contained in the D.O.E. *Library Bulletin*, a fortnightly abstracting journal produced by the Library of the Department. Details of this can be obtained on request from the Library (Room P3/178), Department of the Environment, 2 Marsham Street, London, SW1P 3EB. However, curent information on Property Services Agency publications is given in *Current Information in the Construction Industry,* obtainable from the Property Services Agency Library (Room 018), Lambeth Bridge House, Albert Embankment, London, SE1 7SB.

Foreign and Commonwealth Offices

Sanctuary Buildings, Great Smith Street, London, SW1P 3B7.

There are few non-H.M.S.O. publications available to the public as the majority of the reports and memoranda produced by the F.C.O. are classified confidential.

Forestry Commission

25 Saville Row, London, W1X 2AY.

Publications not shown in H.M.S.O. lists which are issued by the Commission are mostly those with a publicity purpose and are therefore available free. Examples of titles are *Britain's New Forests, Forestry Commission Camping and Caravan Sites,* and *Starting a School Forest.* A catalogue is expected to be published.

produced by other departments of the Administration. The publicity material consists of a series of over twenty fact sheets on all aspects of development, a bi-monthly newspaper *Overseas Development,* and various posters and leaflets. A list of *Material on Overseas Development and Aid* is issued by the O.D.A. Information Department and frequently revised. It also includes details of publications available from H.M.S.O. The bibliographies issued by the O.D.A. Library include a *New Books List* issued twice a month, *Development Index* a weekly list of periodical articles, *Technical Cooperation: a monthly bibliography* which gives details of the official publications of Commonwealth countries received in the library, *Public Administration: a select bibliography* (3rd edn. 1973) and *Select Bibliography on British Aid to Developing Countries* (3rd edn. 1971). Further information about these bibliographies is available in a leaflet *Library services* issued by the O.D.A. library.

Patent Office

25 Southampton Buildings, London, WC2A 1AY (callers); Sale Branch, The Patent Office, Orpington, Kent, BR5 3RD (by post).

A comprehensive price list is available on request, and a deposit account may be opened with the Sale Branch for the supply of British patent specifications or other Patent office publications. The latter include the *Official Journal (Patents), Classification Key, Reference Index, Subject-Matter File Lists, Classification Manuals, Abridgments* and *Name Index.* Many free explanatory pamphlets are available, e.g. *Applying for a Patent, Information for Patentees, Searching British Patent Literature, Applying for a Trade-mark, Protection of Industrial Designs* and *About Patents: patents as a source of technical information.*

Posts and Telecommunications (Ministry)

Waterloo Bridge House, Waterloo Road, London, SE1 8UA.

The Ministry of Posts and Telecommunications publishes papers setting out the appropriate technical conditions necessary for using radio, whether mobile, maritime or land-based etc. Papers are also published giving indivi-

dual performance specifications for different kinds of equipment. Both technical conditions publications *(BR series)* and performance specification publications *(MPT Performance Specification series)* are available free of charge.

Statutory Publications Office

Queen Anne's Chambers, 41 Tothill Street, London, SW1.

Despite its name, the S.P.O. is an editorial and not a publishing office. It does, however, issue a helpful leaflet called *Looking up the Laws.*

Trade and Industry (Department)

Every month the D.T.I. issues a list entitled *Publications not sold by H.M.S.O.: Department of Trade and Industry publications (excluding Patent Office publications).* This includes, for example, publications of the Overseas Technical Information Unit, the Technology Reports Centre and the Treasury. It also gives the addresses from which copies may be obtained. The list is included in the Department's list of new accessions in economics and general subjects, and is also available separately.

Treasury (H.M.)

Treasury Chambers, Great George Street, London, SW1P 3AG.

H.M. Treasury has over the years issued a few non-sale publications, mostly guides to procedure for civil servants and civil service, statistics and so forth. Nearly all of them are now the responsibility of the Civil Service Department (q.v.). The only significant current publication still produced is the monthly *Economic Progress Report* which the Central Office of Information issues on the Treasury's behalf. No catalogue or list is available.

Water Resources Board

See Department of the Environment.

Welsh Office

Cathays Park, Cardiff CF1 3NQ.

Non-H.M.S.O. publications fall into three main groups. Firstly there are those of the Welsh Council, a nominated body set up to advise the Secretary of State on any matters concerning Wales. They are listed in the Council's periodic reports and are available from the Economic Planning Division of the Welsh Office. The second group concerns Welsh Office circulars. Few of these are printed and even then are mainly those issued jointly with the Department of the Environment. The Welsh Office Library produces an annual checklist of circulars. Finally there are a number of publications issued jointly with the Department of Health and Social Security mainly relating to the work of the Central Health Services Council. Such publications usually appear on the monthly *Library List* of the Welsh Office Library.

Index

301